'[This book] is carefully designed as a forceful and concise statement on the artist's innovations . . . There's much more to say about this excellent book and Thomas offers daring interpretations on almost every page . . . Moments such as these underline both Thomas's skill as a historian and Caravaggio's towering genius.' – *Popmatters*

'Thomas is at his best when emphasizing Caravaggio's artifice, the extent to which he went beyond the mere transcription of nature, and in analyzing the ways in which his works provoked an unprecedented visual and intellectual engagement with the viewer . . . His discussion of the art market and of Caravaggio's role in cultivating a new audience of private collectors in Rome, who prized artistic freedom, novelty, and sophistication, is also valuable.'
– *Sixteenth Century Journal*

'This is not a typical chronological overview of the artist's life or a catalog of his works. Rather, the book is thematically conceived . . . This clever format allows Troy to continually circle back to previously discussed paintings but under different terms . . . this affordable book is a fitting complement to more traditional studies; it will help the reader better understand Caravaggio's importance to artistic modernity and the history of art in general.' – *Choice*

'Accessible but sophisticated . . . Building on previous scholarship and also offering some intriguing new interpretations of Caravaggio's remarkable pictures, Thomas argues that the ambiguity of the artist's approach to his subjects, along with his novel realism, psychological penetration, and dynamic immediacy, make Caravaggio a truly modern artist.' – Dr Babette Bohn, Professor of Art History, Texas Christian University

'Thomas's [book] deserves our attention, our respect, and our compliments for it invites us, indeed enables us, to see and understand Caravaggio effectively from a truly different and enlightening perspective, in a way few books on the artist do.'
Franco Mormando, Boston College, Religion and the Arts

'Troy Thomas presents an insightful, well written overview of the life and art of this fascinating painter. His examination of Caravaggio's radical style, eccentric persona, and ambiguous religious works against the background of cultural developments during the Counter-Reformation provides a fresh view of the artist's originality and continuing influence.' – Wendy Wassyng Roworth, Professor Emerita of Art History, University of Rhode Island

CARAVAGGIO

and the Creation of Modernity

TROY THOMAS

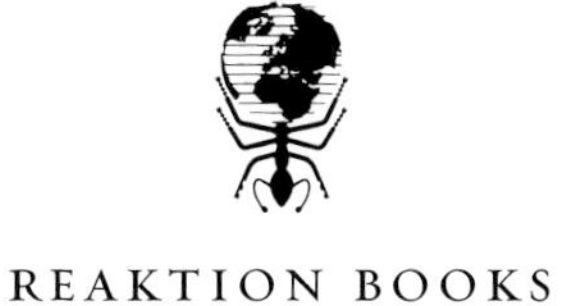

REAKTION BOOKS

Published by Reaktion Books Ltd
Unit 32, Waterside
44–48 Wharf Rd
London N1 7UX, UK
www.reaktionbooks.co.uk

First published 2016, reprinted 2017
Paperback edition first published 2024

Printed and bound in India by Replika Press Pvt. Ltd

A catalogue record for this book is available from the British Library

ISBN 978 1 78914 870 1

COVER: Caravaggio, *Judith Beheading Holofernes*, 1598–9, Galleria Nazionale d'Arte Antica, Palazzo Barberini, Rome.

CONTENTS

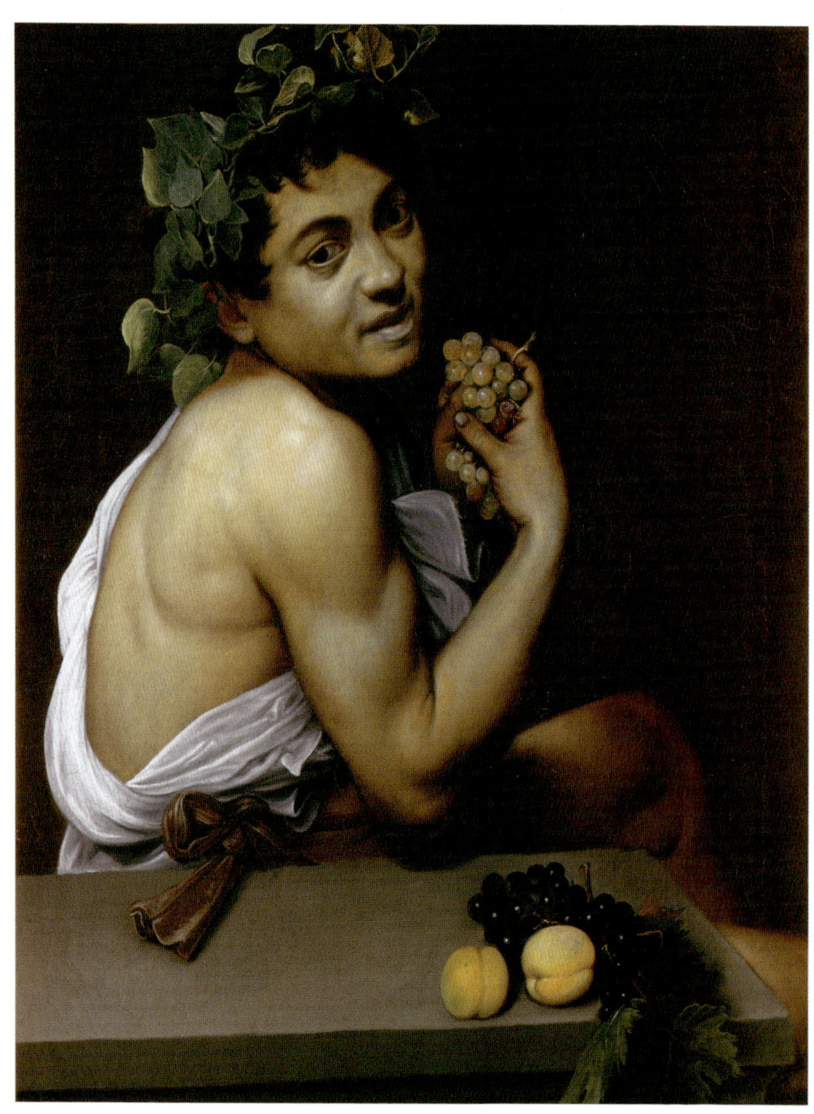

Introduction

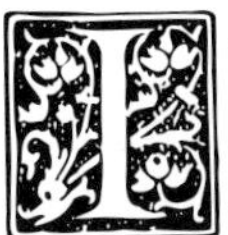N THIS BOOK I lay out the argument that in creating a new kind of art around 1600, Caravaggio went further than any previous painter in establishing characteristics that are today recognized as modern. To claim the truth that he was widely understood in his own time to be the most original artist of his generation is in itself insufficient to assert his modernity. His fame and the modern character of his art were based not merely on realism and tenebrism (his characteristic strong contrast of light and dark) that were widely recognized at the time as new, but on the deeper issue of ambiguity in his works. Indeed, it is the beholder's struggle with meaning that is the clearest indicator of his modernity.

Caravaggio's art does more than merely fall about halfway into the long chronological period known as the early modern era, beginning about 1400 with the rise of Humanism and the Renaissance and extending to the French Revolution. His paintings are characterized by a notable and decisive advance in qualities that are recognized as quintessentially modern: self-consciousness, self-reference, introspection, subjectivity and scepticism; experiments with novelty of form, content and artistic practice; social awareness; contradiction,

1 Caravaggio, *Self-portrait as Bacchus (Il Bacchino Malato)*, c. 1593–4, oil on canvas.

ambiguity, oppositional aspects and loss of certainty; a rejection (or radical reshaping) of tradition along with an emphasis on individualism; and, in his personal life, a fierce search for freedom, equality and higher social status. Such traits appear repeatedly in his art: self-consciousness and self-reference are seen in the self-portraits he inserts into his narrative paintings where he fashions his own persona (illus. 1). Introspection and subjectivity are found in his unexpected approaches to reinventing traditional subjects in art. Scepticism is discerned in his radically human-centred concept of religion, particularly in his protagonists' psychologically ambiguous reactions to the events depicted in his paintings. His experiments with form and content centre on his veristic effects, and his new approaches to artistic practice range from painting without preliminary drawings to introducing genre elements into religious pictures and advancing a new private art market aimed at connoisseurs. Social awareness is found in the plebeian simplicity of the saints and worshippers represented in his canvases. Contradiction, ambiguity, oppositional aspects and loss of certainty emerge in the way he challenges the viewer to ponder and interpret his often cryptic works. He radically reshapes tradition through his rejection of the idealist visual rhetoric of previous art. In the pursuit of freedom and higher status in his personal life, he pulled himself out of poverty by dint of talent and hard work, insisting that, as a celebrated painter, he be treated with respect. In all these ways Caravaggio's art marks a more advanced stage of modernism, where a new realistic and subjective approach informs not only his style of painting but equally the expressiveness and psychological candour of the protagonists in his narratives.

Some of these characteristics first appeared in the arts in embryonic form with the arrival of early modernity in the fifteenth century, most notably in the sculpture of Donatello, and long after Caravaggio's time they reached a sophisticated stage of development in the mature phase of modernism of the nineteenth and twentieth centuries. While his contemporaries who addressed his art had their own way of speaking and writing about its novel characteristics, the modernity of his paintings is clearer to us now than it was to members of his own generation. That is because we have the hindsight of having lived through modernism and postmodernism, and have a greater ability to comprehend how he anticipated expressive qualities that are familiar to us. To put this another way, we are now able to frame his art with our experience of modernity, to engage in a critical examination of it that both reveals its seventeenth-century historical and social context and addresses why his works continue to speak to us today.

A striking feature of Caravaggio's paintings is that as we stand before them, their newness, their radical spirit, can still be felt today: we sense their difference from the works of his contemporaries. The modern, subjective foundations of his art are broad. The self-portraits embedded in his religious narratives may be understood as contrived personas or guises that comment on his pride and his failure as a Christian. The pervasive blackness enveloping his scenes suggests an isolation of humanity evinced in part by the cosmic schemes newly proposed in his own time that put in doubt God's place in the universe and his relation to humankind. In his narrative canvases, Caravaggio establishes a stark psychological expressiveness in his protagonists that evades the ease of interpretation of past art. Because of their psychological realism, his figures are often difficult to construe in their religious context. His sacred works seemed (and still seem) to be marked by conflicting meanings that have resulted in oppositional readings. In his own lifetime, critics began a pattern of debate over the negative or positive religious connotations of his paintings that, in a modified form, has continued to the present time. Some interpreters emphasize the depth of the religious content of his works, while others stress their secular character. He posits a resolutely human and mundane perspective on sacred events, and a contingent and oppositional approach to expression and meaning. This book confronts Caravaggio's polysemic expressiveness, which marks a new stage of modernism.

Working against the grain of late sixteenth-century religious art, in which the inclusion of heavens with choirs of angels, haloed saints and gracefully spiritualized, idealized mortals was standard, Caravaggio conceived his radical realism in which humankind is cut off from the divine world, unable to penetrate its mysteries. Even though divine beings such as Christ or angels might invade the world of quotidian reality, the protagonists in his paintings often fail to comprehend their import. The spiritual realm is inextricably a part of Caravaggio's world, yet human awareness of it is limited; it is a fleeting thing, hard to discern in the painter's world of darkness. For Caravaggio the 'effect of the real', as an inclusive phenomenological concept, requires the presence and consciousness of the divine.[1] But the artist puts divinity, from a human and earthly perspective, in its place, so to speak, as something that his mortals struggle to comprehend. His pictures serve to correct those painted visions of the heavens that are never really part of ordinary human experience.

Caravaggio is famous for having created a revolution in realism by working on his pictures directly from the living model, without preparatory drawings, although it has been demonstrated recently that, in addition to incising lines into wet paint, he used his brush to draw directly on the canvas the outlines of figures and objects.[2] His practice of painting without separate, preliminary drawings or studies, however, did not mean that he recorded the unmediated reality of the living moment. Naively transcribing in paint such an unvarnished record of the studio model was not possible, even if Caravaggio's contemporaries accused him of doing precisely that. Nevertheless, a sense of reality remains in his holy figures expressly because he willed it so; through his self-conscious and mediated vision, his canvases offer the illusion (but only that) of an immediate present. His transformation of his models into saints was hardly convincing to his contemporary critics, since he chose to retain the specific physical characteristics of his sitters and often omitted conventional religious trappings. His articulated vision included emotions and gestures of seemingly real people as they reacted to the sacred dramas in which they took part.

Because Caravaggio desired to convey real rather than artificially graceful gestures, his works seemed hard to read, contradictory and ambiguous to his contemporaries, and they continue to appear so to many of today's observers. It is not always easy to sense the motivation, feelings or intentions of the human figures in his dramas because of their apparent uncompromising realism. The cryptic quality of his protagonists' demeanours was already discerned in about 1620 by Giulio Mancini, who said that Caravaggio's figures lacked movement and expression.[3] Some criticized his protagonists' enigmatic reactions to divine beings such as Christ or angels; enigmatic because they seemed too real, even sceptical. While the expression of Caravaggio's figures may appear to be authentic, they are nevertheless studio contrivances, based on models whose poses the artist controlled while painting.

Unlike previous artists, Caravaggio insisted that his models assume miens that seem genuine, not artificial or forced. His canvases were built upon consciously deployed aesthetic and narrative strategies, historical fictions and artistic intentions and meanings that were most often criticized by his contemporary commentators but were sometimes accommodated as authentically religious. Caravaggio's protagonists show human incomprehension as often as they reveal awareness of the divine world. He created inscrutable figures who show genuine human struggle with the holy mysteries. His visual strategies are not anti-religious; rather, his emphasis on showing humanity's difficulty in comprehending divinity is a time-honoured and legitimate theological position that has been demonstrated throughout the long stretch of Church history, as far back as Christ's Apostles themselves. Caravaggio presents his protagonists from a fundamentally and profoundly human point of view, with the implication that an imperfect humanity is separated by a deep divide from the divine realm and from a full understanding of the biblical events in which it plays a role.

Natural settings, including landscape or interior backgrounds, as they are normally conceived hardly exist in

Caravaggio's mature works, which instead show a pervasive and impenetrable blackness. The murky settings of his religious paintings suggest analogically that humankind exists in an isolated world with only the barest knowledge of a distant divine empyrean. Even though Caravaggio's pictures are punctuated by an intense light entering from an outside source, and his protagonists are visited by such divine figures as Christ and angels, humans' awareness of divinity is limited. His empty backgrounds seem to take on a cosmic significance. In Caravaggio's time many new, competing and contradictory theories were proposed about the heavens, variously calling for an earth- or sun-centred system, some finite and others infinite. Caravaggio's umbral paintings express anxiety about the cosmos and humankind's place within it, since the new science made God and the traditional celestial heaven seem more remote than ever.

The dark spaces of Caravaggio's pictures are penetrated by preternaturally strong light that cannot be explained in ordinary terms. Light in many of his mature works appears to be at once earthly and divine, and even within his radical emphasis on tangible reality, he treats light as an element in which the natural and spiritual dimensions cannot be separated. (In every aspect of his pictures, except his depiction of light and of holy figures such as Christ, Caravaggio conceives of a radical separation between the divine and the earthly, with a focus on the latter.) The source of light in many of his pictures may be interpreted as the sun, but even then it would retain divine connotations, for in Caravaggio's time the light of the sun was understood by theologians and natural philosophers as being simultaneously physical and spiritual.[4] His approach to light reflects larger philosophical, ideological and religious beliefs of the late Renaissance, when the spiritual and secular spheres were not always easily distinguishable. It was in his paintings of the life of St Matthew in the Contarelli chapel of the church of San Luigi dei Francesi in Rome that Caravaggio first articulated the synthetic and unifying character of his light. In the *Calling of St Matthew* (see illus. 18), the light is divine but also part of the natural world, and comes from a single source. Against the blackness of the background, strong illumination falls on the protagonists from above and to the right, and is also discernible in the diagonal shaft of light that rakes across the back wall. This light accompanies Christ as he calls Matthew to become his Apostle.

Caravaggio's modernity grows not directly from the social sphere, but from the religious domain in which the social is embedded. He demonstrated his empathy for the poor through his depiction of plebeian saints and simple peasants, garbed in tattered clothes. He went to the trouble of painting their dirty fingernails, which served as a barometer by which to judge his proletarian sympathies. Later in his Roman career, he lost public commissions for altarpieces in churches owing to his continued insistence on depicting indecorous figures, including the poor. Sometimes, as with the crude and startled simpleton of a saint in his first version of the *Inspiration of St Matthew* (see illus. 36), Caravaggio incorporated irony into his scenes, testing the limits of what was acceptable in religious representation, in order to be audacious and bold. He engaged the viewer at a deeper level of meaning and, on a personal level, aimed to succeed in making a name for himself in the

Roman art world. Because of his oppositional approach, the positive meanings implicit in his religious works were not always apparent to the viewers of his paintings, resulting in harsh criticism and, in the process, through his antinomic strategies, making him both famous and infamous, a fact that is equally part of his modernity.

The problems of interpreting Caravaggio's complex art also apply to his early secular works, such as his suggestive pictures of androgynous boys making music, and to his relatively few profane paintings after 1600, such as the salacious *Victorious Cupid* (see illus. 32). Canvases such as these were coveted by a new breed of private collectors in Rome starting in the late 1590s (illus. 2). Caravaggio capitalized on what he had learned in painting secular pictures of this sort and on appealing to this kind of audience as he turned his attention to making large-scale religious works. His sacred canvases, too, had special appeal for the same collectors when they were rejected by churches and put up for sale. His experience as a painter of secular images had a decisive effect on his revolutionary strategies for creating religious pictures. His novel approach in placing highly realistic human figures before unlit backgrounds grew in conceptual strength as he imagined focusing in his religious paintings on the mundane world of ordinary mortals set against an implied divine realm indicated solely by light. In developing his sense of how to create sacred narratives, Caravaggio responded both to the taste of his familiar secular audience of private patrons and to important debates within the Roman religious community over subjects such as grace and free will. The oppositional quality of his pictures and their revolutionary reconceptualization of

how to make penetrating sacred images may have been calculated by him to have special appeal to cultivated patrons and
collectors, who were shaping new kinds of taste in art around
1600, and by whom novelty and sophistication were prized
as much as new and audacious ways of expressing religious
meaning.

Caravaggio's paintings may be characterized as embracing a 'culture of dissent' through his use of irony, eroticism,
lowbrow figures and indecorousness; and, even if his works
are not overtly political (nor could they have been in his
historical moment), in his dissent he is much like Gustave
Courbet two and a half centuries later. Multilayered interpretive strategies are required to decipher Caravaggio's art,
which is like Courbet's in its contingent and complex character. In the complexity of his artistic enterprise, Caravaggio
had no immediate followers, and indeed it could be argued
that one has to wait until Courbet for a similar pictorial sensibility to arise. The *Caravaggisti*, his followers across Europe,
failed to notice the polysemy of his religious art. They either
redirected their subject matter towards secularism and genre
painting (where appeal to the emerging art market was more
overt) or normalized their religious scenes, by deleting (or
not detecting in the first place) the disturbing features of the
master's sacred works.

The traits in Caravaggio's art that make it modern embrace
the oppositions of the divine and the natural, belief and
doubt, religion and science, the transcendent and the earthbound, grace and free will, wisdom and ignorance, wealth
and poverty, and the positioning of the attentive viewer
caught within this polarizing web of forces. The oppositions

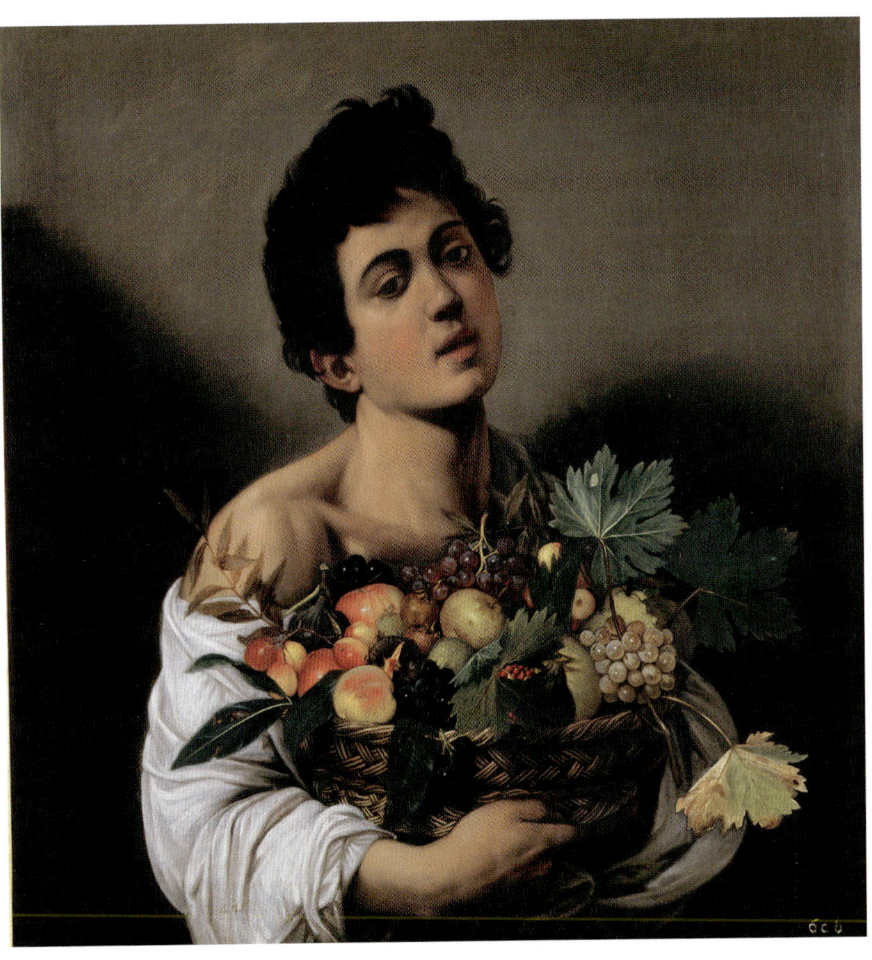

between the mundane and spiritual sides of his art, and the
negative and positive aspects, remain held in tension, never
entirely resolved, and it is this conflict, in part, that makes him
a modern artist.

I should say a word about the organization of this book. It is
arranged both chronologically and thematically. Caravaggio's

2 Caravaggio, *Boy with a Basket of Fruit*, c. 1593–4, oil on canvas.

life and works in his early (up to 1599) and late (1606–10) periods are treated chronologically, but the canvases of his mature Roman period (1599–1606) are discussed thematically. In the middle section of the book his life, works and historical frame are integrated into the thematic chapters. This arrangement permits a more detailed and conceptual focus on the important innovations that are found in Caravaggio's mature Roman paintings.

ONE

Early Life: Milan–Rome, 1571–99

FTER HIS ARRIVAL in Rome Michelangelo Merisi was known as Caravaggio, the name of the town near Milan that was his ancestral home. A document discovered recently shows that he was born not in Caravaggio but in Milan, on 29 September 1571, the feast day of St Michael the Archangel, who became his name saint.[1] Relatively little is known of Caravaggio's early life, although some suppositions may be drawn on the basis of documents conveniently gathered together by Stefania Macioce.[2] Among the records – largely legal transactions dealing with his family – a few mention Caravaggio himself. Old biographies give some useful information, even if written by critics hostile to him, such as his contemporary and rival Giovanni Baglione, a painter whose life of Caravaggio appeared in 1642. Others from the period penned his biography, as well, most importantly the writer and art theorist Giovanni Pietro Bellori, in his *Vite* of 1672.[3] Based on the early biography of the artist written in about 1620 by Giulio Mancini, a physician, art dealer and collector, it was previously thought that Caravaggio's father, Fermo, was architect and major-domo to Francesco I Sforza, the Marchese of Caravaggio.[4] In fact, documents discovered some years ago corroborate Baglione's old report that Fermo was actually a stonemason; as such he served the Sforza in both Milan and Caravaggio.[5] He was able to keep his family in modest comfort, but he was far from wealthy. The father of the artist's mother, Lucia Aratori, owned a large house in Caravaggio. Although probably not of noble stock, her side of the family was closely allied with the powerful Colonna and Sforza families. Costanza Colonna, the wife of Francesco Sforza, was one of a series of nobles who provided Caravaggio with protection later in life.

Thus the young Caravaggio, whose family had close ties with local nobility, would have had first-hand knowledge of the lifestyle of the wealthy class. Many of his problems in later life, including his scrapes with the law, centred on his pretentions to superior class status and presumed privilege. At the same time, he was painfully aware of his relative poverty, which became even worse when his father died at Caravaggio, probably of the plague. The boy was just six years old, and his mother, left with four small children and a step-daughter, was obliged to rely on relatives for support; she herself was dead by the time Caravaggio was nineteen.

As a child Caravaggio was quite aware of the lot of the poor, who readily succumbed to the repeated ravages of the plague and who in the 1570s were starving in the streets of Milan. He would have known of the efforts of the Archbishop of Milan, St Carlo Borromeo, to minister to the needy poor. Later, in his religious paintings, Caravaggio revealed a strong sympathy for the lowly, a circumstance that in part may have derived from his childhood memories of their widespread suffering in Milan. He may have recalled positively Borromeo's spiritual and physical aid to the indigent, but was less influenced by the stern archbishop's autocratic ways, constant suspicions of sin and efforts to suppress it, zeal in rooting out heretics and draconian efforts to round up the destitute and homeless during an outbreak of plague.

When in the early 1580s Caravaggio set himself the goal of becoming an artist, he was apprenticed to the Bergamese painter Simone Peterzano in Milan. Claiming to be a pupil of Titian, Peterzano indirectly made Caravaggio aware of the Venetian style, which the latter evoked in the landscape of his *Rest on the Flight into Egypt* (see illus. 14). In his *Deposition of Christ* (illus. 3) in the church of San Fedele, Milan, Peterzano painted his figures boldly in strong light against a shadowy background in a manner that would be echoed clearly in the works of Caravaggio.

The simplicity and clarity of Peterzano's realism show that he had fallen under the spell of Borromeo, who in his *Instructiones fabricae et supellectilis ecclesiasticae* (Instructions on Church Buildings and Furnishings) of 1577 had included a chapter on 'Sacred Images and Pictures'. Borromeo's faith was rooted in the visualization of the sacred stories, much like Ignatius Loyola's in his *Spiritual Exercises* (1548). Borromeo called for a clear and direct art showing proper decorum that induces the viewer to piety; his teaching inspired Milanese artists to develop a stark, emotional painting devoid of sensual niceties.

This kind of concrete, plain-spoken painting was also partly the result of the strongly continuing influence of Leonardo da Vinci on art in Milan. Leonardo had lived in the city for about 22 years (1482–99/1500; 1508–13), and left an enduring legacy of forthright realism with figures

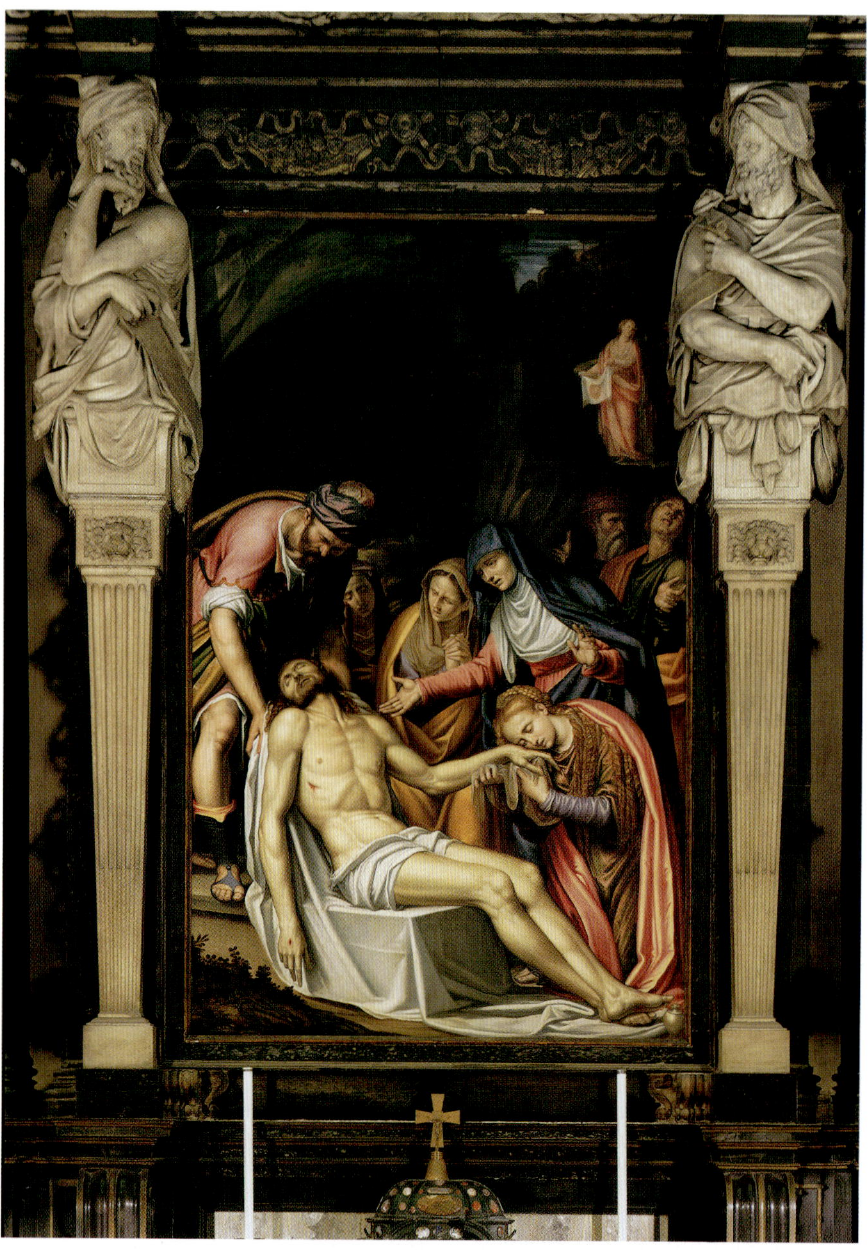

3 Simone Peterzano, *Deposition of Christ*, 1584, oil on canvas.

boldly modelled in *chiaroscuro*. His style was continued by his Milanese pupils, Bernardino Luini, Giovanni Antonio Boltraffio and others. The Lombard tradition of dark realism likewise characterizes the works of the Brescian artist Girolamo Savoldo, whose *Inspiration of St Matthew* (in the Metropolitan Museum of Art, New York) is often compared with Caravaggio's. The popular, pious naturalism found in the painted free-standing groups of the Modenese sculptor Guido Mazzoni and others also had a share in Caravaggio's formation as a spare, theatrical and visceral realist. In the mid- to late sixteenth century Antonio Campi, from the Lombard town of Cremona, painted religious scenes with figures set against unlit backgrounds. His brother Vincenzo specialized in pictures of figures with fruit, another genre that strongly influenced the young Caravaggio (illus. 4). A third, older, brother, Giulio, was known for paintings of musicians and gaming, subjects likewise painted by Caravaggio in his youth. These latter trends had nothing in common with the austere religious style promulgated by Borromeo, but nevertheless exercised a strong hold on Caravaggio, revealing another, secular aspect of his developing art. Such approaches to style and subject, sacred and secular alike, would later emerge fused in his religious paintings, a synthesis that revealed the ambiguity, contradiction and complexity for which he would be both praised and damned. In common with the works of other artists, Caravaggio's paintings did not emerge in a vacuum. But in spite of the formative sources mentioned here, it is his novelty that must be stressed. He was not a passive follower of tradition, but a radical innovator who shaped past art into something entirely new.

During the years between his mother's death and 1592 Caravaggio sold off much of his inheritance, in the form of landholdings, apparently to extricate himself from legal problems. He seems to have had a contentious and troublesome life from the very beginning. According to terse, handwritten notes by Mancini and Bellori, Caravaggio was involved in a murder in Milan, perhaps as an accomplice, precipitating his sale of land and his journey to Rome. In spite of recently found documents suggesting that the artist may have arrived in that city as late as 1595 or early 1596, in fact the long-held supposition that he was there as early as 1592 is probably correct.[6] For one thing, his surviving pictures, even the earliest ones, seem to have been painted in Rome. An arrival there in 1596 would make it difficult to account for his artistic development, which can be traced clearly in

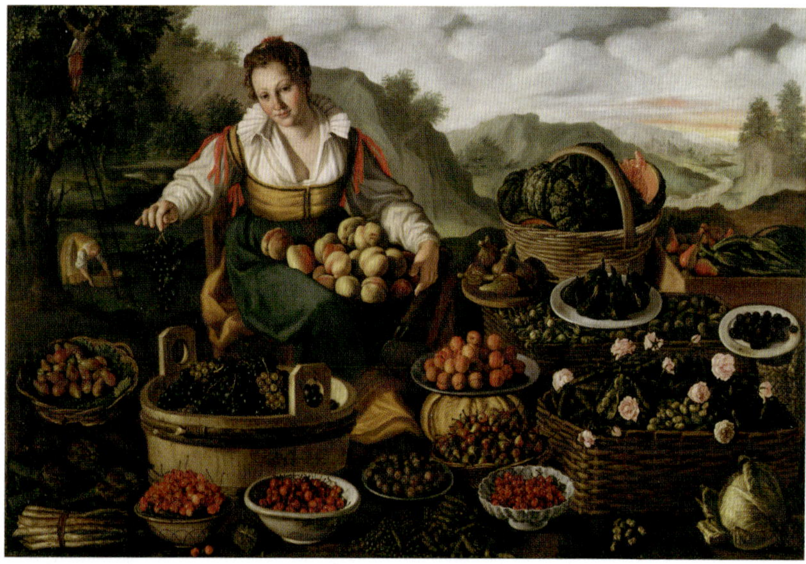

4 Vincenzo Campi, *Fruitseller*, c. 1580, oil on canvas.

his canvases and which almost certainly was stretched out over a number of years rather than confined to just a few in the late 1590s.

Charles Dickens's characterization of the eve of the French Revolution, that it was the best and worst of times, may be applied aptly to the Rome of Caravaggio's day, where the divide by wealth and poverty was enormous. Those fortunate enough to belong to the nobility or to be attached to it in the upper echelons of service enjoyed affluence and a renewal of culture and comforts following the austerities of the Counter-Reformation. The nobles not only luxuriated in their palaces but supplied the Church with its ruling elite, the cardinals, bishops and others, who often were not immune to earthly gratification. Meanwhile the many thousands at the bottom of the social ladder endured hard lives, living a hand-to-mouth existence often only days from starvation. Late sixteenth-century popes wavered in their treatment of the poor, including prostitutes, gypsies and cheats, sometimes providing them with food and shelter and at others expelling them from Rome. In the 1580s and '90s a major building programme had begun in the city, under which fountains, churches, *palazzi* and new, straight streets were constructed in surprising numbers. Caravaggio's arrival coincided with the beginning of the papacy of Clement VIII, whose reign was marked by a delicate balance between political expediency and Counter-Reformation fervour. He was less hostile than previous popes to the intellectuals, poets and artists who investigated antique culture; on the other hand, he could be merciless in stamping out heresy and dissent. At times, Clement was austere and proscriptive, like his predecessors. Caravaggio himself may have been a victim of papal disfavour, for he received no Vatican commissions until Clement's successor, Paul V Borghese, became pope in 1605.

One of the outstanding men of Rome in the later sixteenth century was St Filippo Neri, the head of the Oratorians, who devoted himself to the poor, led a simple life, possessed a playful wit and gave informal sermons of great popularity. By the time of his death in 1595 he had achieved a huge following, and it is likely that Caravaggio was affected by his dedication to the poor. We see in Caravaggio's religious paintings a sympathetic treatment of the low and humble, and later, under Cardinal Cesare Baronio, head of the Roman Oratory after Neri's death, he received from Girolamo Vittrici a commission for an *Entombment of Christ* (see illus. 47) for Santa Maria in Vallicella, the impressive, recently built church of the Oratorians.

Few distinguished painters worked in Rome in the late sixteenth century, apart from Annibale Carracci, the creator of a new classical style in Baroque painting. He and his brother Agostino were called to Rome in 1595 to fresco the gallery ceiling in the Palazzo Farnese (their cousin Ludovico, also an artist, remained in Bologna). By Caravaggio's time Federico Zuccaro had retired, leaving as the most prominent painters Giuseppe Cesari (Caviliere d'Arpino), Cristoforo Roncalli and Scipione Pulzone. Cesari was a Mannerist whose accessible, graceful style was so widely admired that he was in constant demand for new commissions. He painted both frescoes and small pictures in oil, sometimes creating dramatic contrasts in lighting but more often working his colours

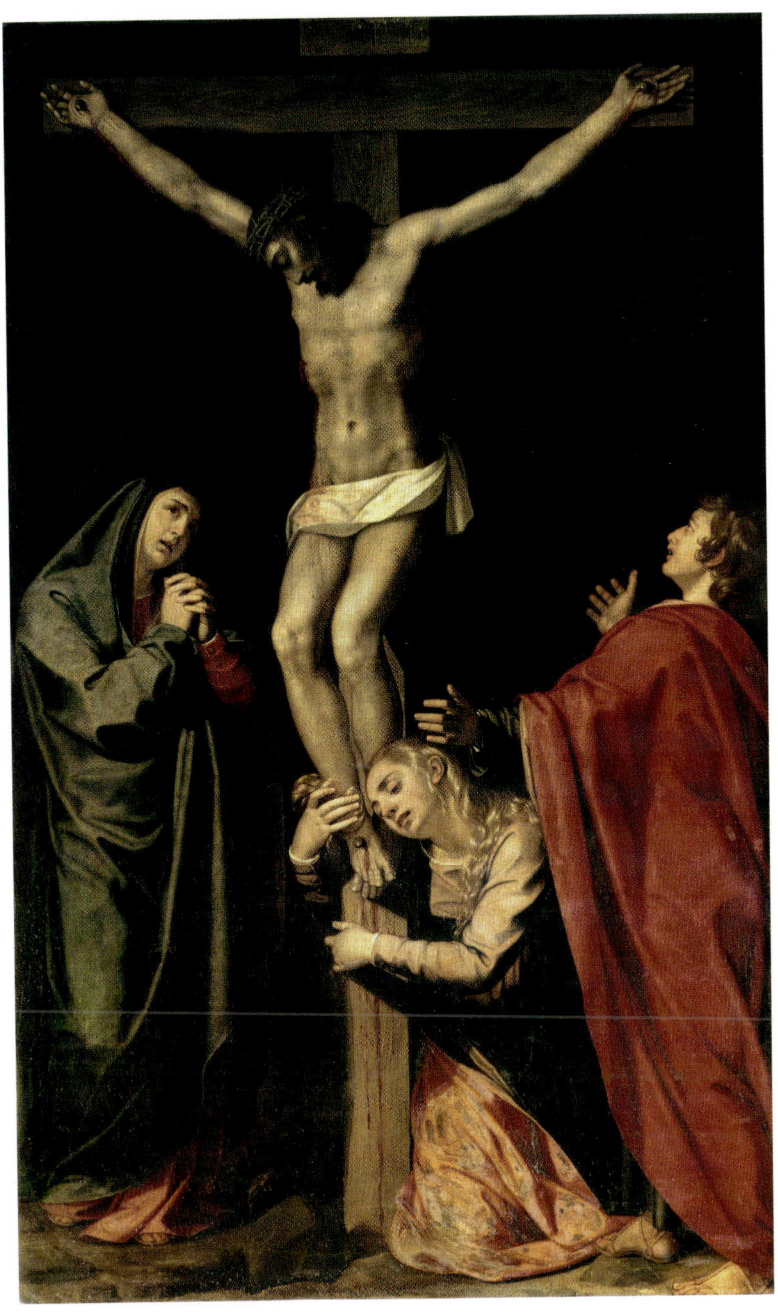

5 Scipione Pulzone, *Crucifixion with Saints*, c. 1588–90, oil on canvas.

delicately (see illus. 52). He used Caravaggio as an assistant for a short while. Roncalli, also a Mannerist specializing in fresco, made animated, elegant and sometimes dramatic works that were much admired by Cardinal Baronio. Pulzone was a 'counter-*maniera*' painter whose simple, unembellished naturalism answered the call for an accessible, devotional style by churchmen such as Borromeo and Cardinal Gabriele Paleotti in his *Discorso intorno alle immagini sacre e profane* (Discourse on Sacred and Profane Images) of 1582. Pulzone's approach seemed an appropriate response to the Church's stress on the need in painting for piety and naturalness (illus. 5). Since he probably noticed that there was room in this conventional artistic environment for innovation, Caravaggio determined to make a name for himself by dint of ambition and novelty.

When Caravaggio arrived in Rome he was poor but not entirely without connections. Costanza Colonna, the wife of the Marchese of Caravaggio and daughter of the famous Marcantonio Colonna, who had led the papal fleet to victory over the Turks at Lepanto, may have introduced the young painter to those members of her powerful family who lived in Rome. Shortly after his arrival, Caravaggio lodged in the house of Monsignor Pandolfo Pucci, steward to Camilla Peretti, the sister of Pope Sixtus V, who had close ties with the Colonna family. After a little while the young artist found living with Pucci unsatisfactory, since the latter offered him only salad to eat, resulting in the painter's famous, acerbic name for his host, 'Monsignor Insalata'. As a young painter who was not particularly precocious, he found himself unnoticed, hardly able to sell his pictures or find a patron to protect and promote him. He resorted to doing hackwork for established masters and painting pictures of single figures and fruit for the owners of shops and stalls.

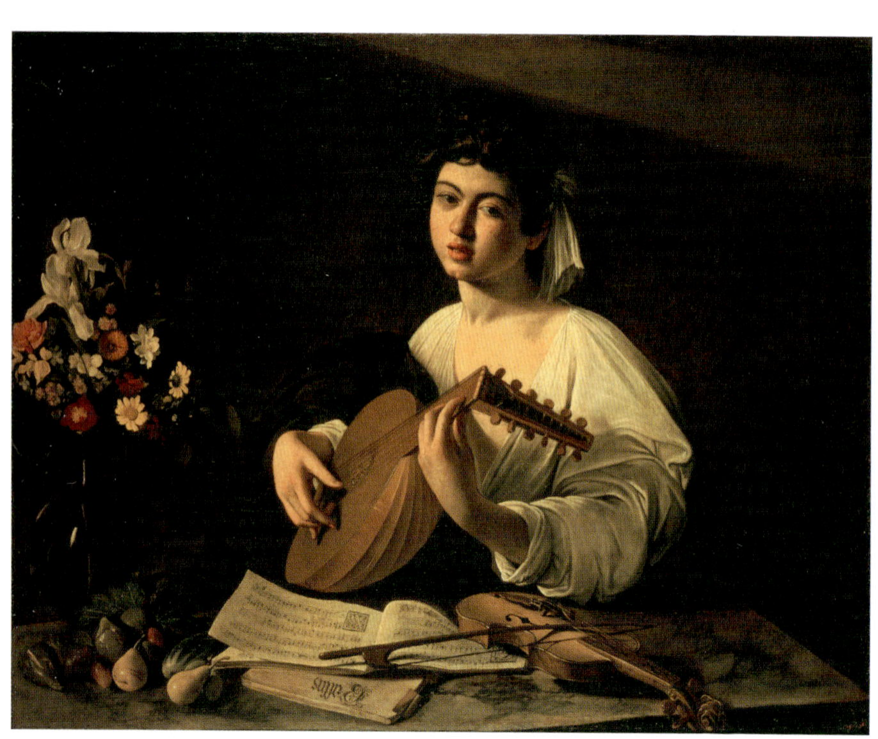
Bassus

TWO

The Modern Art Market; Early Patronage

FTER SHORT STINTS working in the studios of Lorenzo Carli, an obscure Sicilian who mass-produced paintings, and Antiveduto Grammatica, who was known mainly for his portraits, Caravaggio was determined to work his way up the artistic ladder. He laboured for increasingly well-known painters, finally gaining employment in the shop of Giuseppe Cesari, probably in 1593. Cesari – who was the most fashionable fresco painter in Rome – hired Caravaggio to paint independent cabinet pictures, typically of flowers and fruit. The master was a *maniera* painter, but his young assistant already worked more naturalistically. Giovanni Pietro Bellori mentions that while in the shop of Cesari, Caravaggio painted still-lifes in oil, including 'a vase of flowers with the transparencies of the water and glass and the reflections of a window in the room, rendering flowers sprinkled with the freshest dewdrops'.[1] It is uncertain to which pictures Bellori refers, but his remarks certainly may be applied to details of paintings done a few years later, such as the vases and flowers or fruit in the St Petersburg *Lute Player* (illus. 6), Florence *Bacchus* (see illus. 11) and London *Boy Bitten by a Lizard* (see illus. 51). Bellori both condemned Caravaggio's artistic project of imitating

6 Caravaggio, *Lute Player*, c. 1596, oil on canvas.

'common and vulgar forms' (*'forme umili e vulgari'*) and admired his realistic effects, which he described lovingly.[2] Bellori's contradictory approach reveals one of the oppositional layers within Caravaggio's art. In less than a year Caravaggio left the studio of Cesari, determined to strike out on his own and establish an independent reputation.

Probably in 1593, while in Cesari's employ, Caravaggio met Prospero Orsi, an indefatigable dealer and promoter who dedicated himself to launching the young painter's career. In helping to establish Caravaggio, Orsi aided in the advertising and sale of his works, provided introductions to dealers and wealthy collectors, and laid the foundation for the emergence of the followers of Caravaggio, the *Caravaggisti*.[3] Bellori mentions the crucial acclaim of Caravaggio by Orsi that attracted the interest of well-placed patrons.[4] A painter himself, Orsi traded in originals and copies, including replicas after Caravaggio, and imitated the latter's style in his own canvases. He was an operator in the art market at a time when shops selling paintings had only recently begun to appear in Rome.

The selling of works on the open art market, through shops or stalls or directly through dealers, was considered beneath the dignity of established artists, but for a few years Caravaggio found himself doing just that. Giovanni Baglione mentions that early in his career Caravaggio sold paintings on the street at San Luigi dei Francesi through a vendor named Valentino, whose real name we now know was Costantino Spata (or Spada).[5] No ambitious Italian artist wanted to work for low prices in the open market, but rather on commission, where pictures were more expensive and painted to order. Later Caravaggio made that transition successfully, and he readily found important private and public commissions once he became established as a religious painter, but in his first years he had a hard time finding buyers. He had so much trouble selling his half-figures that he was forced to endure the embarrassment of disposing of his beautiful *Boy Bitten by a Lizard* (see illus. 51) for 1½ *scudi*, and his equally impressive *Gypsy Fortune Teller* (illus. 7) for 8 *scudi*.

Gradually, Caravaggio's secular works of the mid- to late 1590s were sought after by the new audience of private collectors in Rome. The idea of building a private picture collection featuring the works of notable artists was new to the city. Francesco Maria Del Monte and a few others, including Pietro Aldobrandini and Ciriaco Mattei, were responsible for introducing this concept of collecting. By 1600 a rich secondary market had emerged for Caravaggio's early works, which continued to be sold, resold and copied.[6] By this time the paintings he had made a few years earlier were fetching steadily higher prices, and the market became flooded with replicas and variants. Because of the developing wide appeal of his art, and since his production was limited thanks to his practice of not using assistants, Caravaggio was one of the artists most frequently copied. Less than scrupulous purveyors of paintings tried to sell copies of his works as originals; indeed, there were many high-quality replicas of his works in circulation. Among his canvases copied and sold by other artists were the *Cardsharps* (illus. 9) and *Gypsy Fortune Teller*, replicated by Carlo Magnone. According to another report, a tailor sold half-figures painted in imitation of Caravaggio's by Guido Reni.[7]

Before 1600, Caravaggio apparently judged those who made or sold copies of his works as beneficial to his

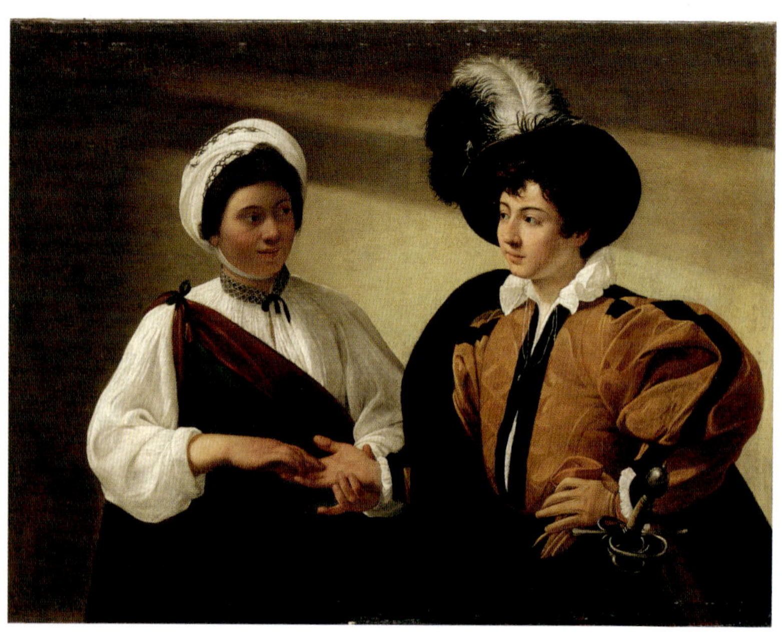

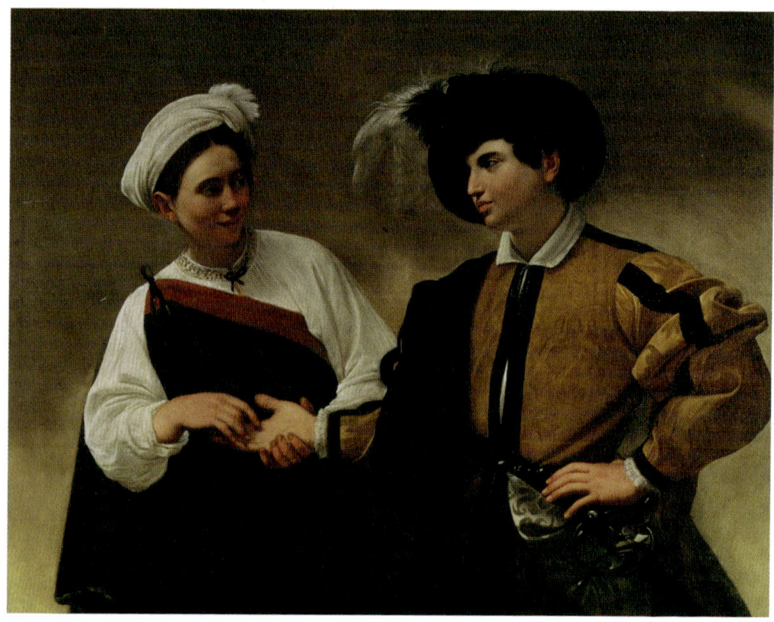

7 Caravaggio, *Gypsy Fortune Teller*, c. 1594–5, oil on canvas.
8 Caravaggio(?), *Gypsy Fortune Teller*, c. 1594–5, oil on canvas.

career, since they drew attention to his art at a time when he was still largely unknown. Such was the reason, in part, for his friendship with Orsi. Giulio Mancini, Caravaggio's biographer, was himself involved in having copies made after the painter's works as early as 1606, including once again the *Cardsharps* and *Gypsy Fortune Teller*. After 1600, once he was famous, Caravaggio became known for resenting his imitators, whom he perceived as stealing his *invenzioni* as well as potential commissions, and whose copies were having a negative impact on his prices. Eventually, his fame became so great that collectors competed to obtain any work of his, regardless of subject matter. Later, after his death in 1610, prices for high-quality copies of his works rose, in some cases dramatically. In 1613 a copy of his *Gypsy Fortune Teller* sold for

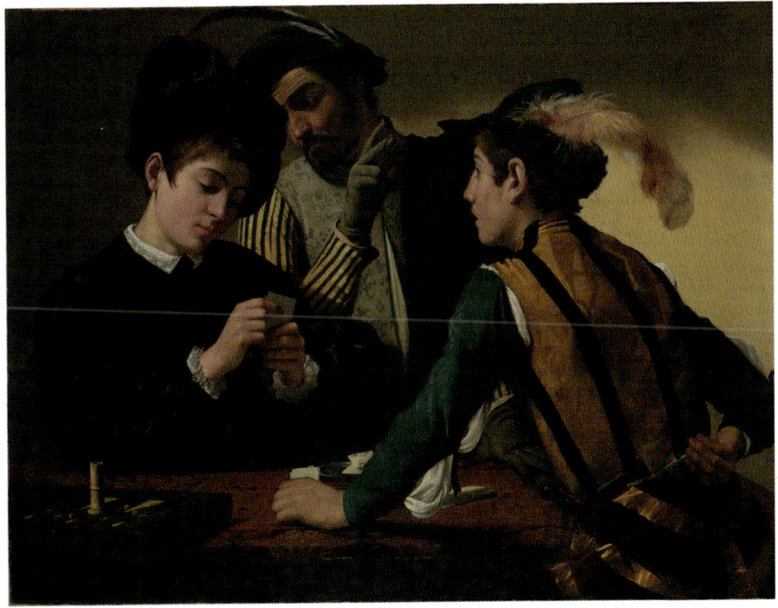

9 Caravaggio, *Cardsharps*, c. 1594–5, oil on canvas.

300 *scudi*, almost twice what Caravaggio himself had earned for each of his famous canvases of the life of St Matthew in San Luigi dei Francesi in Rome.[8]

From the very beginning, Caravaggio's works showed striking originality. In his earliest canvases he made his own unique contribution to the popular genres sold in stalls and shops, by specializing in pictures of young boys in vaguely antique garb holding fruit, such as his *Boy Peeling Fruit* (c. 1592–3, Rome, Longhi Collection); *Boy with a Basket of Fruit* (see illus. 2); and *Self-portrait as Bacchus* (also known as the *Bacchino Malato*, illus. 1). His low-life scenes of cheating and gambling, the *Gypsy Fortune Teller* (see illus. 7, 8) and *Cardsharps* (see illus. 9), introduced Rome to a kind of subject matter not seen there before.

It was Orsi who put the young painter in touch with the art dealer Costantino Spata, who in turn made the fateful, life-changing move of introducing him to his important first patron, the diplomat and art connoisseur Cardinal Francesco Maria Del Monte. By late 1595 Caravaggio was living in the cardinal's palace. This kind of arrangement must have been his goal, since a place in the household of a prince or cardinal would give him the security of painting pictures for a principal patron but also put him in touch with other members of the aristocratic elite who might want to buy his art. Living with Del Monte gave him the opportunity to become known among the powerful and eventually to receive public commissions.

Del Monte was a polymath enamoured with music and art who also dabbled in natural magic, which today would be called science. He had further interests in theatre, literature, history and archaeology. His rise to pre-eminence was ensured when he became a principal advisor to Cardinal Ferdinando de' Medici, son of Grand Duke Cosimo I of Florence. On his father's sudden death, Ferdinando renounced his vows and assumed power as Duke of Florence. Del Monte was made a cardinal through the duke's influence, and subsequently watched over his interests in Rome. In 1589 the new cardinal moved into the Palazzo Madama, the Medici palace in Rome, just across the street from the church of San Luigi dei Francesi.

When Caravaggio was introduced to Del Monte, the cardinal bought the *Cardsharps* and perhaps also the Capitoline version of the *Gypsy Fortune Teller* (illus. 8). Del Monte and his wealthy associates were fascinated by the poor, the alien Other, as represented in these pictures, even if the urban vagrants and gypsies who devised endless schemes to rob and cheat people were a constant source of frustration to the Roman populace and the popes. Such characters were the stock-in-trade of the popular theatre frequented by the cardinal. He was struck by Caravaggio's innovative subjects and style and encouraged him to paint scenes with young boys. Such pictures include *Boy with a Basket of Fruit* (see illus. 2), *Self-portrait as Bacchus* (see illus. 1), *Concert of Youths* (illus. 10), *Lute Player* (see illus. 6), *Bacchus* (illus. 11) and *Boy Bitten by a Lizard* (see illus. 51). These paintings have been interpreted variously as allegories of love or *voluptas*; of *vanitas* or the *memento mori*; of the senses or seasons; or of the temperaments or deceit. The boys holding fruit and playing music clearly have homoerotic overtones.[9] In the second quarter of the seventeenth century evidence came to light that suggested Del Monte was himself a homosexual.[10]

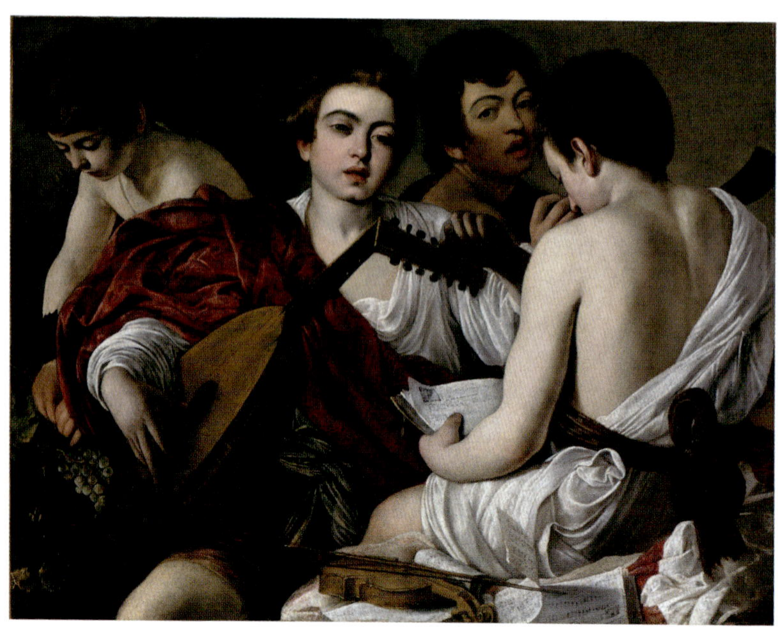

Even if the cardinal's critics, such as Dirck van Ameyden, who said so were hostile and unreliable, it is certainly true that Del Monte enjoyed parties and good company, and had a zest for life and its pleasures. Some judged that he delighted in amusements more than was seemly, but others thought his reputation spotless. Even those who defended him by emphasizing his modesty, rectitude and uncalculating simplicity admitted his love of enjoyments and leisure.[11] An anecdotal account mentions a party at Del Monte's Palazzo Madama where boys wore girls' clothing.[12] The controversy over Del Monte's sexual life undervalued the importance of political activity at his palazzo and overlooked the cardinal's real service to Ferdinando de' Medici and Florentine and French interests at the papal court. He was known for working

10 Caravaggio, *Concert of Youths*, c. 1594–5, oil on canvas.

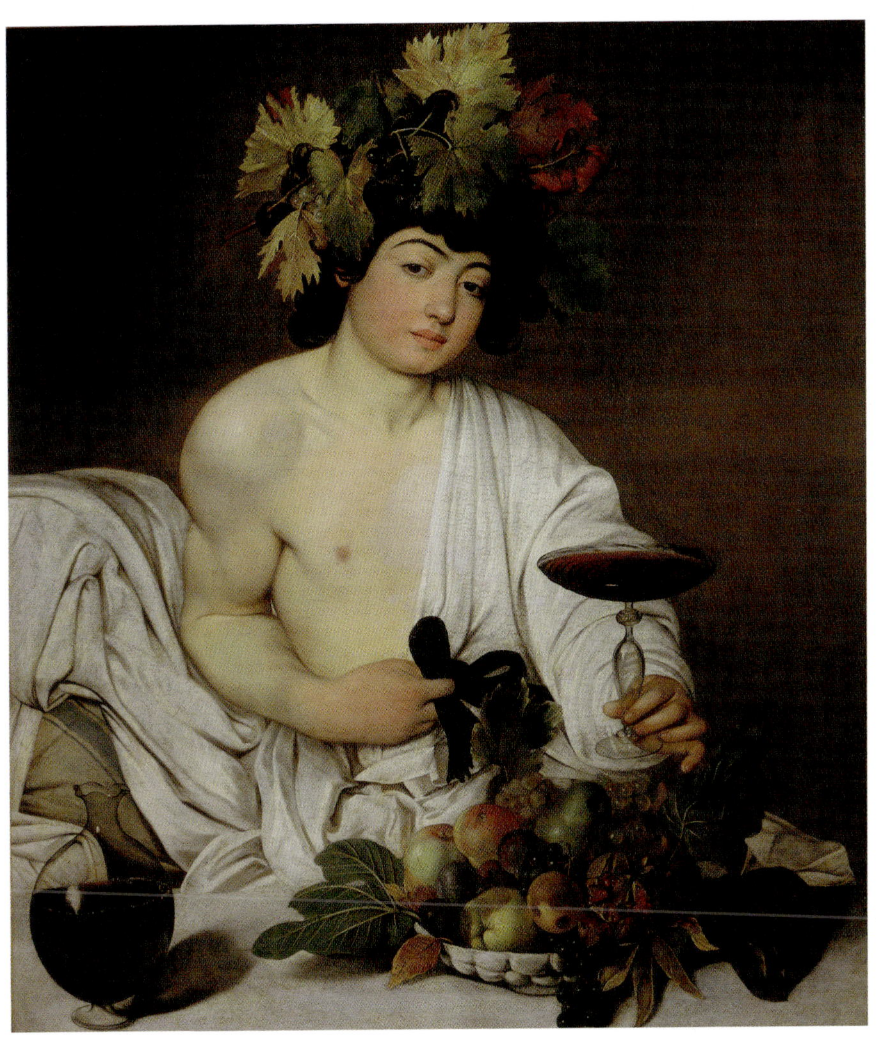

11 Caravaggio, *Bacchus, c.* 1596–7, oil on canvas.

behind the scenes as a negotiator in the informal atmosphere of his palazzo, hosting parties for both those supporting French interests and their adversaries.[13]

The claim that Caravaggio's pictures of boys are homo-erotic is one of many conflicting assertions about the propriety of his art. Certainly, these paintings are provocative and were calculated to be so, according to the artist's desire to make a name for himself. He may have been playing a dangerous game if he intended his paintings to be explicitly homoerotic, since such pictures might have raised suspicion and encour-aged the authorities to investigate his private life. Caravaggio may have been bisexual, and sodomy in Rome at that time was a crime punishable by death. A little later his religious paintings were likewise called indecent, and were thought by many to be too secular in character.

In ignoring distinctions between genres and in intro-ducing new ones, Caravaggio was supported enthusiastically by his patrons. While living in Palazzo Madama, Caravaggio would have crossed paths with the Roman elite who were the cardinal's friends. These included the physician Giulio Mancini, who wrote one of the earliest biographies of Caravaggio; Cardinal Pietro Aldobrandini, nephew of Pope Clement VIII; Cardinal Alessandro Montalto, Pope Sixtus V's nephew; Cardinal Benedetto Giustiniani and his brother the banker Vincenzo, who bought pictures from Caravaggio; and Cardinal Girolamo Mattei and his brothers Ciriaco and Asdrubale, avid collectors and owners of works by Caravaggio. Del Monte also counted among his friends the banker Ottavio Costa, who likewise acquired works by Caravaggio and Giovanni Battista Crescenzi, a painter whose father, Virgilio, and brother Giacomo had been charged with overseeing the completion of the Contarelli chapel in the church of San Luigi dei Francesi in the years before Caravaggio was hired to paint there. The artist continued to live with Cardinal Del Monte until 1601, shortly after the time his paintings in this church made him famous.

Stocky and dark in appearance, Caravaggio was described by a barber in 1597 during testimony in a criminal case as 'a large young man . . . with a thin black beard, black eyes with bushy eyebrows, dressed in black, in a state of disarray, with threadbare black hose, and a mass of black hair, long over his forehead'.[14] In contrast to the atmosphere of sophistication and learning in which Caravaggio was steeped in the household of Del Monte, on his own on the streets of Rome he was acquiring a reputation as a haughty and belligerent troublemaker. He spent time with friends who were known for getting into scrapes and brawls, including the architect Onorio Longhi and a fellow painter, Orazio Gentileschi (father of Artemisia). Caravaggio started getting into trouble with the law. His police record, which begins in 1598, documents a litany of offences ranging from fighting with fists or swords to breaking the window of his landlady to throwing a plate of artichokes at a waiter.

Caravaggio was becoming increasingly well known for his hot temper, for asserting his rights and for defending his art. He began to imagine himself privileged and above the law, stating when arrested for carrying a sword without a licence that 'I wear a sword because I am the painter of Cardinal Del Monte because I have the cardinal's support for myself and my servant.'[15] In this arrogant response he appeals to his prerogatives as an employee of a cardinal and makes the point that he has the superior status of one whom a servant follows through the streets. In spite of his unpleasant personal qualities and irascible nature, however, under the influence of his cardinal he continued to paint pictures of the utmost sophistication, delicacy and novelty.

Although Caravaggio's earliest canvases were not religious in subject matter, they show approaches to art that would fully emerge in his mature works, which are almost exclusively sacred, beginning in 1599. His early secular works establish and refine not only his realism, psychological expression of character and dark settings, but a subtle and clever ambiguity of genre and meaning.

THREE

Early Roman Works, c. 1592–9

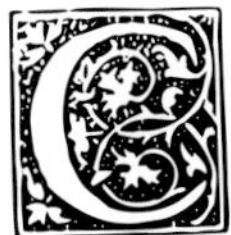CARAVAGGIO CREATED a new and provocative kind of painting in two of his earliest canvases, *Boy with a Basket of Fruit* (see illus. 2) and *Self-portrait as Bacchus* (see illus. 1). Pictures containing human figures and fruit were not uncommon in northern Italy, Flanders and Holland at the time, but they were more prosaic in conception, often depicting vendors selling food, as in Vincenzo Campi's *Fruitseller* (see illus. 4). By contrast, Caravaggio creates works that are ambiguous in subject, difficult to pin down in time or place, and sexually suggestive. The boys in these two pictures look vaguely antique, with a shirt or robe pulled down over the shoulder, but also – despite being crudely painted by the still-young artist – remarkably contemporary, conveying the sense that they are posing as we watch. The young man in *Boy with a Basket of Fruit* looks directly at the observer with his head thrown back and lips parted, as if he is deliberately adopting a sexy pose exclusively for the viewer's benefit. In his life of Caravaggio, Giovanni Baglione claimed that the *Self-portrait as Bacchus* was painted from a mirror, suggesting that the artist merely copied what he saw.[1] Both Baglione and Giovanni Pietro Bellori overstate the imitative function of Caravaggio's pictures, ignoring their artifice, strangeness and contrived

personas. The boy, crowned with ivy, focuses his attention on the viewer, looking out over his right shoulder, seeming to imply an intimacy and a story that we can only guess at. The art historian Roberto Longhi named this picture the *Bacchino Malato* because of the boy's sickly, green-yellow complexion. His expression conveys both melancholy and confidentiality. Such pictures would have appealed to sophisticated Roman collectors, who were open to ambiguity and suggestive symbolic possibilities.

In the *Bacchus* (see illus. 11), the fleshy deity proffers a glass of wine to the viewer, unwittingly breaking the barriers between painting and reality, and between antiquity and the present. This is the god not of divine rapture, but of drunken dissipation, who holds out the glass with glazed eyes, inviting the viewer to escape with him into a strongly suggested erotic degeneracy. The observer is encouraged to be complicit, to become part of the pretence, the clever charade. Through such devices the young Caravaggio makes a forceful visual statement and creates an unforgettable image.

Baglione, who was usually hostile to Caravaggio, could not help admiring the exquisite realism of the *Lute Player* (see illus. 6), noting the fine conception of such details as the reflections of the window and room in the carafe and the dewdrops on the flowers and fruit.[2] The music in this picture is readable: it is not antique but a song from the sixteenth century by the Franco-Flemish composer Jacques Arcadelt, 'Voi sapete ch' [io v'amo]' (You know that I love you).[3] Similarly, the part books and instruments of the boys in the *Concert of Youths* (see illus. 10) are modern, while the costumes suggest antiquity, giving rise to an ambiguous encounter of timelessness and immediacy. Such pictures had special appeal for Cardinal Del Monte, who delighted in musical performances and owned a large collection of instruments. The eroticism is unmistakable in the looks of the youths, in their dress and in the symbolism of the music and singing. The boys in all these paintings are androgynous, implying homosexuality. The gender of the youth in the *Lute Player* is especially equivocal: Baglione called it a boy, but Bellori thought it a young woman.[4] The mixture of genres and times, typical of Caravaggio, would also be found later in his religious paintings that were criticized for seeming too secular.

In about 1596–8 Caravaggio introduced two novelties that would profoundly affect his mature works of the next decade. The first is the dramatic *chiaroscuro* of the *Boy Bitten by a Lizard* (see illus. 51), with highlights raking over the youth's face and body from an acute angle at the side so that much of the figure is lost in deep shadow. In addition, a strong diagonal shadow interrupts the light falling on the back wall, an example of Caravaggio's famous 'cellar lighting', first seen in his *Boy with a Basket of Fruit* (see illus. 2). The other innovation is the artist's capturing of an instant in time, revealing the boy's sudden reaction in pain at the reptile's bite. Like his other early works featuring youths, this one is contrived and erotically charged, especially through the pout-ing expression, the delicate fingers (it is the middle one that is bitten), the exposed shoulder and the rose behind the boy's ear. With this precious but humorous subject, the art-ist's satirical side emerges. Drama, emotion and the instant are all brought together for the first time in his art.

Probably made just after the *Boy Bitten by a Lizard*, the *Medusa* (illus. 12) startlingly intensifies the emotional pitch of that picture. Painted on canvas glued over a convex wooden panel, it is three-dimensional, similar to the real shields with Medusa heads that served as apotropaic warnings to the enemy. Baglione tells us that it was a gift from Cardinal Del Monte to Grand Duke Ferdinando I of Florence. As such, it would have flattered the duke by bestowing upon him the

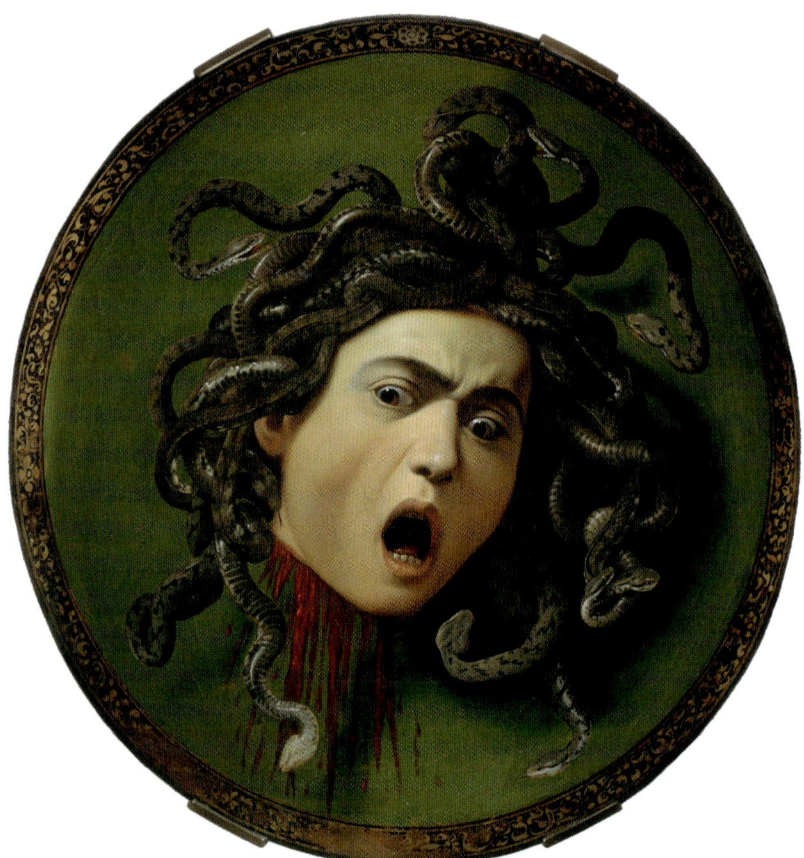

12 Caravaggio, *Medusa*, c. 1597, oil on canvas on wooden shield.

symbolic protection and powers of Medusa. Through semi-otic slippage the viewer is aware that this painting, a visual form, may suggest another medium, sound, by the scream of Medusa. Because she seems to be alive – a fact suggested by her astonishing expression and heightened by the ana-tomically accurate snakes writhing on her head – Medusa appears to break down the barrier between painting and reality. But she simultaneously seems dead, like a lifeless picture, because of her severed neck gushing with blood. When writing of paintings, bards of the period ceaselessly repeated the trope of how paintings seem alive; they did so especially in poems about Caravaggio's art. The picture plays with terror and humour simultaneously when the viewer fears being turned to stone under Medusa's gaze, but then takes comfort in recalling that she is only a painting. While he is often caricatured as a crude and brazen man of the streets, sword in hand, Caravaggio had an intellectual side into which this painting gives us insight. Even though he knew nothing of semiotics and little of art theory, he must have been aware when painting this work of its suggestive elision of art and life, life and death, terror and humour, the visual and the aural.

Caravaggio also invented new subjects in his scenes of con artists, the *Cardsharps* (see illus. 9) and *Gypsy Fortune Teller* (see illus. 7). While northern Italian precedents existed for images of card playing, he was the first to make cheating the theme of a large, independent painting. *Cardsharps* appealed to Del Monte not only because of its humorous yet deca-dent and even dangerous subject, but for the striking clarity of its strongly contrasting colours and its detailed textures and surfaces. The pleasures offered by the painting encompass both its exposure of deceit and its aesthetic attractions. *Gypsy Fortune Teller* is likewise novel, for the first time showing this scene as an exclusive subject, even if the type derives from details of Italian and northern European genre pictures. Caravaggio presents the gypsy woman flashing her eyes at the gullible youth while relieving him of his gold ring. The artist based some of his lowbrow types, such as gamblers and *bravi* (swordsmen or soldiers of fortune), on characters from Italian treatises and theatre, particularly the *commedia dell'arte*.[5] The gypsy (*zingara*) fortune teller was a staple in theatrical performances, sometimes aimed at the sort of elite audience that would include Del Monte.[6] In spite of her assimilation and defusing through a humorous approach by the artist, the *zingara* remained deeply ambiguous: she could still be demonized as the evil Other by privileged social groups.[7]

Bellori's assertion that Caravaggio simply imitated what was in front of him is invalidated by the artist's thoughtful reimagining of low-life types seen in both popular prints and theatre. The dozens of variants of these picture types by Caravaggio's followers over the next thirty years in Italy, France and the Netherlands make it difficult to appreciate the novelty of these two canvases, which are unique in his *oeuvre* (the variant *Fortune Teller*, illus. 8, which Del Monte had made for his collection and which is now in the Capitoline Museum in Rome, may be a copy by another artist). Later in the century Bellori, the champion of classicism, admired Caravaggio's early secular pictures most of all, precisely because of their difference from and structural opposition to large-scale narrative painting.

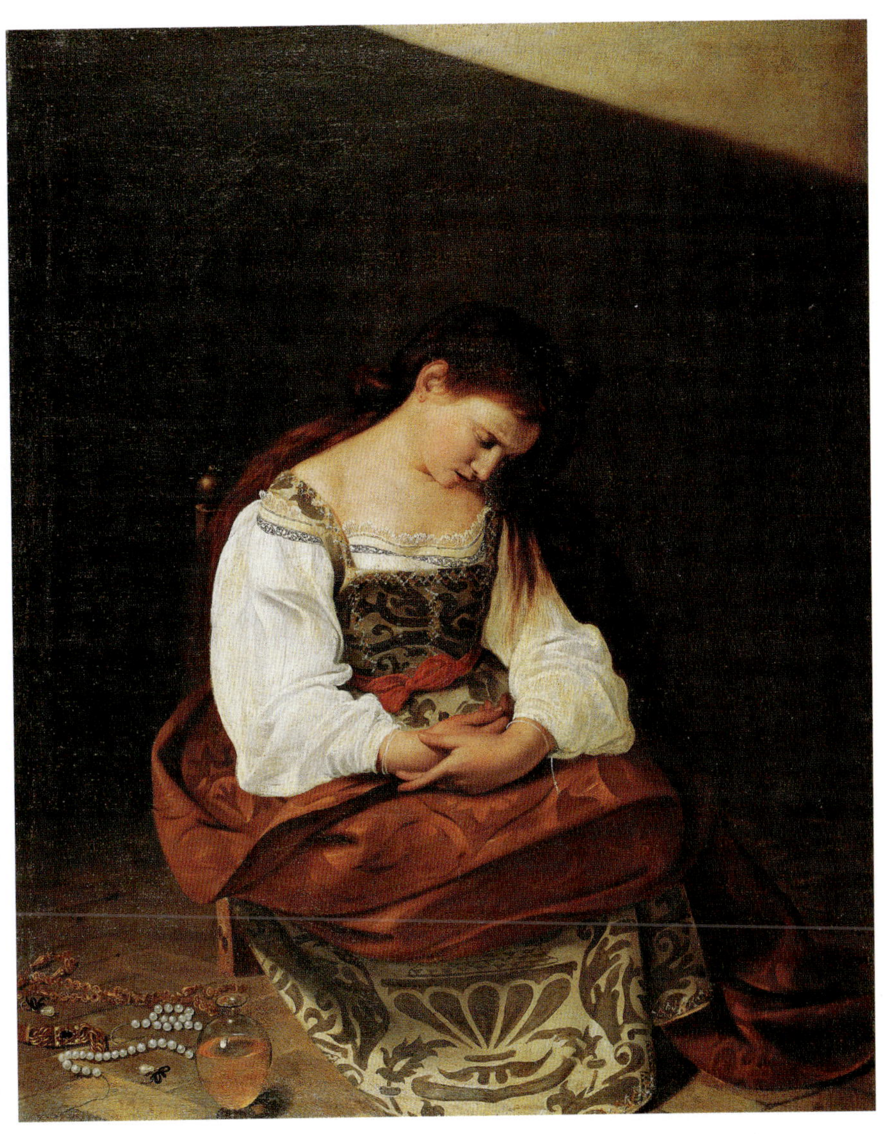

13 Caravaggio, *Penitent Magdalen, c.* 1595–6, oil on canvas.

At this time Caravaggio began making his first religious canvases. The *Penitent Magdalen* (illus. 13) could be mistaken for a genre scene featuring a contemporary girl; Bellori says that Caravaggio 'painted a girl drying her hair . . . adding a small ointment jar, jewels and gems on the floor, pretending that she is the Magdalen'.[8] In showing Mary Magdalen as ordinary, contrite and modest, with her head lowered and hands folded, wearing an embroidered blouse, damask dress and cape gathered over her knees, his picture is very different from previous artistic conceptions, in which she was often shown nude or nearly so. In the *Penitent Magdalen*, Caravaggio recasts a religious text as living drama. He would carry this revolutionary idea – painting figures directly from life, without preliminary sketches – into his mature religious works, with controversial results that would bring him fame.

The *Rest on the Flight into Egypt* (illus. 14) shows a partly nude angel seen from behind, playing music for the Holy Family. Mary cradles the Christ Child in her arms as she falls asleep, while Joseph holds the angel's music. A donkey, whose head appears between those of Joseph and the angel, seems to listen to the music, too. The barren foreground at the left is rocky, while oversized plants appear at the right, forming a partly dry and partly verdant symbolic landscape that stretches into the hazy distance. This landscape is one of few painted by Caravaggio, whose backgrounds became increasingly obscure. The provocative aspect of the angel and the playing of music are themes that similarly appear in his contemporary secular pictures of young boys. The sensuous angel exemplifies the 'dangerous unpredictability' of Caravaggio's paintings, which allow 'space for the unregulated responses of the viewer's

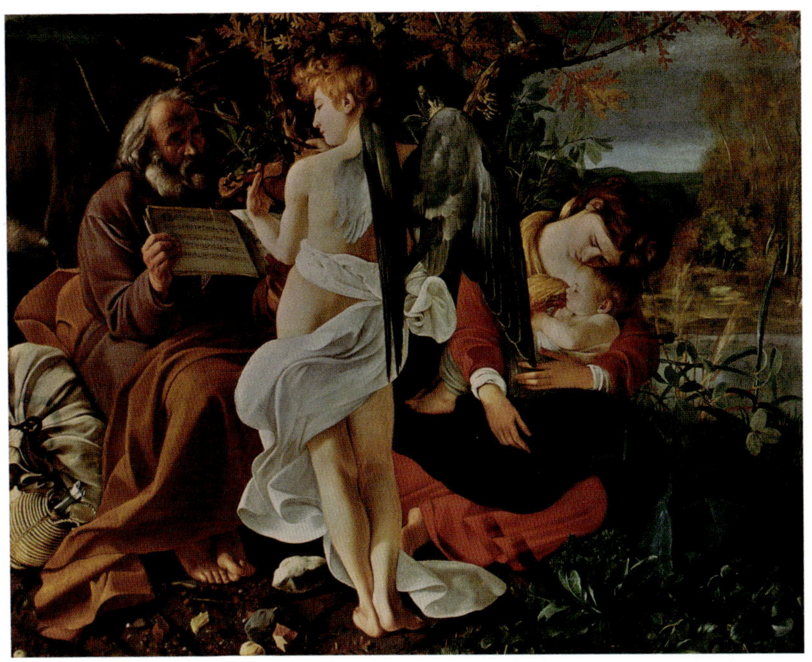

wandering eye'.[9] The angel's perversity is enhanced when its visual source is understood: it was modelled on the recently painted figure of Vice in Annibale Carracci's *Judgement of Hercules* of c. 1596.[10] The motif of Joseph, an old, simply dressed man with bare feet sitting next to an erotic, standing seraph, will appear later, transformed into the more controversial figures of Matthew and the angel from Caravaggio's first version of the *Inspiration of St Matthew* (see illus. 36).

Caravaggio's *Ecstasy of St Francis* (illus. 15) is innovative and unique in showing the saint lying down, with eyes nearly closed and head thrown back, supported by a partly nude angel. Luminous streaks on the distant clouds reveal that dawn is just beginning to break, and in the landscape at the

14 Caravaggio, *Rest on the Flight into Egypt*, c. 1595–6, oil on canvas.

left a few small figures around a fire point eagerly to the left, to the source of a miraculous, intense light that floods over the saint and the angel. Caravaggio omits the traditional seraph who imprints the signs of Christ's wounds on Francis's body. The stigmatization is de-emphasized and expressed in the saint on a personal and internal level by virtue of the power of divine light. In treating the subject in this way, Caravaggio sets the stage for his later religious paintings in which he hides the source of heavenly illumination and chooses to focus on a profoundly human view of miracles, callings and saintly deaths.

The precise role of Martha in the *Conversion of the Magdalen* (see illus. 50) is ambiguous. She was once thought to count the sins of Mary Magdalen on her fingers while exhorting her sister to renounce her wicked ways, but more recently she

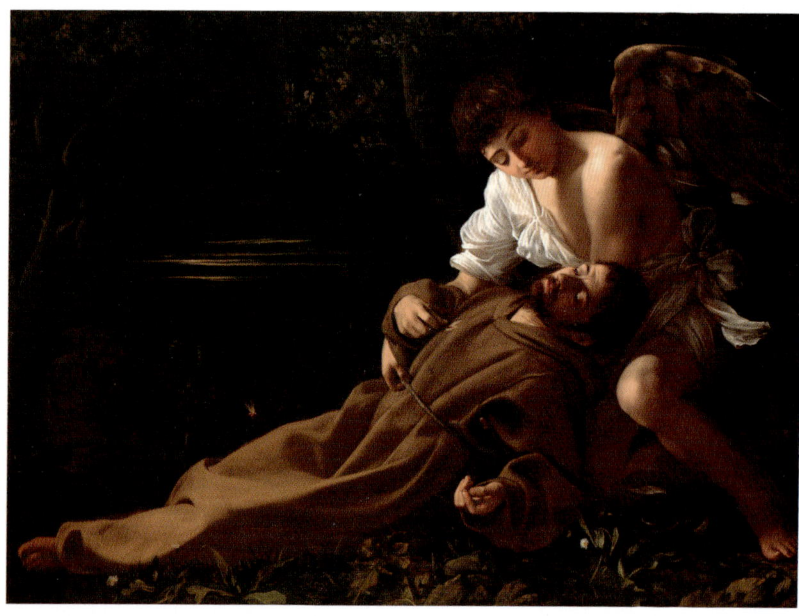

15 Caravaggio, *Ecstasy of St Francis, c.* 1595–6, oil on canvas.

has been interpreted as enumerating the miracles of Christ, since she was a Christian, like her sister (Luke 10:38–42). An inventory of 1606 describing this painting states that Mary 'is being converted', perhaps alluding to Martha's role in encouraging her sister to accept Christ.[11] At the point of her conversion, Mary seems to look through rather than at her sister, with her thoughts directed inwards. Her left hand rests on a prominent convex mirror that Caravaggio owned as part of his studio equipment. The mirror, normally a symbol of vanity, here reflects a strong light entering an unseen window at the left, symbolizing the divine illumination of grace. Even so, the picture might be mistaken for a secular portrait rather than a devotional work. It points to the future direction of Caravaggio's religious art, with a focus on a radically earthly view of sacred events.

Caravaggio's dazzling, large canvas *St Catherine of Alexandria* (illus. 16) also looks like a portrait, but the broken wheel, sword, palm branch, cushion and halo indicate that it is indeed a picture of a saint. The artist had now almost fully developed his *tenebroso* style, to striking effect. The face and blouse of Catherine stand out sharply against the background, and the brocade on the dress is a marvel of freely slashed strokes of paint. So compelling is the realism that the religious trappings seem iconic rather than part of an integrated sacred vision. This realism is deepened and rendered perversely contemporary through the model, the courtesan Fillide Melandroni, and the rapier, which is bloodied and almost certainly the one that Caravaggio used in his duels.

Judith Beheading Holofernes (illus. 17) shows a grisly scene from the apocryphal Book of Judith (13:1–12), in which the daring

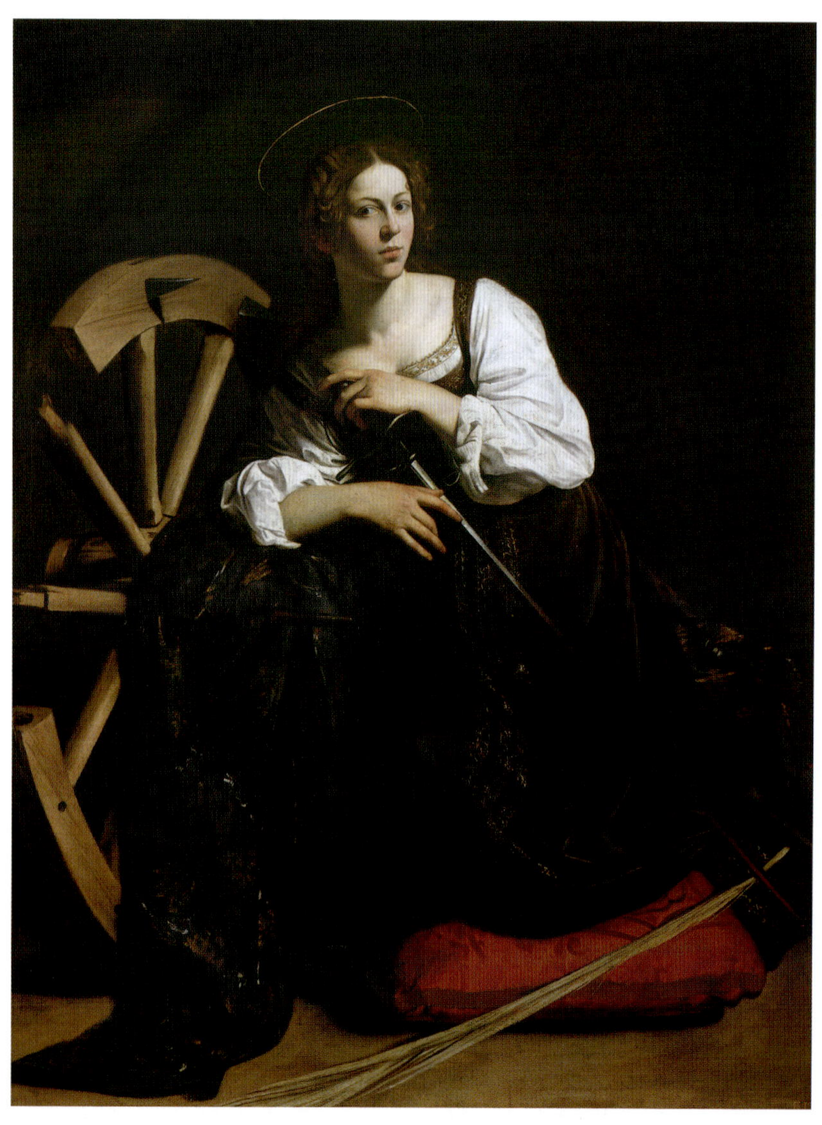

16 Caravaggio, *St Catherine of Alexandria*, c. 1598–9, oil on canvas.

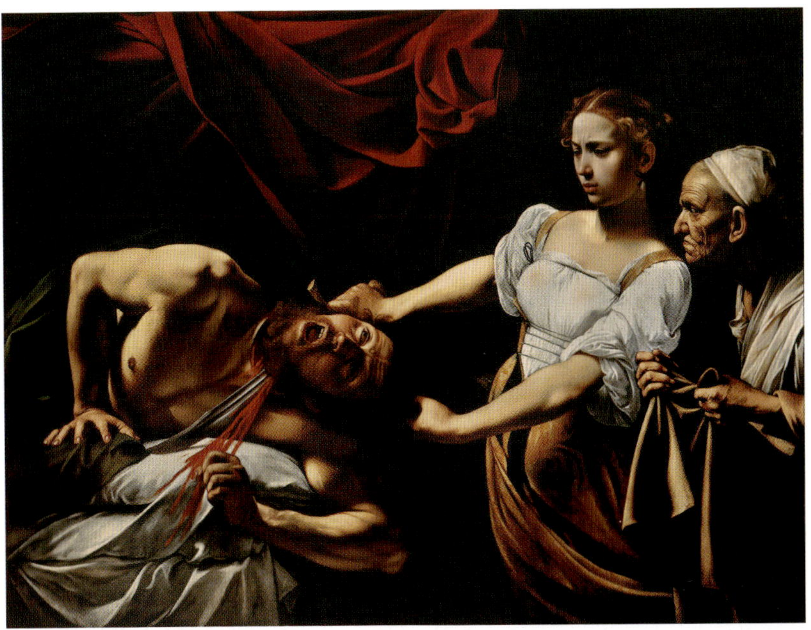

Jewish widow saves her people from an invading Assyrian army led by Holofernes. Judith reaches out, undertaking the gruesome business of cutting off Holofernes' head, while her grim, steely-eyed maidservant at the right readies a cloth in which to wrap it. Jets of blood shoot out from Holofernes' neck as Judith cuts with one hand and with the other wrenches his head in clockwise rotation. Judith's awkward pose, in which she tries to maintain her distance from the general, indicates that Caravaggio was not yet a fully mature artist. But emphasis on the tangible surfaces, the startling subject conceived as an integrated narrative, the moment, the dramatic light and the black background results in the kind of striking imagery that Caravaggio capitalized on in his mature Roman work.

17 Caravaggio, *Judith Beheading Holofernes*, 1598–9, oil on canvas.

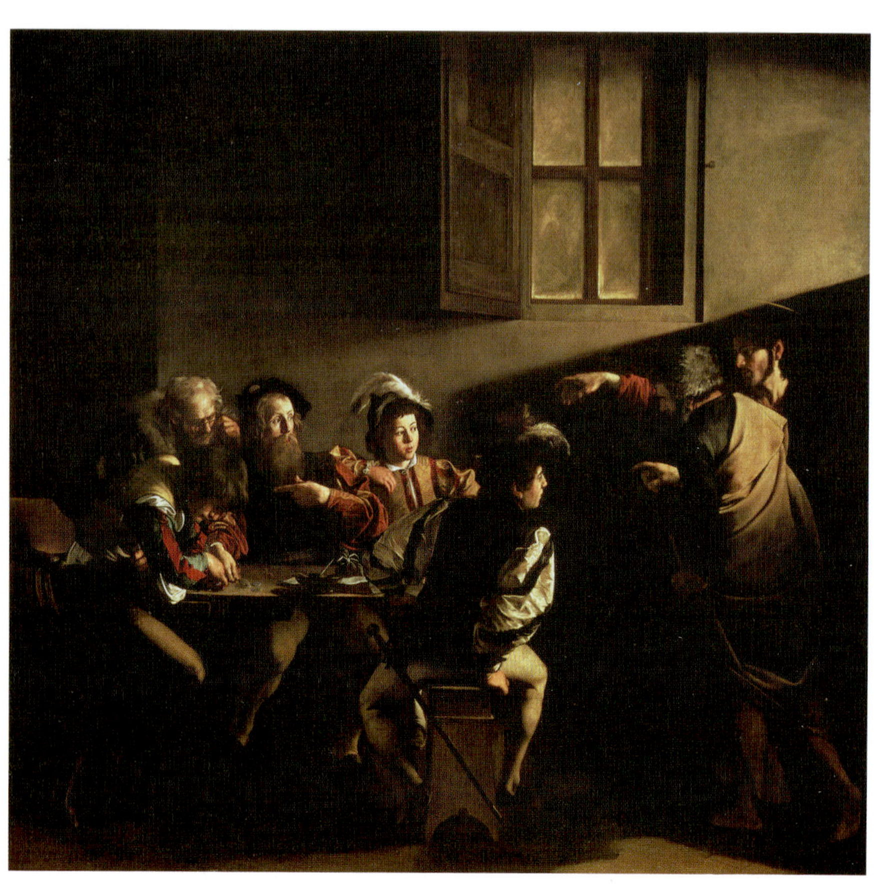

FOUR

A Stark Reality: Life and Mature Roman Works, 1599–1606

STANDING AT THE beginning of a new phase of modernity, Caravaggio invented a stark realism in his first major commission for public paintings in the church of San Luigi dei Francesi, Rome. He obtained the chance to make his breakthrough canvases because of the preceding decades of near inactivity in the church's Contarelli chapel. Previously the Mannerist Giuseppe Cesari, too busy with other commissions to finish the chapel frescoes he had been assigned, had managed to complete only the ceiling (see illus. 52). As a result of complaints from the French priests, in 1597 Pope Clement VIII ordered Abbate Giacomo Crescenzi to surrender responsibility for the Contarelli chapel to the Fabbrica (building committee) of St Peter's. These circumstances led to Caravaggio being commissioned to produce the chapel's paintings. According to Giovanni Baglione, Caravaggio got the job 'with the support of his cardinal [Del Monte]'.[1] In his *Calling of St Matthew* (illus. 18), one of the lateral paintings in the chapel, Caravaggio breaks with tradition by presenting his religious drama as if it is happening right in front of the viewer, on a contemporary Roman street. He replaces the graceful figures normally seen in historical

18 Caravaggio, *Calling of St Matthew*, 1599–1600, oil on canvas.

pictures with the raffishly dressed boys who had appeared in his previous secular works. Christ and St Peter, dressed in simple antique garb, seem to fall into a scene of a late sixteenth-century tax-collector, an old man and the three somewhat suspect youths, one of whom is a swordsman protector. Such *bravi* also inhabit the *Martyrdom of St Matthew* (see illus. 31), the other lateral painting, fleeing from the savage scene.

In 1602 Caravaggio completed his first altarpiece for the chapel, the *Inspiration of St Matthew* (see illus. 36), and then, after it was rejected, a second version (see illus. 35) later the same year. By now his forthright realism had reached a stage of maturity. His works in the Contarelli chapel established him as a great innovator in the creation of large-scale religious paintings. The controversial content of his pictures increased and took on new forms now that he was focusing almost exclusively on religious subjects.

Caravaggio's earth-centred approach is clearly visible in his *Calling of St Matthew*. As Christ and St Peter enter the scene from the right, the former extends his hand towards the tax-collector Matthew, calling him to Apostleship. Two of the young *bravi* gathered at the counting table turn to look cautiously but curiously at the divine intruders, while Matthew is so stunned by Christ's call that he remains seated, pointing to himself as if to say, 'Do you mean me?' We do not see Matthew eager to follow the Lord, but a man as yet unmoved by religious impulse. The expressions of the actors in this drama are equivocal, suggesting a psychological disquiet and inner complexity that are quite modern. Their reactions are strikingly different from the dignified and elevated visual rhetoric of past art.[2] In the first version of his *Inspiration of St Matthew* (see illus. 36, 37), the intended altarpiece for this chapel, Caravaggio depicts the Apostle as an unlettered peasant struggling to write his Gospel with the help of an angel, who guides his hand. Here, too, the artist focuses on Matthew's resolutely human reaction of surprise and his earthly ignorance. The *Martyrdom of St Matthew* shows the saint afraid and ineffectually defending himself from his assassin instead of dying nobly. Caravaggio's protagonists often evince incomprehension, fear, astonishment or impassiveness more than they disclose divine understanding.

The manner in which Caravaggio seems to present his saint as a dullard in his first *Inspiration* cannot be dismissed as an unintended consequence of his famous method of working from live models; that is, the imagery cannot be explained away by asserting that the artist was simply copying in some naive way what he saw before him, in this case a humble model. What we see in this picture is the result of expressive decisions made by the artist – the way he chose to pose and paint his models – and not simply an indirect effect of working from living models in the first place. His detractors assumed incorrectly that he did nothing more than copy in an unedited fashion what he saw in his studio.[3] Giulio Mancini, for example, thought the lack of expressiveness he perceived in Caravaggio's figures was a by-product of his working from live models:

> This school . . . is closely tied to nature, which is always before their eyes as they work . . . in narrative compositions and in the interpretation of feelings, which

are based on imagination and not direct observation of things, mere copying does not seem to me to be satisfactory, since it is impossible to put in one room a multitude of people acting out the story . . . having to laugh or cry . . . while having to stay still in order to be copied. As a result, [Caravaggio's and his followers'] figures, though they look forceful, lack movement, expression and grace.[4]

In Caravaggio's *Inspiration*, Matthew is not merely forceful (Mancini would grant that), but compelling in his expressive power, showing his astonishment as he reads of Christ's ancestry and legitimacy as Messiah while the angel guides his hand in writing the Gospel. As for movement, the artist was interested in capturing a distinct moment in time, not in suggesting continuous, flowing motion. Besides, he had his own way of representing movement, as in his Christ in the *Calling* (see illus. 18) with his feet turned to exit the picture. Caravaggio's method of working from live models was not a defect, but rather allowed him to achieve the expressiveness he wanted. Since no drawings are known to have come from his hand, he seems to have managed to get his model for Matthew in the first *Inspiration* to pose for an extended period of time with eyes wide open in the way he imagined him.

To Mancini, it seemed that the Mannerists or the new brand of seventeenth-century classicists, such as Annibale Carracci, were more successful in capturing 'movement, expression and grace', but the formulas they used to represent these qualities are exactly what Caravaggio wanted to avoid. He desired the physicality and gestures of his figures to be real and personal, a new approach that reveals why he painted studio models directly from life: in order not only to study anatomy and gestures, but to adjust facial expressions finely and to depict psychological states with uncompromising realism. Caravaggio's new kind of expressiveness failed to register with traditionalists like Mancini, who were simply incapable of seeing meaning in his novel approach.

Contemporaries who wrote about Caravaggio's paintings occasionally misinterpreted or maliciously misread them. The historian and painter Joachim von Sandrart, who lived a few doors from the church of San Luigi dei Francesi, at the Palazzo Giustiniani, between 1629 and 1635 and was clearly familiar with the Contarelli chapel paintings, mistakenly thought the *Calling* showed 'rogues playing cards and throwing dice and drinking'.[5] Money is indeed on the table, as tax proceeds, but no cards, dice or drinks, only Matthew's ink pot and paper to record duty transactions. The frankly commonplace individuals in Caravaggio's paintings were ironic in that they seemed designed to undermine the reverential manner in which holy personages were normally represented, a fact that perhaps led to Sandrart's misperception.

After completing the side canvases for the Contarelli chapel, Caravaggio repeated his remarkable performance in the *Crucifixion of St Peter* (illus. 19, see illus. 49) and *Conversion of St Paul* (illus. 20), painted for the burial chapel of Pope Clement VIII's treasurer-general Tiberio Cerasi in the church of Santa Maria del Popolo. In his job as papal treasurer, Cerasi had occasion to work with Vincenzo Giustiniani, a friend of Cardinal Del Monte and supporter of Caravaggio, and it may have been Giustiniani who suggested that Cerasi employ the

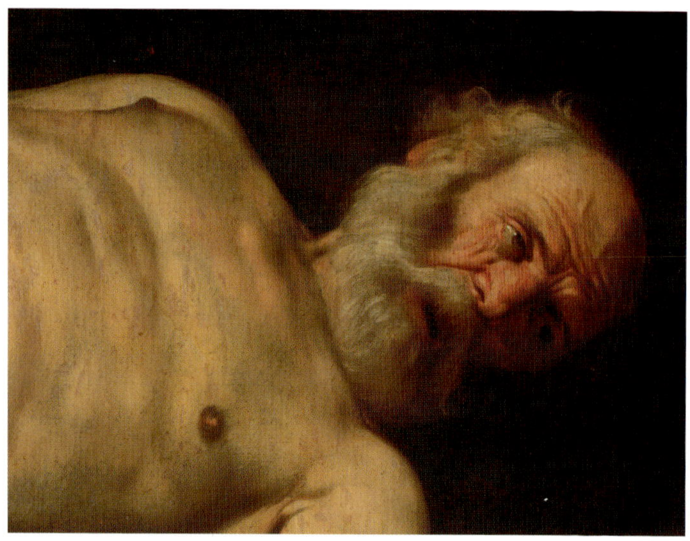

painter. The Augustinian friars of Santa Maria del Popolo may
also have endorsed Caravaggio; they had connections with his
native Lombardy and no doubt approved of the Augustinian
content stressing grace and conversion in his paintings of
St Matthew in San Luigi dei Francesi near by. The same pair
of subjects – Peter and Paul – to be painted in the Cerasi
chapel had been frescoed by Michelangelo in the Pauline
chapel at the Vatican in the 1540s, and surely Cerasi intended
Caravaggio's new works to be compared with those. Cerasi
also set up a competition between Caravaggio and Annibale
Carracci, the other most talented painter in Rome, whom he
employed to paint the altarpiece in his chapel. Carracci had
just completed his stunning frescoes of the loves of the gods
on the Palazzo Farnese gallery ceiling, so the Cerasi chapel
would be the stage for a notable rivalry between his altarpiece
and Caravaggio's laterals.[6]

19 Detail of head of St Peter, from Caravaggio, *Crucifixion of St Peter*,
1600–1601, oil on canvas (illus. 49).

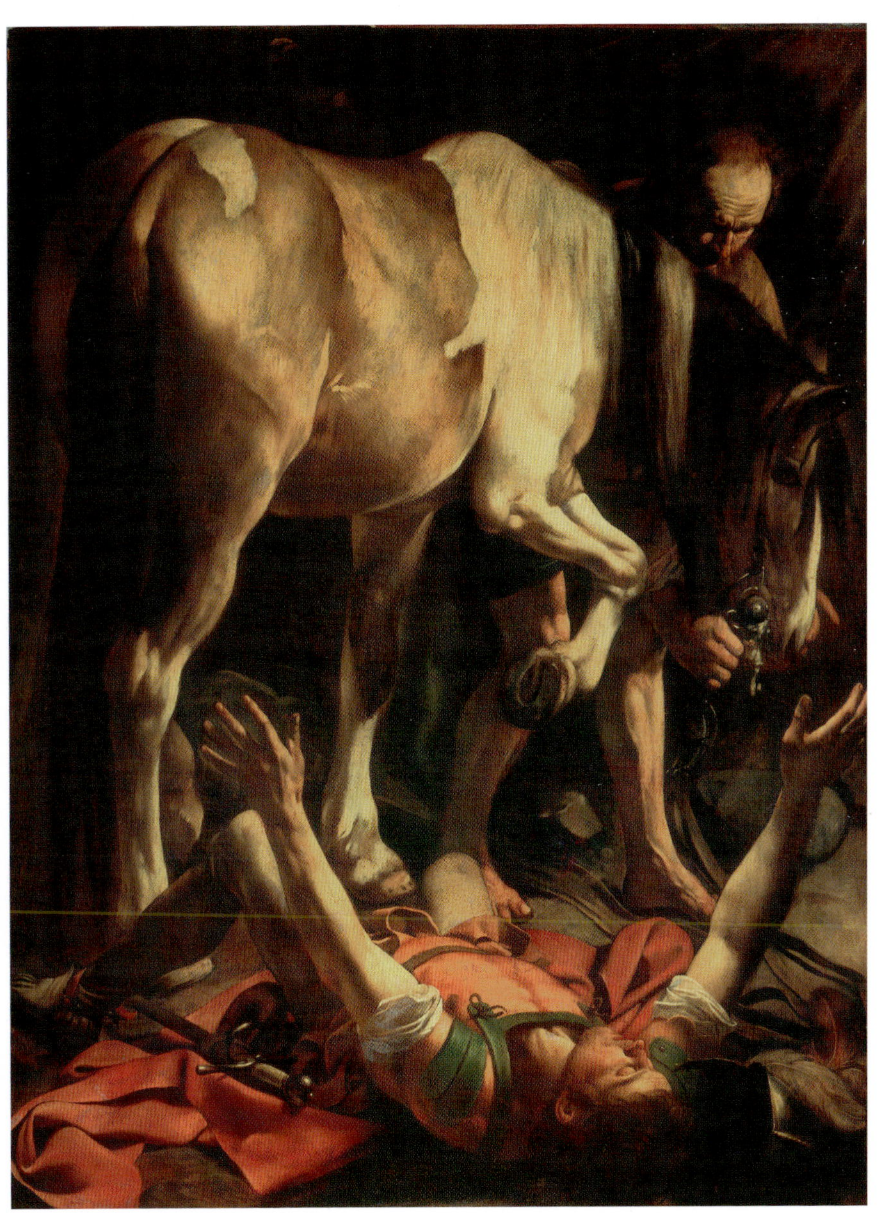

20 Caravaggio, *Conversion of St Paul*, 1600–1601, oil on canvas.

In his *Crucifixion of St Peter* Caravaggio shows the saint's enigmatic expression as he is raised on the cross: his stoic face lays bare the immediacy and harsh reality of strain and pain, with perhaps more of a sense of abandoned hopelessness than firmness of faith. Two poor and indifferent workmen struggle to heave Peter's cross into position with the saint already nailed to it, upside down, as he wished. In this picture we see no halo, no martyr's palm, no angels awaiting the saint's arrival in heaven, and Peter is disturbingly physical in his near-nakedness. The Apostle looks seriously and intently out of the painting towards the real altar before him in the Cerasi chapel, but with a stark expression that is ambiguous in its communication of religious faith. Caravaggio was aiming at another kind of expressiveness in Peter, one where doubt, fear and a questioning of faith were not only possible but part of a more profoundly human understanding of religion. In his unflinching look at the altar as he faces certain death, Peter reveals complex emotions that reflect his determination but also his doubts, as recorded in the Bible (Luke 22:54–62) and in the apocryphal Acts of Peter, where he at first flees Rome but then returns to face crucifixion.

Caravaggio's sombre portrayal of Peter's death could not have been more different from Carracci's altarpiece for the chapel, a noble *Assumption of the Virgin* (illus. 21) painted in bright, saturated colours, with classicized figures and an ideal, lofty tone. In his spare, gritty style, Caravaggio makes no distinction between saints and ordinary humans; their humanity is all that is important to him. In this respect, heightened by his minimal settings, his stark, emotionally immediate works are different from many Counter-Reformation paintings and

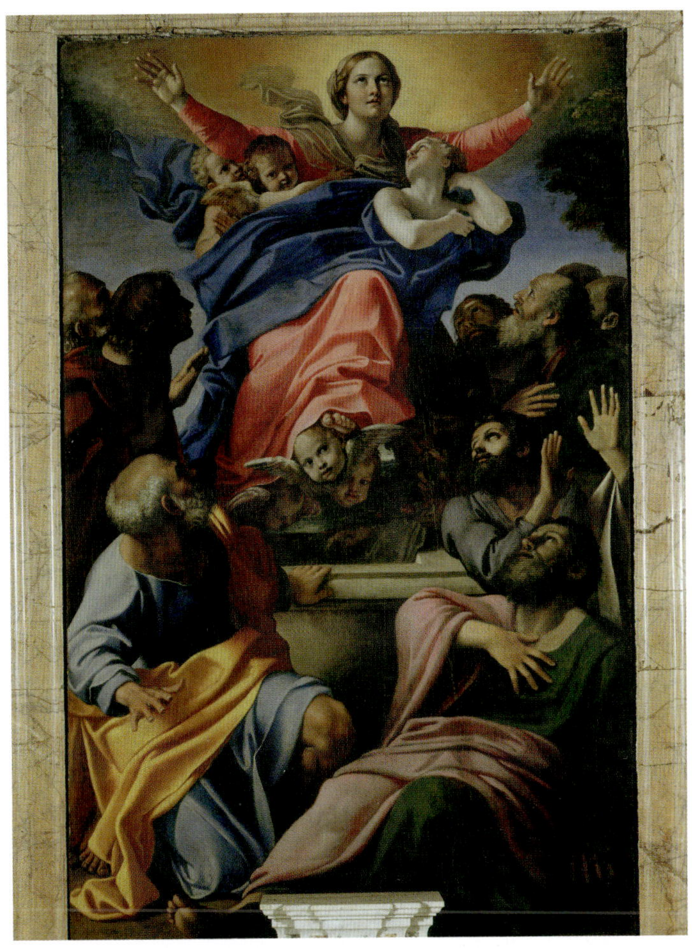

prints created in the late sixteenth century and highlighting the cruelty of Catholic martyrdom. In such examples as Circignani's grisly frescoed scenes at Santo Stefano Rotondo in Rome (illus. 22), the martyrs are identified by their attributes and elaborate ancient settings, with a focus on outward cruelty rather than inner emotion.

21 Annibale Carracci, *Assumption of the Virgin*, c. 1600–1601, oil on wood.

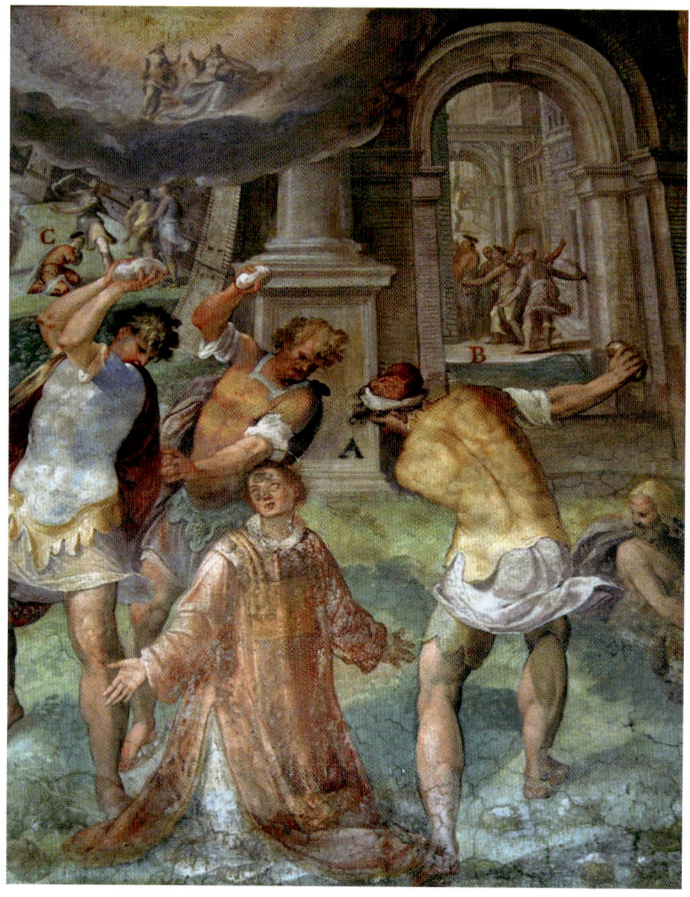

These didactic pictures are more illustrations than works of art, and even include captions to explain the scenes. By contrast, Caravaggio's martyrdoms and crucifixions seem more immediate and real than these laboured *maniera* works; his are more disturbing not only because of their unvarnished realism, but by virtue of his subtle expressive power. The isolation of his martyrs is more pronounced, with their bodies

22 Niccolò Circignani (Il Pomarancio), *Stoning of St Stephen, c.* 1583, fresco, Santo Stefano Rotondo, Rome.

forced near the picture plane, and the umbral settings surrounding them emphasizing their desolation. His modernity
resides partly in the psychological depth of his scenes of
martyrdom, as with his St Peter, shaken to his core as he starkly
confronts pain and death.

Other works, too, reveal Caravaggio's artistic subtlety
in depicting scenes of pain and torture, not merely his bra-
vado and spectacular effects: his *Sacrifice of Abraham* (illus.
23), painted in 1603, conveys the reality of Isaac's terror
because the artist is able to capture convincingly the way
the young boy screams, like a real child, as his palpable flesh,
soft and luminous, is threatened by the knife of his father.
Elsewhere Caravaggio reveals a continuing fascination with

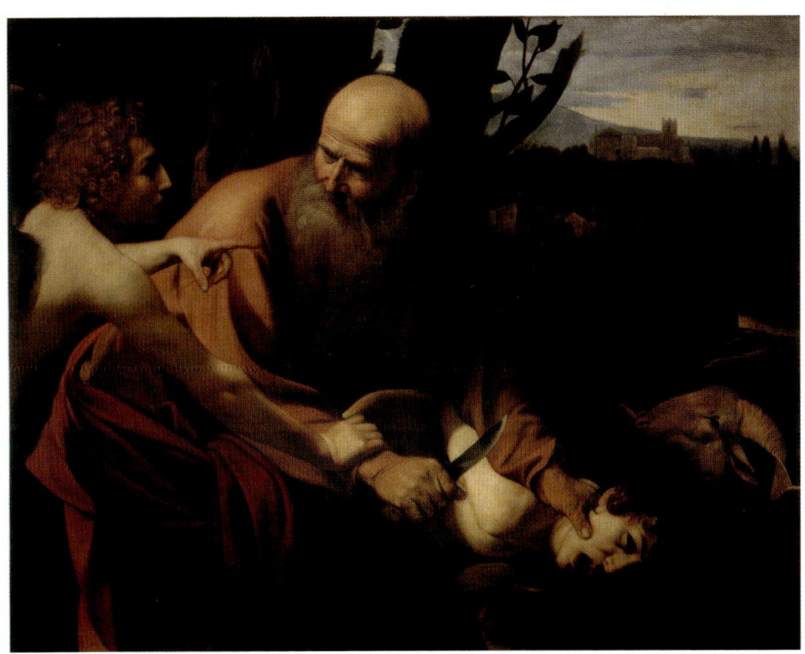

23 Caravaggio, *Sacrifice of Abraham*, c. 1603, oil on canvas.

the expressive possibilities of decapitation or its aftermath, stretching from early pictures – his *Medusa* (see illus. 12) and *Judith Beheading Holofernes* (see illus. 17) – to such later works as his *Beheading of St John the Baptist* (see illus. 61), *Salome Receiving the Head of John the Baptist* (see illus. 67) and *David with the Head of Goliath* (see illus. 40). Emphasizing the borderline between life and death in scenes of martyrdom and beheading provided him with the opportunity within realist painting to fascinate his viewers and hold them spellbound. He exploited the expressive possibilities of these themes to the full, creating images of impending or actual death more convincingly than any artist before him.

The *Conversion of St Paul* (see illus. 20) from the same chapel as the *Crucifixion of St Peter* continues Caravaggio's earth-centred focus. As he undergoes conversion, St Paul's emotion is directed entirely inwards, his eyes closed in an image of unprecedented stillness; he avoids any showy, rhetorical demonstration of faith addressed to the viewer. In seeming to convey the truth of Paul's experience, Caravaggio embraced a self-conscious artlessness (in a positive sense), as if he could re-create the immediacy of the scene directly, without artifice. The narrative conception of his pictures seemed so unmediated that many questioned his works, perceiving them as lacking art (in a negative sense), but they were accepted by some as true to religious experience; indeed, his paintings never suffered a want of willing collectors ready to acquire them.

Paintings such as the *Conversion* resulted from the artist's carefully conceived narrative strategies, with story situations that were thoughtfully created, not merely imitated from the model, as his critics claimed. Caravaggio imagines that Paul's conversion is driven by an inner psychological force, not by a majestic image of the Lord in the sky, as was traditionally shown in paintings of this subject. The saint, fallen unceremoniously from his piebald horse, lies flat on the ground, his arms outstretched in the orant position of early Christian prayer towards a shaft of light that penetrates the darkness. Paul's horse lifts a hoof to avoid stepping on him, while the uncomprehending groom holds the horse's bridle to steady the animal and looks down, averting his eyes from the intense light. This painting had a reality and directness previously unknown in religious art.

Even before the completion of these works, Caravaggio's fame was clear to all in Rome. His notoriety had been established by the lateral canvases he made in the Contarelli chapel. In the contract for the Cerasi chapel he was called 'egregius in Urbe Pictor' (illustrious painter in the city); similarly, in a letter of 1604 Lancillotto Mauruzi, a nobleman from Tolentino, identified Caravaggio as the best painter in Rome.[7]

Caravaggio's instant stardom brought out his worst instincts, and his police record became ever longer.[8] When he was thrown into prison, which now happened regularly, his powerful patrons inevitably came to his aid. He became if anything more belligerent and suspicious once he had achieved fame, continually getting into scrapes and brawls – sometimes with clerks, guards and rivals over girlfriends, at other times with those who criticized his paintings. Such censure was the reason for his assault on the young art student Girolamo Spampa, who had dared to disparage his Contarelli chapel paintings.[9] Caravaggio selectively attacked painters who he deemed were imitating his style, which he guarded jealously. He was proud of his prominent position as the leading artist in Rome and was known for begrudging painters who copied his style or questioned his supremacy.

Caravaggio nevertheless tolerated some followers more than others, maintaining good relations with the established painter Orazio Gentileschi. Caravaggio's new realism had a magnetic attraction for younger artists, such as the Bolognese Guido Reni, the Venetian Carlo Saraceni and the Lombard Bartolomeo Manfredi, all of whom arrived in Rome and began to imitate his style. Having a particular hatred for Baglione, Caravaggio became furious when that mediocre painter launched a visual critique of his own *Victorious Cupid* (see illus. 32) in his *Divine Love*, and won a commission that Caravaggio had wanted for an altarpiece in the important Roman church of Il Gesù. He wrote scurrilous verses against Baglione, who in turn sued him in 1603. During the ensuing trial, Caravaggio was confined in prison; it was the French ambassador, Philippe de Béthune, one of many rich and noble supporters of his art, who arranged his release. One of few statements on art by Caravaggio was recorded during this libel trial (not the most favourable venue for an extended discussion of the fine points of painting). He called the painters he admired *valenthuomini*, good artists who 'paint well and imitate well natural things'.[10] He listed the painters then working in Rome whom he regarded favourably, all of whom – Mannerists, classicists and naturalists alike – were distinguished by the qualities he found most admirable: they had a real understanding of painting, practised their style well and were famous and successful. They included the Mannerists Giuseppe Cesari,

Federico Zuccaro and Cristoforo Roncalli, and the reforming classicist of the new Baroque style, Annibale Carracci. Caravaggio mentioned these artists because he wanted to align himself with respectability.[11]

In developing his new kind of religious painting just after 1600, Caravaggio turned to a gritty realism, not naturalism: nature as it is usually understood is omitted from his paintings, lost to his umbral backgrounds. In both the Contarelli and Cerasi chapels he declared a new, forthright kind of religious expressiveness, focusing on a veristic and unflinching, if ambiguous, presentation of gesture and emotion. His protagonists are characterized by startlingly real reactions to the narrative situations in which they find themselves, with a psychological depth and directness heretofore unseen in religious paintings. The figures seem so real that they appear to be painted exclusively from the model, but in fact they are simultaneously sophisticated creations sometimes based on antique sculpture and Michelangelo's art, the same sources as those used by the Mannerists. Caravaggio's *St John the Baptist in the Wilderness* (see illus. 33), painted about the same time as his works in the Contarelli and Cerasi chapels, has a *contrapposto* pose seen from the side, recalling Michelangelo's *ignudo* to the upper left of the *Sacrifice of Noah* in the Sistine chapel ceiling (illus. 24); Caravaggio's concurrent *Victorious Cupid* (see illus. 32), with legs splayed salaciously, was most probably inspired by that same *ignudo* as well as by St Bartholomew in Michelangelo's *Last Judgment* (illus. 25) and by his sculpture of *Victory* in the Palazzo della Signoria, Florence. The summoning hand of Christ in the *Calling of St Matthew* (see illus. 46) was modelled on Adam's in Michelangelo's *Creation of Adam*.

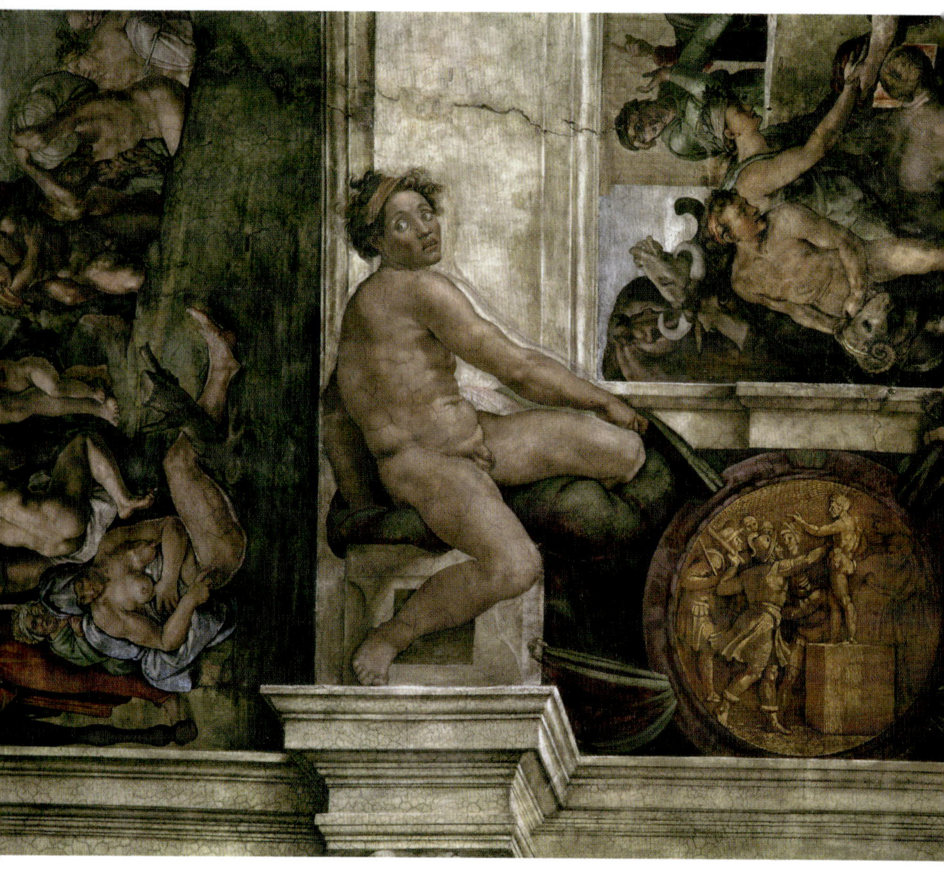

Caravaggio's approach is very different from Michelangelo's, however: his figures have nothing in common with the latter's heroic, platonic nudes, which were understood in his own time as metaphors for the soul's aspiration to rise to God. Nor are Caravaggio's figures like those of the Mannerists. In place of their elegant figures, he fashioned his subjects with a candour that seemed baffling to some observers of his pictures. His St John the Baptist and Cupid are young boys,

24 Michelangelo, *ignudo* to upper left of *Sacrifice of Noah*, 1509–10, fresco, Sistine chapel ceiling, Rome, Vatican.
25 Michelangelo, St Bartholomew from *Last Judgment*, 1534–41, fresco, Sistine chapel, Rome, Vatican.

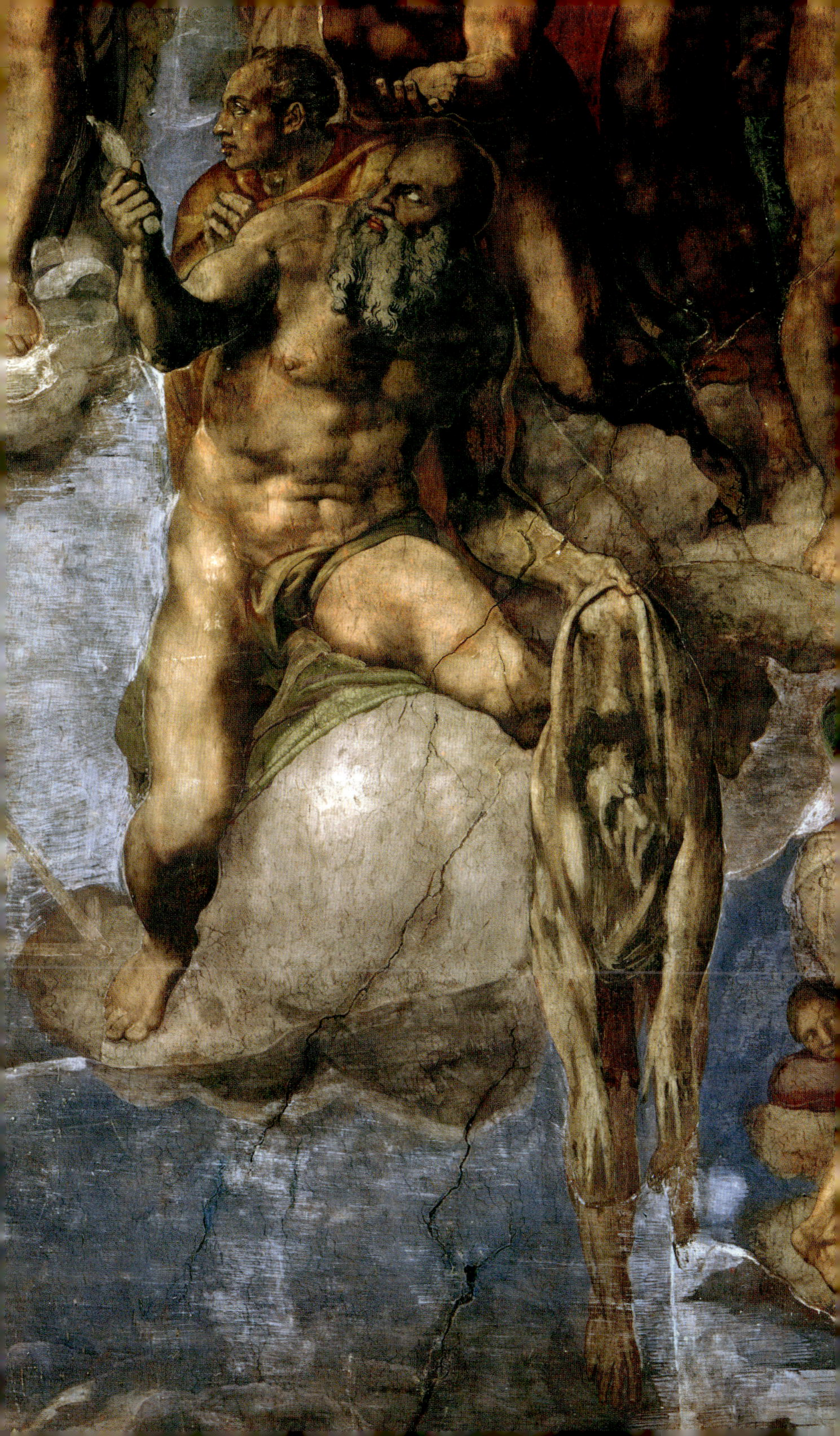

not Michelangelo's adult males, and hint at pederasty in their provocative, exhibitionist poses. His works are marked by parody and perversity. The contradictions and ambiguity found in these paintings are signs of his modernity, where tradition is eschewed in favour of conflict and where the viewer is called upon to interiorize and interpret.

While he followed the same visual sources as the Mannerists, Caravaggio used them differently, rejecting his predecessors' idealism in a renunciation not only of stylistic abstraction but of rhetorical elitism. The artificial poses found in Mannerist paintings, often anatomically impossible, embodied the idea of a studied grace as described in French and Italian books of manners. These manuals contained recommendations for deportment that in the sixteenth century were meant to imply an educated and courtly elegance.[12] Such contrived attitudes for figures continued to be used by painters into the seventeenth century, but Caravaggio's work went a long way towards eliminating their use. In conceiving of his protagonists in this new way, he aimed to replace the shopworn figures of previous religious art with more ambiguous subjects, who demonstrate psychologically believable reactions to divine events from an earthly point of view as they struggle with sacred mysteries. In their boldly realistic expressions, Caravaggio's figures often seem bluntly stunned or puzzled in their reactions to Christ or angels.

Through his realism, Caravaggio isolates his subjects, clarifying and intensifying them in narratives that are both original and startling but still resonate with centuries of religious tradition. His novelty, which centred principally on his realistic figures and tenebrism, held immediate appeal for young artists all over Europe, who wholeheartedly imitated his manner. Giovanni Pietro Bellori wrote that the young artists of Rome 'looked on his works as miracles', and began searching the piazzas and streets for their models.[13] More traditional critics and artists of a classical bent hated his style: later in the century Nicolas Poussin said that Caravaggio had 'come into the world to destroy painting'.[14] Bellori the arch-classicist found much to criticize in Caravaggio's work: 'He did not know how to come out of the cellar [referring to Caravaggio's murky settings] . . . [he lacked] *invenzione* and *disegno* . . . decorum or art . . . but such accusations did not stop the flight of his fame.'[15]

Bellori had no serious objection to the realism in Caravaggio's early secular works; he greatly admired the detail in his still-lifes of flowers and fruit in his youthful pictures. So did Baglione, who was normally withering in his criticism of Caravaggio. It was the artist's mature works they particularly disliked, his large-scale religious paintings with realistic protagonists enclosed within obscure backgrounds. What they found objectionable in his religious canvases was not merely the high degree of realism in his figures, but their conception as uncompromisingly mundane, low-class and even vulgar. Caravaggio's critics often failed to read the psychological expressiveness of his figures correctly. In his *Cours de peinture par principes* (1708), Roger de Piles gave Caravaggio a score of 'o' for expression because, he declared, he merely copied nature and therefore this aspect of art was not important to him. In fact, Caravaggio's artistic expression is powerful, as such later critics as Denis Diderot recognized, but also subtle, anti-classical and quite intentional.[16]

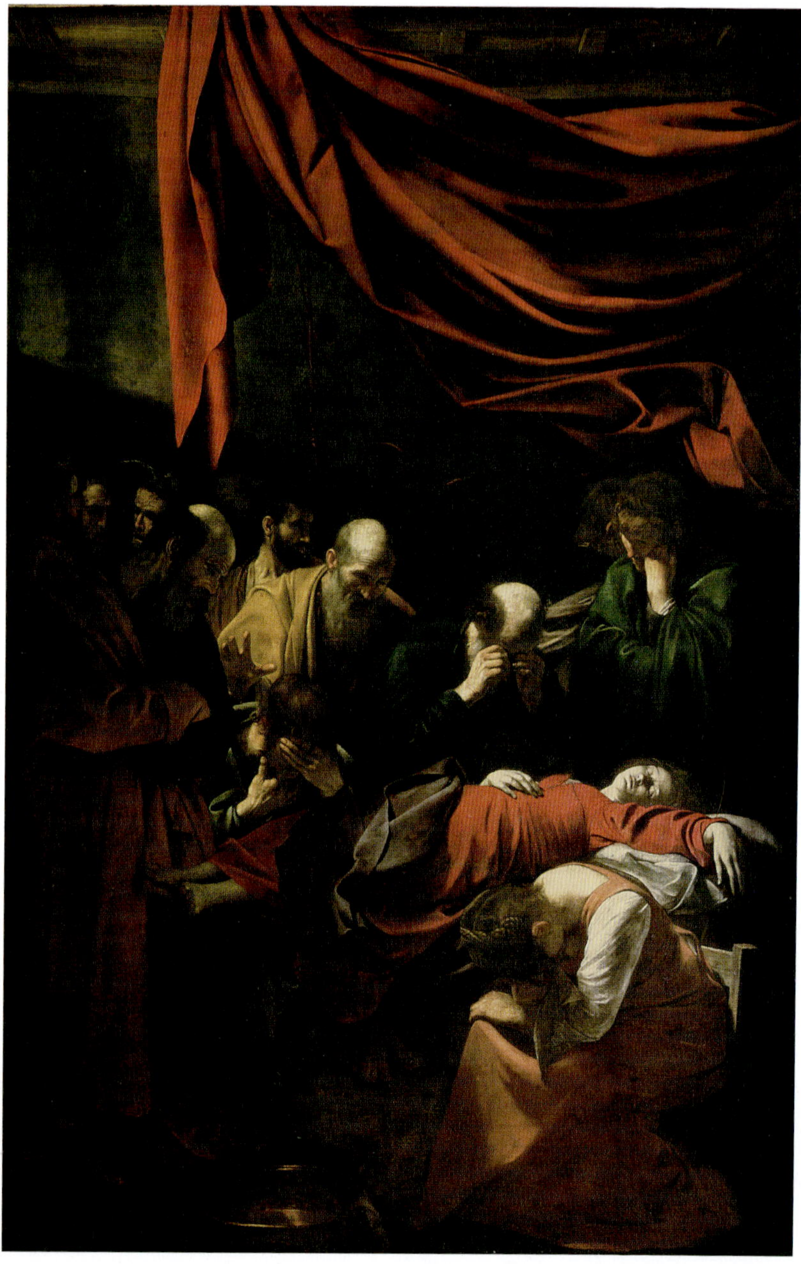

FIVE

The Divine and the Human

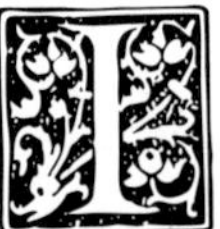N HIS PLAIN-SPOKEN new style, Caravaggio is modern in making clearer than earlier artists the gulf between the mundane and heavenly worlds. He viewed existence from a resolutely human perspective, candidly depicting the difficulty his mortals had in recognizing divinity. More so than most of his peers, he invited the viewer to ponder the relationship of the human and heavenly domains through his failure to depict the latter. He declined to paint the heavens not because he merely recorded what he saw in front of him; rather, he avoided painting divine visions because of a conscious choice to suppress them.

This unknowability of the heavens was part of Caravaggio's constructed world, his mediated vision; it was not the result of a naive *Dasein*, of his own 'being here' in Martin Heidegger's phenomenological sense of total focus on his own existence in the immediate present of the studio.[1] Rather, he articulated his black backgrounds to stand symbolically for humanity's incomprehension of things beyond immediate earthly experience. Some saw him as a secular artist who was openly impious in his paintings; he sometimes represented saints in ways that appeared unseemly to his contemporaries, in scenes that often hinted at ambiguity and irony. In about 1620, a

26 Caravaggio, *Death of the Virgin*, 1604–6, oil on canvas.

decade after Caravaggio's death, Giulio Mancini objected to Caravaggio's *Death of the Virgin* (illus. 26) for its perceived violation of doctrinal propriety. Mancini called his unidealized model for Mary a 'dirty prostitute from the Ortaccio', and explained that 'the good Fathers rejected [the picture] for that reason.'[2] In the marginal notes to his life of Caravaggio, Mancini added that the model for the Virgin was the courtesan lover of the artist. Here Mancini refers to a real woman, perhaps even knowing her name, although it has been suggested that his intention was metaphorical, using the term 'meretrice sozza' (dirty prostitute) as a rhetorical figure, in order to comment on the lowly and inappropriate style of the painting.[3] In either case, Caravaggio's Virgin seemed to Mancini nothing more than a bloated corpse, her blank face lit disagreeably from below and revealing nothing beatific. Her simple bier is surrounded by Mary Magdalen and the barefoot Apostles, all quietly weeping and grieving over the loss of her companionship.

Caravaggio is known to have used prostitutes as models in his religious works. In earlier paintings these had included Anna Bianchini, who probably posed as Mary Magdalen in his *Penitent Magdalen* (see illus. 13) and as the Virgin Mary in his *Rest on the Flight into Egypt* (see illus. 14), and Fillide Melandroni, who appears as Mary in his *Conversion of the Magdalen* (see illus. 50) and in *St Catherine of Alexandria* (see illus. 16). It may be that the sword in the latter painting was perceived as a phallic symbol, and Fillide's running her finger along it taken as a sexual pun. It would not have been at all unusual for wags of the time to see sexual imagery in sacred pictures, and here Caravaggio seems to have invited such an interpretation. The ambiguity of images such as these arose from the viewer's uncertainty as to whether such figures were saints at all, or low-life types inappropriate for religious paintings.

The *Death of the Virgin* typifies Caravaggio's radically modern conception of the relationship of human experience to divinity. Instead of imagining, as his predecessors had done, that a natural or 'normalizing' relationship exists between the mundane and celestial worlds and that the latter may readily be depicted in painting as having easy intercourse with the former, he perceives the impossibility of giving concrete form to a heaven beyond. For Caravaggio, the Apostles and saints, including Mary, belong to the world of unidealized mortals. His stark, unflinching presentation of Mary's mortality in this painting could not have been more unlike Carlo Saraceni's second, conventional version of this subject, which was chosen to replace Caravaggio's rejected work at the Church of Santa Maria della Scala. Saraceni's altarpiece (illus. 27) shows the Virgin very much alive as she sits up in bed, surrounded by adoring Apostles and worshippers, praying and looking up towards the heavens, which reveal a vision of angels making music and carrying flowers among clouds and golden light. Caravaggio chose to represent the Virgin dead, whereas Saraceni synthesized the subject of her death with her assumption. Clearly, in 1607, the year in which the Carmelite fathers rejected Caravaggio's work that had been commissioned six years earlier, they decided that they would have preferred a conflation of death and assumption, the *transito* or *dormitio*, the deathbed scene that shows the revivified Virgin about to ascend to the waiting heavens.[4] Caravaggio refused to speculate in paint about what he could not see,

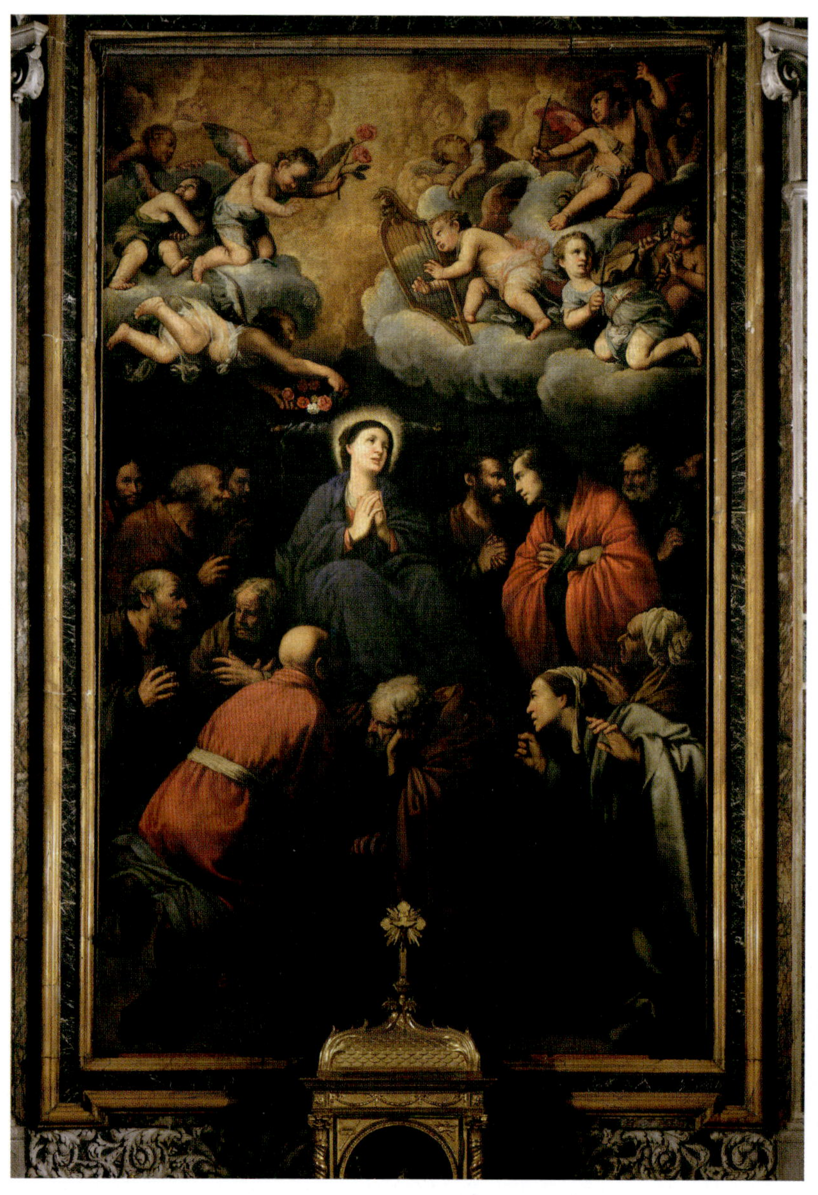

27 Carlo Saraceni, *Dormition of the Virgin*, 1607, oil on canvas.

insisting that the transcendent zone remain beyond human explanation or understanding.

In Caravaggio's other paintings, too, the customary signs of divinity are absent as the subjects are reconceptualized in earthly terms. None of the figures in his *Entombment of Christ* (see illus. 47), for example, have haloes. Caravaggio imagined that the majesty of Christ is sufficiently visible in his earthly embodiment, without halo, in almost all his representations of him. But even when Christ does have a halo, as in the *Calling of St Matthew* (see illus. 18, 46), the tax-gatherer Matthew is still caught unawares, uncertain how to react. Artists were expected to show Matthew's willingness to follow Christ, since the biblical story requires that he immediately accompany him, as indicated in Caravaggio's instructions for this painting: 'St Matthew . . . rises from the counter with the desire of following Our Lord.'[5] But by showing his puzzlement, Caravaggio reveals Matthew's human weakness, which Christ must overcome through the bestowal of an undeserved grace (see illus. 29). Caravaggio used Matthew's hesitancy as a means to create productive tension in his scene and to focus on the power of grace to overcome human indecision.[6] The artist is not working here from a secular impulse, but wishes to stress the tax-gatherer's modern and natural reaction by showing the foreignness of divinity from ordinary human experience as well as the potency of grace.

Another painting with a similar approach, *Doubting Thomas* (illus. 28), shows protagonists at first unaware that they are in the presence of divinity. Here, coarse peasant Apostles are surprised to discover sacred meaning in their narrative. Thomas and his two companions relinquish their disbelief and instantly become followers when the sceptical disciple probes Christ's wound with his finger. Caravaggio made the painting shortly after completing his work in the Cerasi chapel, for the wealthy banker and intellectual the Marchese Vincenzo Giustiniani. Vincenzo and his brother Benedetto, who were known for their art collection, probably asked Caravaggio to paint the *Doubting Thomas* because, through their close association with the Roman Oratory, they had ties to San Tommaso in Parione, a church dedicated to this saint. In the painting, the artist contrasts the celestial (in the person of a halo-less Christ) with the rough Apostles. The distinction is subtle, for his Christ, hardly spiritualized, has a realistic torso and an unsavoury wound. Thomas's graphically probing finger is disturbing in the depth of its insertion into this wound. His digital penetration was important to Catholic reformers, who used this act as proof of Christ's Resurrection and divinity, thus providing a powerful message of faith in a story about doubt.[7] Most interpreters of the painting see Christ as grasping Thomas's hand and drawing his forefinger into the wound in his side. But the Lord's concerned expression may indicate that Thomas has penetrated his flesh too far, causing him pain, and that with his left hand he prevents his follower from pushing further. In either case, physical tangibility is given privilege over divine otherworldliness.

Caravaggio's art makes clear the gulf that separates humanity and divinity. This division is achieved both psychologically, through his earthly protagonists, and physically, as when he isolates his all too real angels at the top of his canvases, or avoids representing God the Father altogether. An understanding of his new kind of painting required a sophisticated viewer,

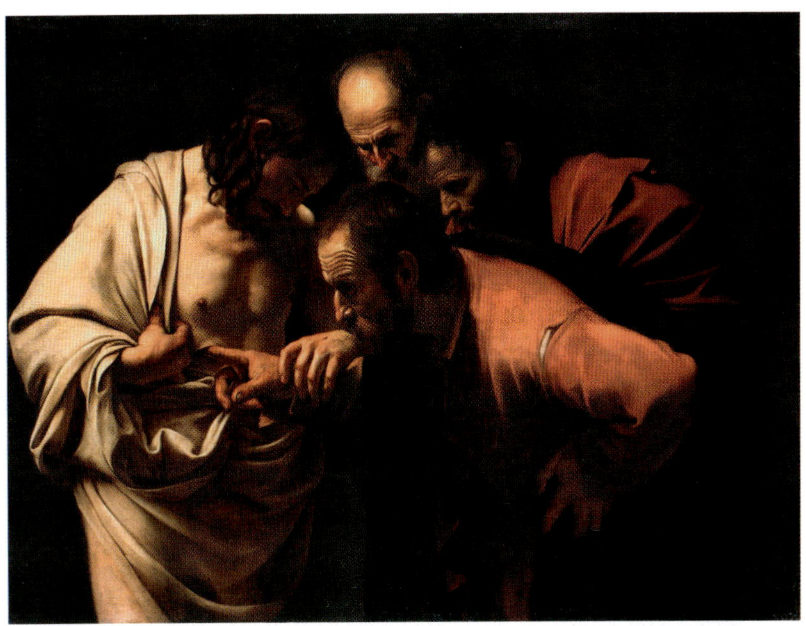

knowledgeable about the long-established theological concept of humanity's ignorance of the divine world. In conceiving this gap between human experience and an unknown divine domain, Caravaggio was still working from a religious impulse. His figures, while entirely human, struggle with faith, and the ironic depiction of a saint may indeed be justified by appeal to Church traditions of biblical exegesis.

For example, Caravaggio puts the viewer of his first *Inspiration of St Matthew* (see illus. 36, 37) in a position to be amused by the Apostle's intense effort to understand the text before him, since the observer may already be familiar with the opening lines of Matthew's Gospel and the way they link Old and New Testaments. The artist shows the awkward and massive Matthew as a simpleton to underline the idea that

28 Caravaggio, *Doubting Thomas*, 1601–2, oil on canvas.

he freely accepts divine aid from the angel in order to write his Gospel. A parallel may be drawn between Caravaggio's simple-minded Matthew and certain qualities prized by Filippo Neri, the leader of the Oratorians in Rome, who was famous for his love of playing jokes and would hide the seriousness with which he took his devotions. Pietro Giacomo Bacci, who completed his life of Neri in 1622, made the point that the Roman founder of the Oratorio liked to be considered a man of little worth, and that he engaged in foolish behaviour to mask his wise humility. Bacci notes that Neri always kept in mind the maxim of the Apostle: 'If any man among you seems to be wise in this world, let him become a fool, that he may be wise' (1 Corinthians 3:18).[8] A similar point is made by St Ignatius Loyola in his *Spiritual Exercises*, when he states that he is 'willing to be considered as worthless and a fool for Christ', echoing a passage from the Bible (1 Corinthians 4:9–10): 'We [Apostles] are fools for Christ's sake.'[9] Such passages justify from a theological point of view Caravaggio's conception of Matthew's simple appearance.[10]

Even though ceiling frescoes of prophets and of *St Matthew Resurrecting the Daughter of the King of Ethiopia* (see illus. 52) by Giuseppe Cesari were already in place in the Contarelli chapel vault when Caravaggio painted there, he conceived a thematic unity centring on Matthew's reaction to divine aid in his three paintings, independent of Cesari's frescoes. The emphasis is psychological more than religious, and Matthew is passive before divinity. The three canvases reveal steps or stages in Matthew's access to divine power: his call to grace, inspiration to write and entry to heaven. But what we see is merely the struggle of the mortal Matthew to understand in the *Calling* (see illus. 18, 29) and first *Inspiration* (see illus. 36, 37), or, in the *Martyrdom* (see illus. 31), his helplessness in protecting himself. Caravaggio privileges the human over the celestial realm, and man's incomprehension or fear over divine revelation. As with his angel resting on a small, all too solid cloud set against the black background of the *Martyrdom*, Caravaggio allows virtually no escape to the grander supernatural realm. In emphasizing what he thought of as the proper relationship between the earthly and the divine, his conceptions came dangerously close to parody. Such is the case when Matthew in the first *Inspiration* seems a simpleton whose projecting foot appears to threaten the officiating priest in the chapel with a kick, or when in the *Calling* he questions Christ.

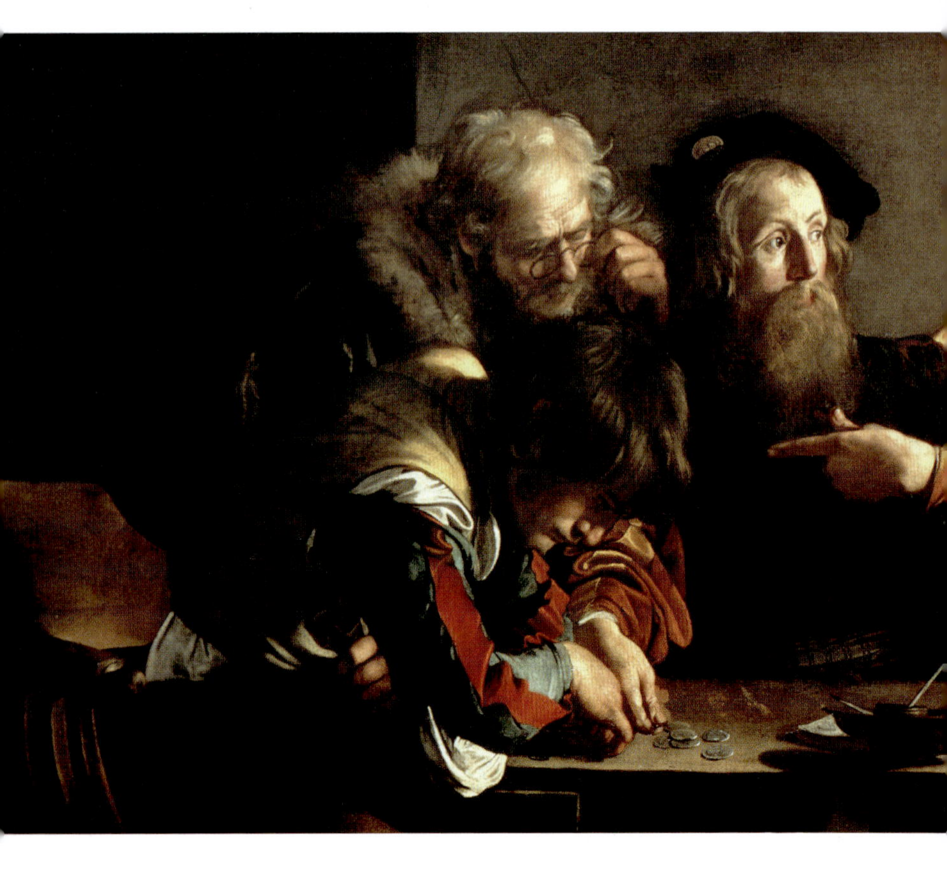

SIX

Ambiguity

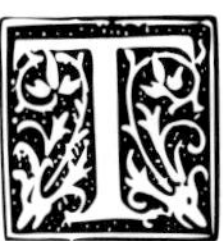

HE PRESENCE OF ambiguity in Caravaggio's art has been noticed by observers both in his time and in our own. One of the striking conundrums about his paintings is that, because of their rough realism and cryptic expressiveness, they admit of differing interpretations, sometimes seeming to undergird deep religious meaning, sometimes apparently undermining the same, and sometimes doing both at once. Ambiguity, a quintessentially modern aspect of Caravaggio's art, is part of his complex pictorial rhetoric that cannot be described as conventionally natural because of the wilfulness of his realism and his polysemous and unusual expressive choices. One finds it difficult to read his figures, to interpret his protagonists' emotional states and meanings. The viewer wonders what, for example, St Peter's stark, impenetrable expression really means as he is lifted on to his cross (*Crucifixion of St Peter*, see illus. 19, 49); why the Virgin is depicted as a bloated corpse laid out on a mortuary table (*Death of the Virgin*, see illus. 26); or whether the bug-eyed stare of St Peter Martyr at the right in the *Madonna of the Rosary* (see illus. 39) should be considered serious or parodic. The ambiguity of Caravaggio's paintings is thus highlighted, and their meanings remain in play.

29 Detail of St Matthew, old man and boy at left, from Caravaggio, *Calling of St Matthew*, 1599–1600, oil on canvas (illus. 18).

Caravaggio's ambiguity is partly a by-product of his insistence on 'real-world' attitudes and gestures for his figures, and of his refusal to use the stock reactions found in the visual rhetorical tropes of the immediate past that would have made their meanings more readable. His lack of clarity may also be built on the idea of creating deliberate ambiguity for reasons of reception, in order to engage the viewer in sensual and intellectual play, to present visually rich semantic puzzles and to encourage the observer to ponder deeply the mysteries of faith.[1] The conundrums to be found in his pictures may have been calculated by him to have particular appeal to private collectors and the sophisticated Roman intelligentsia, who could be counted on to create a buzz about his works.

The ambiguity in Caravaggio's paintings is far-reaching and foundational; the debate about which figure represents Matthew in the *Calling of St Matthew* (see illus. 18) has been sufficient for a few scholars to see it as undecidable.[2] Some interpreters have insisted that the bearded man seated at the centre of the table cannot be Matthew (illus. 29), because pointing to himself and questioning Christ would betray the whole point of his call to Apostleship and pervert the religious significance of the scene.[3] The boy at the left-hand end of the table has instead been identified as Matthew, but he has also been interpreted as a taxpayer or alternatively as a thief.[4] Caravaggio deliberately made it difficult for an observer visiting the Contarelli chapel for the first time to pick out Matthew among the figures at the table, in order to engage the viewer's interest and attention. It is highly likely that the traditional identification of Matthew as the bearded man in the centre of the table is correct. The artist's choice to depict Matthew before he follows Christ both stresses the suddenness of the latter's appearance and creates a dramatic, psychological tension between the two chief protagonists. While Caravaggio's Matthew, the bearded man, shows a certain interest in Christ through his alert eyes, he remains neutral, not animated in his readiness to follow the Lord, but less positive and more ambiguous in his pointing to himself in disbelief and uncertainty. Caravaggio's tax-gatherer is more realistic, less rhetorically fashioned than other artists' renderings of the saint in their paintings of this subject. For example, Matthew is shown humbly and devoutly ready to follow Christ in Ludovico Carracci's version (illus. 30), or he protests his unworthiness in Giuseppe Cesari's study and in Cristoforo Roncalli's fresco of this scene.[5]

If the setting in the painting across the chapel, the *Martyrdom of St Matthew* (illus. 31), is indeed a baptistery, Caravaggio exhibited his characteristic strangeness in hardly showing the baptismal water in the pool at the bottom. This is an important oversight if he wanted to make a point about the sacramental mixing of Matthew's blood with the water, recalling Christ's baptism, sacrifice and Resurrection and alluding to Matthew's death and spiritual rebirth. Whatever hint of water Caravaggio may have painted has darkened with age into an unrecognizable blackness. As it is, the artist put so little stress on the pool that some modern commentators are uncertain if the semi-nudes in the foreground are really neophytes awaiting baptism. Recently these figures have been interpreted as cripples healed by Matthew, but they are most probably candidates for baptism preparing to enter the pool.[6]

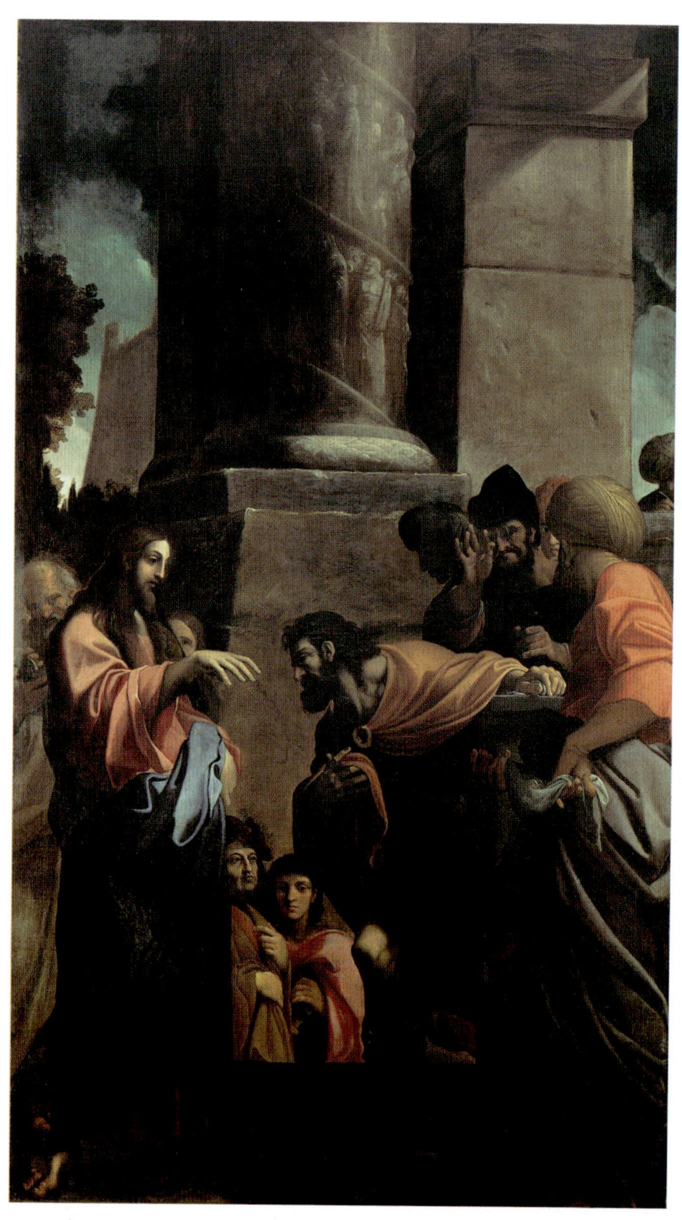

30 Ludovico Carracci, *Calling of St Matthew*, c. 1610, oil on canvas.

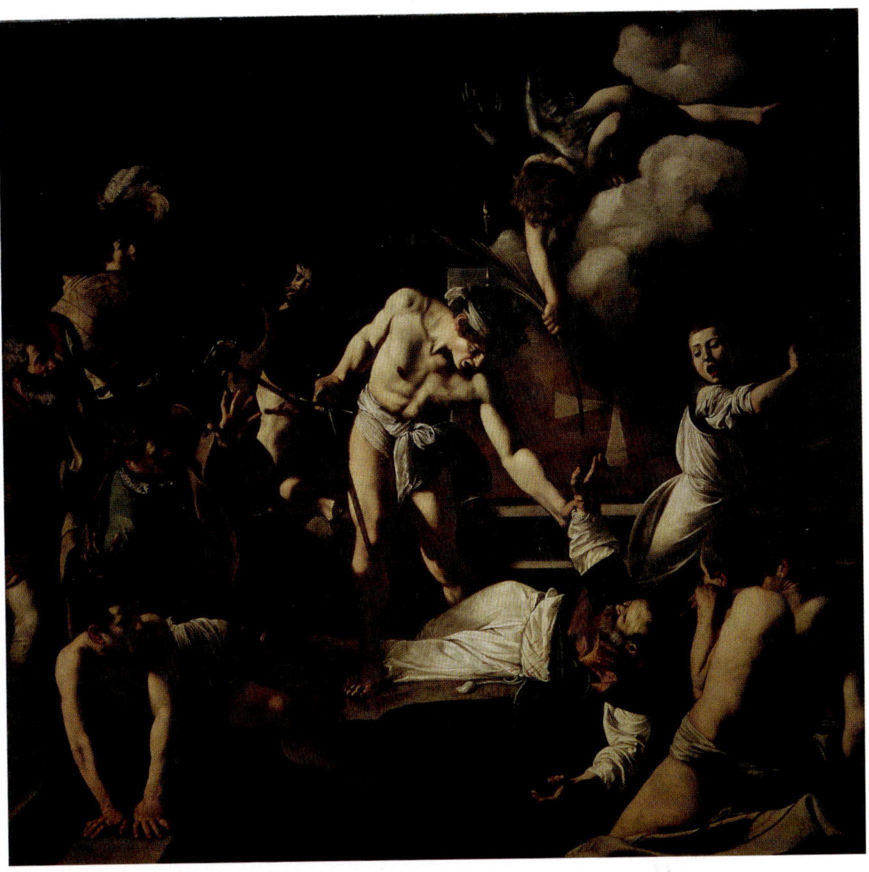

The angel in this painting is meant only for Matthew to see, and is unnoticed by the other figures, but in fact the saint himself shows no sign of recognizing the divine messenger. Even though Matthew's head is seen from above, it is clear that his gaze is fixed on his executioner. The saint is so preoccupied with the attack that he ignores the angel offering him the palm branch. He seems to protect himself from the executioner with the gesture of his right hand, which

31 Caravaggio, *Martyrdom of St Matthew*, 1599–1600, oil on canvas.

is actually turned (or wrenched by his killer) towards the angel and palm branch, suggesting – perhaps inadvertently, or perhaps with Caravaggio's characteristic strangeness – that Matthew is rejecting the palm rather than reaching for it, thus undermining the religious importance of God's grace and salvation. Once more, Caravaggio arranges his protagonist so that he fails to perceive the divine world, and the viewer is left to face a visual conundrum.

The ambiguity of Caravaggio's first *Inspiration of St Matthew* (see illus. 36, 37), intended as the altarpiece for this chapel, is twofold: first, rather than depict Matthew as suitably learned in writing his Gospel, the painter shows him as a coarse individual apparently incapable of composing the Hebrew text in front of him.[7] This characterization of the saint led Giovanni Pietro Bellori to perceive a lack of decorum in this painting, a view based on religious grounds as much as on the figure's want of classical idealization. Caravaggio's point here seems for once to align with the ideas of the conservative and ever-watchful Cardinal Gabriele Paleotti, who in his *Discourse on Sacred and Profane Images* states that the books of Holy Scripture were written not by men but by God through the hands of men.[8] Caravaggio's angel guiding the hand of the befuddled Matthew makes that point especially well.

The other ambiguity of this painting centres on the angel, whose sensuality seems out of place in an altarpiece. Indeed, the picture was rejected by the priests of San Luigi dei Francesi, then bought by Vincenzo Giustiniani, the wealthy banker, intellectual and ardent supporter of Caravaggio. It was Giustiniani who probably convinced Matteo Contarelli's executors to give Caravaggio a second chance to paint the

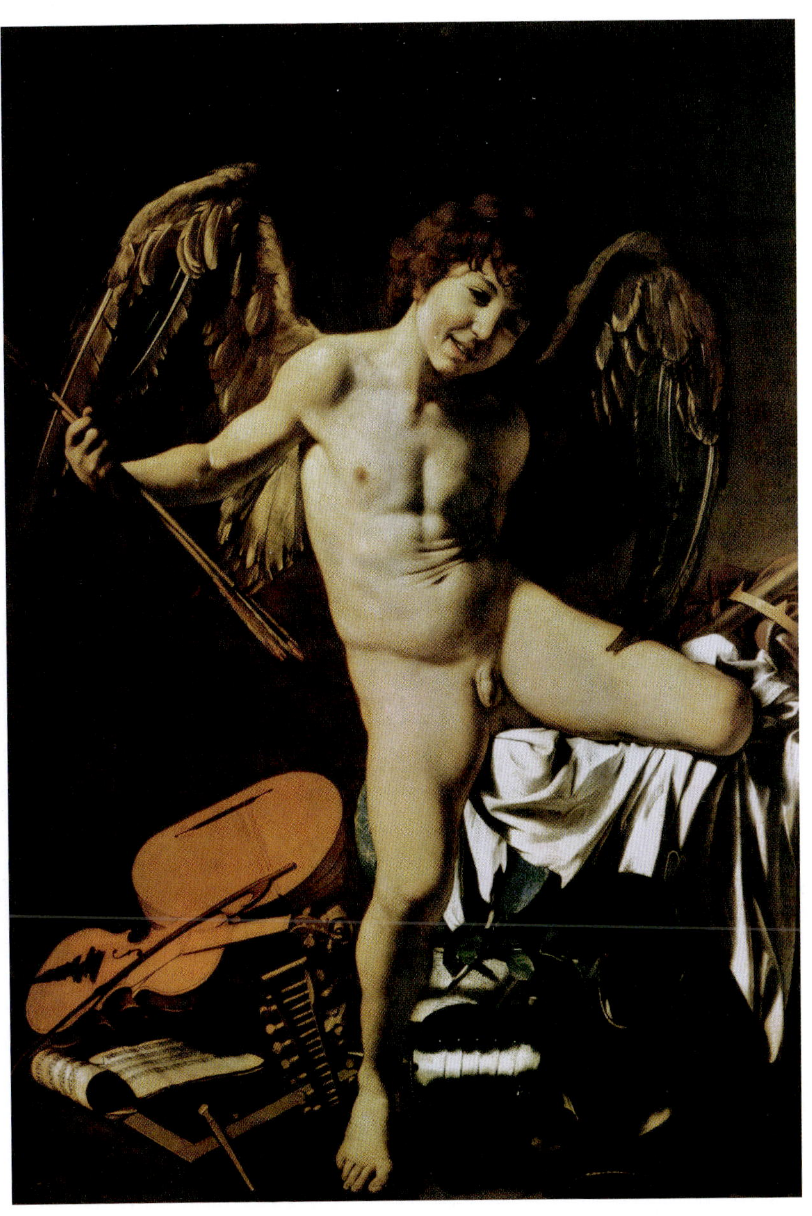

32 Caravaggio, *Victorious Cupid*, 1601–2, oil on canvas.

altarpiece for the chapel; he also probably helped the painter to get the commission for the two Cerasi chapel canvases. He had Caravaggio paint the *Doubting Thomas* (see illus. 28) for him, and the *Victorious Cupid* (illus. 32).

Deprived of its stable religious function, the first *Inspiration* once rejected would have been subjected to the patterns of secular discourse and exchange attendant on private patronage. The painting's sensuous young angel, in many ways similar to the Cupid in Giustiniani's *Victorious Cupid*, would inevitably be compared to the latter. In the *Victorious Cupid*, the love god displays his provocative and indeed sexual victory over the sublimation of desire that accompanies serious humanist endeavour, as represented through its emblems strewn below the boy: instruments symbolizing politics, architecture, music, war and fame. In such a comparison, the eroticism of the angel in the first *Inspiration* would have been magnified, and Cupid in the other picture would be seen to relish his own outrageous seductiveness hinting at pederasty and his defeat of decorum.[9] The ambiguity of the *Victorious Cupid* has led to opposing interpretations, ranging from the triumph of flagrant sexuality to the metaphorical evocation of *amor divino* (divine love). The latter alternative seems difficult to imagine; conceiving of the angel in the first *Inspiration* as representing divine love is equally challenging. Caravaggio must have meant something else: most probably he savoured the idea of using an ironic, sensuous kind of allure as a stand-in for a divine beauty that was beyond human capacity to represent. He sometimes sacrifices religious or sombre allegorical meaning in favour of ironic and aesthetic play, through which he generates a sense of surprise, richness and complexity in his characters.

In the first few years of the seventeenth century Caravaggio had what seemed to be an endless stream of new and important public commissions. By June 1601 he had moved out of Cardinal Del Monte's palace to live with Cardinal Girolamo Mattei, probably staying with him until 1603. As Cardinal Protector of the observant Franciscans, the strict branch of the order, Mattei may have influenced Caravaggio to paint harsh and simple pictures, including the two canvases in the Cerasi chapel.[10] Next door to the cardinal lived his two brothers, Ciriaco and Asdrubale, eager collectors of ancient Roman sculpture as well as contemporary art. For Ciriaco Caravaggio painted several pictures, including *St John the Baptist in the Wilderness* (illus. 33), *Supper at Emmaus* (see illus. 45) and the *Taking of Christ* (see illus. 42). Ciriaco's *St John the Baptist in the Wilderness*, like Giustiniani's secular *Victorious Cupid*, seems a salacious, even lewd painting, apparently lacking the propriety called for by Carlo Borromeo or by Gabriele Paleotti in his proscriptive book on sacred painting. The ambiguity of this work is so pronounced that the identity of the boy as St John has been questioned: he has been called variously the mythological character Phryxus, the shepherd Paris or Abraham's son Isaac.[11] By showing the boy naked, without a reed cross, and with a ram instead of a lamb, the artist seems deliberately obfuscatory. At first puzzling, the ram is not necessarily an irrelevant distraction, since the sacrificial ram is a symbol of Christ. The ram and the grapevines in the background may indicate that, after all, the boy is probably St John the Baptist, who smiles because of his vision of the death of Christ and the salvation of humankind.[12] This sort of Christological interpretation of the boy, taken together with his frank and

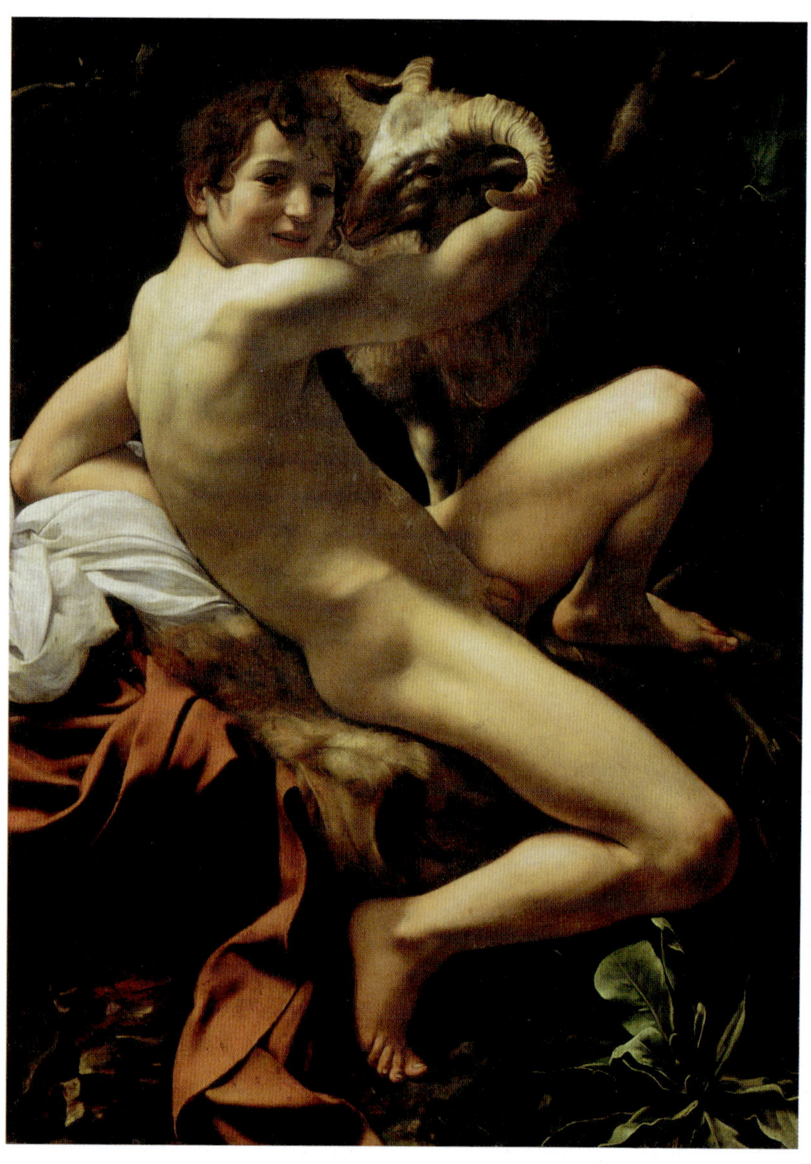

33 Caravaggio, *St John the Baptist in the Wilderness*, 1601–2, oil on canvas.

sensual nakedness, indicates the dichotomous, complex nature of Caravaggio's art.

It may be that the indirect quality of Caravaggio's paintings was deliberate. His pictures undermine clear readings and generate contradictory meanings; furthermore, the ambiguous gestures and demeanours of his figures make it difficult to determine their roles and actions in his paintings. One of his strategies may have been to establish a 'resistance to didactic clarity' in his pictures to underline for the viewer the limitations of human sight or reason for apprehending divine revelation, to reinvigorate for the beholder of his paintings a sense of religious mystery.[13]

Caravaggio used a visual language different from the norm of his time, so much so that his pictures are characterized by an effective multi-level alterity, originality and unconventionality where he transgressed the standards of a rules-based artistic system. At the same time that his sophisticated patrons noticed his violation of artistic codes for devotional reasons, they also respected his works for their aesthetic or intellectual character or as specimens of their genre. In terms of reception theory and viewer response, therefore, Caravaggio allowed for the observer's cerebral and aesthetic sense where a play of meaning was encouraged that created intellectual and sensual engagement. Caravaggio's unconventionality involved an ironic subversion of the previous norms of decorum and artistic expression that had lost their orientating power and failed any longer to provide a sense of novelty or astonishment.[14]

Ambiguity was such a dominating topic in his paintings that while some observers saw positive religious meaning in them, others read them negatively. My arguments above suggest that the artist's ambiguities were at times intentional and fully conscious, but sometimes also unconscious and a result of his idiosyncrasies. In either case, uncertainty of meaning as an end in itself could not have been his goal with respect to the central Christian beliefs. His ambiguity was a means of engaging the viewer's attention, intended to draw the beholder into a serious and protracted engagement with the picture and the complexities of faith as experienced in reality.

In his religious pictures Caravaggio often represents, unexpectedly and audaciously, an intellectual or emotional comprehension in his figures more than a wholly spiritual reaction (see, for example, the *Inspiration of St Matthew*, see illus. 36; *Supper at Emmaus*, see illus. 45; *Doubting Thomas*, see illus. 28). Caravaggio may have flirted playfully with potentially negative religious ideas in his canvases in order to create tension and provocative richness in the mind of the beholder during the interpretive act. The thoughtful viewer wrestles with these ideas. This novel tactic opens up the crucial importance of the reception and interpretation of his work, an essential part of his modern approach. Caravaggio created a new kind of sensibility that can only be called modern because of its contingent and complex character. The viewer's perception remains dialectical and conflicted; indeed, the deep ambiguity of his art remains one of the most fascinating aspects that draws people to it.

A different kind of ambiguity is found in the Contarelli chapel, where Matthew's physical appearance in the first version of the *Inspiration of St Matthew* (see illus. 36, 37) departs markedly from the lateral canvases. In Caravaggio's earlier

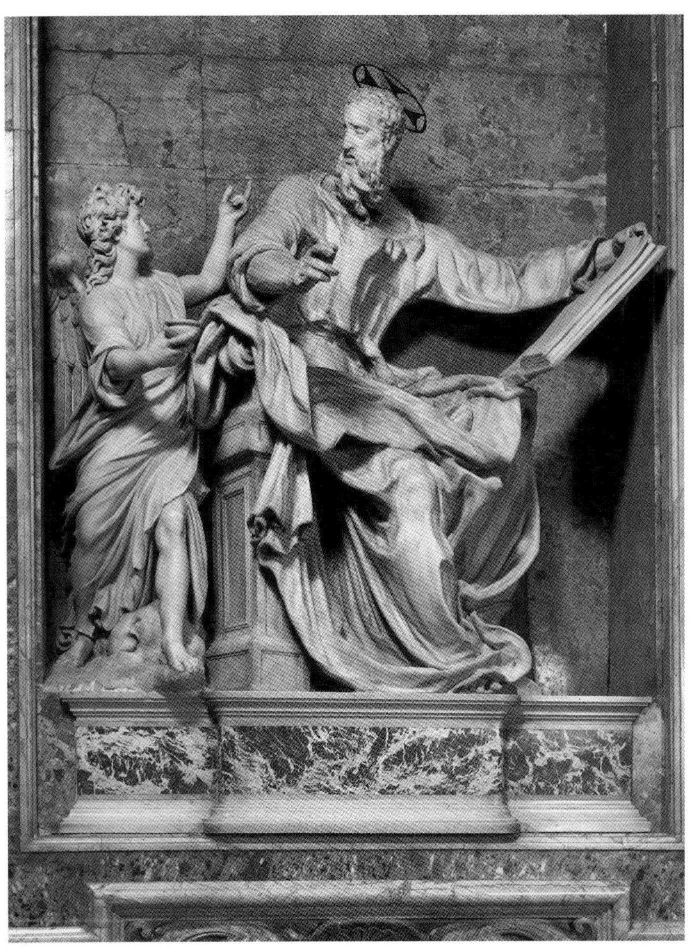

laterals (1599–1600), Matthew is slender, with a long face and pointed nose (see illus. 29, 31), whereas in the later *Inspiration*, painted in 1602, he is stocky and round-headed. No one has provided a convincing explanation as to why Caravaggio changed the appearance of the saint so radically. In 1587 the Flemish sculptor Jacob Cobaert had been commissioned to

34 Jacob Cobaert, *Inspiration of St Matthew*, 1587–1602, marble.

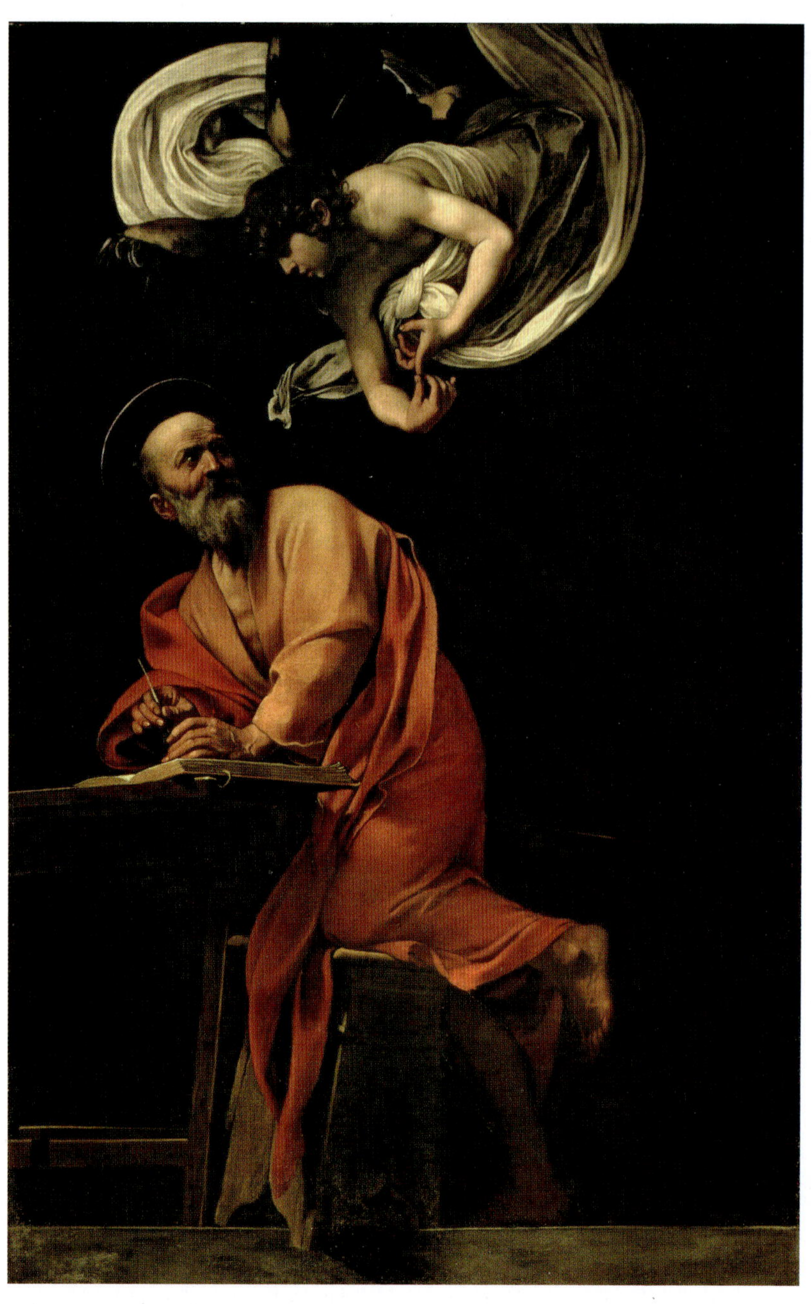

35 Caravaggio, *Inspiration of St Matthew*, 1602, oil on canvas.

make a marble sculpture of the *Inspiration* as the altarpiece for the chapel (illus. 34).[15] In January 1602 Cobaert's sculpture was finally installed on the altar and immediately rejected by the priests of San Luigi dei Francesi, probably on the basis of insufficient aesthetic interest, paving the way for Caravaggio's commission to paint an altarpiece to replace it.[16]

The very fact that Cobaert was still working on his marble sculpture in 1602 is an impediment to the argument for a date as early as the late 1590s for Caravaggio's first *Inspiration*, as some scholars have claimed in order to account for Matthew's different appearance from the laterals.[17] According to this theory, Caravaggio's first *Inspiration* was a temporary trial piece, to be replaced later. The contract of February 1602 for Caravaggio's first *Inspiration* was discovered in the 1960s, indicating that this work was begun after Cobaert's statue was found unsuitable.[18] Thus why Caravaggio so dramatically changed the physical appearance of the saint in his first *Inspiration*, after he had established another facial and bodily type in the *Calling* (see illus. 29) and *Martyrdom* (see illus. 31), is a puzzle that art historians have not solved. The saint's appearance is consistent in Caravaggio's laterals, and also in his second version of the altarpiece, painted later (see illus. 35). In the first *Inspiration* (see illus. 36), Matthew is as different as he could be from the saint depicted in the side paintings. The Matthew of Caravaggio's laterals and his second *Inspiration* is similar in appearance to the thin, long-nosed saint as represented in Jacob Cobaert's sculpture. The reason for the change could be that Caravaggio wanted to distance himself from the saint's physiognomy as established by Cobaert in his marble.

Cobaert's saint was in a relatively finished state by 1599, and had no doubt been seen by Caravaggio before he started his laterals. When painting them, Caravaggio had most probably been asked to follow the physical characteristics of Cobaert's saint. An artist deeply committed to originality, Caravaggio must have resented being asked to follow a precedent established by another artist, and a not very prominent sculptor at that. Once Cobaert's statue group was rejected, Caravaggio wasted no time in discarding Matthew's features as envisioned by the sculptor. In creating a new physical type for Matthew in his first altarpiece, Caravaggio appears to have valued his artistic freedom and creativity more highly than the consistency of the saint's appearance in the chapel. The reason for the rejection of the painter's first attempt at the altarpiece, probably in late 1602, may have been, in addition to the problem of indecorousness, the fact that Matthew did not look like the man in the laterals. Caravaggio found that a solid man of proletarian stock was more expressively apt for his idea of a simple person who is instructed like a backward schoolchild by an overbearing angel; he was so insistent in rejecting Cobaert's conventional approach that he was willing to rupture the unity of the chapel's imagery.

SEVEN

Oppositional Meanings

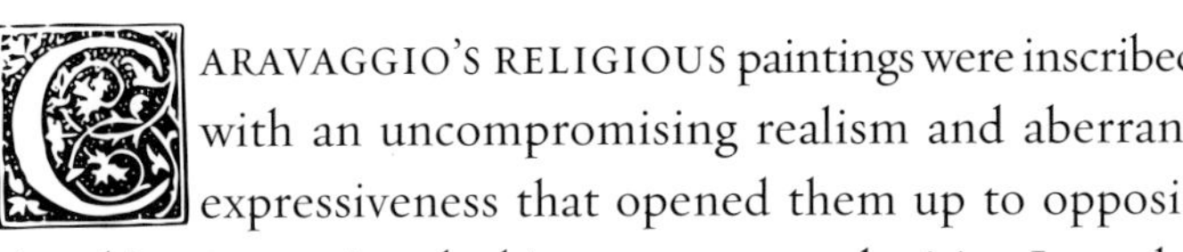

CARAVAGGIO'S RELIGIOUS paintings were inscribed with an uncompromising realism and aberrant expressiveness that opened them up to oppositional interpretations by his supporters and critics. I use the word 'oppositional' to mean that his paintings permit both positive and negative readings of their religious content. Some critics asserted that the artist had a profane approach to sacred art, while others claimed for him an authentic religious expression, giving rise to antonymic or oppositional evaluations of his work. Indeed, his pictures seem to elicit either positive or negative interpretations, based on their elusive, bold realism and the anomalous expressive choices made by the artist, often centring on protagonists who fail to exhibit clear signs of faith. In their reception, his works have proven to be unstable and heterogeneous, with antipodal meanings suggested particularly through his figures' stark demeanours and their puzzled reactions to Christ or angels. Through the course of this chapter I will show how, up to a point, such oppositional interpretations may be explained or reconciled.

The oppositional (positive or negative) religious readings of Caravaggio's paintings have been instrumental in shaping the artist's mixed reception, starting in his own time and continuing to today. Many observers of his canvases in his own era were unable to perceive their positive aspects, and the dialectical reception of his pictures' content persists. On the one hand, Caravaggio's paintings seem devoid of religious content, by their insistent realism, by their stress on humanity's isolation from the divine realm, by their depiction of his protagonists' apparent lack of spiritual understanding and by their strong *chiaroscuro*, implying emptiness. The painter's contemporary biographers, most of whom were biased in favour of classicism, rejected his frank realism, maintaining that his pictures lacked propriety and were devoid of religious feeling. On the other hand, some few argued that his paintings were deeply expressive in religious terms. To those attuned to his works, he succeeded almost overnight in banishing the abstracted and idealized effects of later sixteenth-century Roman art, making them seem instantly outdated. For the faithful who responded positively to his new style, his paintings renewed the apparent truth of images. Rather than exemplifying secularism, the realism found in Caravaggio's works points to the way that the divine may be concretely and vividly imagined by human beings, constrained as they are by the limits of corporeal understanding.

One of Caravaggio's chief oppositional strategies was to think through the style and content of religious painting in terms of genre painting, which was just emerging in Rome during his early years there. He revealed his modernizing impulse by secularizing religious painting, but also, by incorporating it into sacred works, sacralizing genre painting. It is this secular impulse, as seen in the *bravi* from his *Cardsharps* (see illus. 9) inserted into his *Calling of St Matthew* (see illus.

18), taken together with his commonplace realism, that lies at the root of the controversy over Caravaggio and informs his oppositional approach to sacred art. He quickly found that his strategy of inventing an antinomic form of religious art, including such blunt protagonists as his reluctant Matthew in the *Calling*, created both controversy and fame for himself.

An oppositional approach to Caravaggio's art continues among critics today; some scholars define him as a secular realist devoid of religious expression, and others find deep religious conviction in virtually every one of his works.[1] What I see in Caravaggio's art as a whole is a dialectical process in which both the negative and positive aspects of his religious expression are implicit, but in which the positive aspects are seen to predominate once his religious conceptions are carefully considered.

For example, each of Caravaggio's three canvases (omitting for the moment the second version of the *Inspiration*) made for the Contarelli chapel has qualities that seem problematic, even negative, in terms of religion and propriety, focusing on Matthew's hesitation in the *Calling* (see illus. 29), bewilderment in the first *Inspiration* (illus. 36, 37) and distress in the *Martyrdom* (see illus. 31). Such images support the contention among his critics of Caravaggio's strangeness and his contrary approach to religious subjects, as Giovanni Pietro Bellori and others tell us.

But, positively, these three Contarelli paintings show intervention by superior forces holding the promise of divine grace, predominating over weak human volition or understanding. Matthew is acted upon positively by divinity: in the *Calling* by Christ, who bestows grace, and in the first *Inspiration*

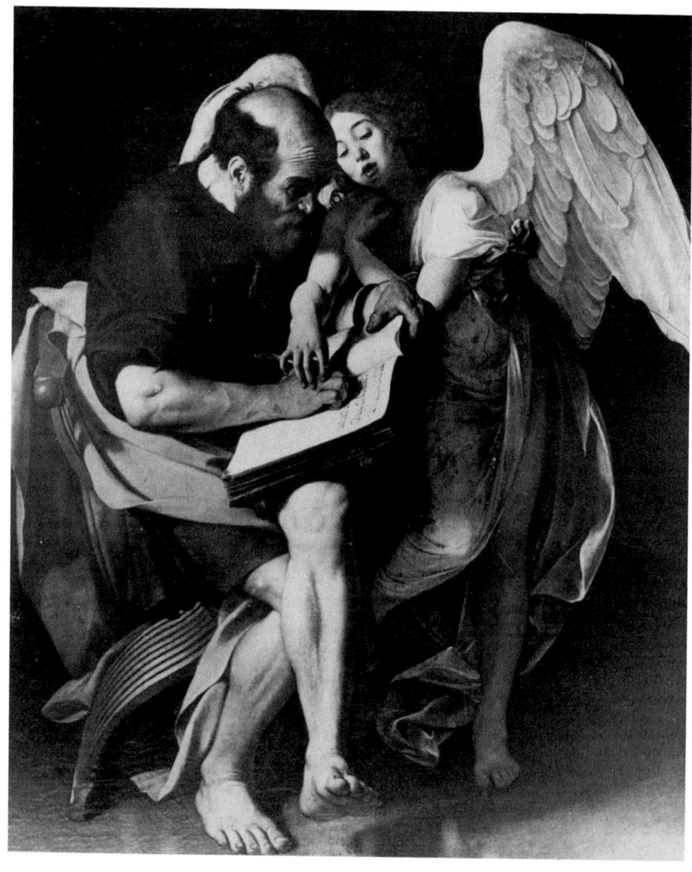

and the *Martyrdom* by angels, who offer divine aid and access to heaven. Up to a point, the problems of negative or positive religious interpretations of Caravaggio's art may be resolved by examining more deeply his expressive and sacred purposes and how those are entwined with the writings of his ecclesiastical contemporaries and forebears. Nevertheless, the opposition between the mundane or secular side of his art and the spiritual side remains in play and is never entirely

36 Caravaggio, *Inspiration of St Matthew*, 1602, oil on canvas. Destroyed.

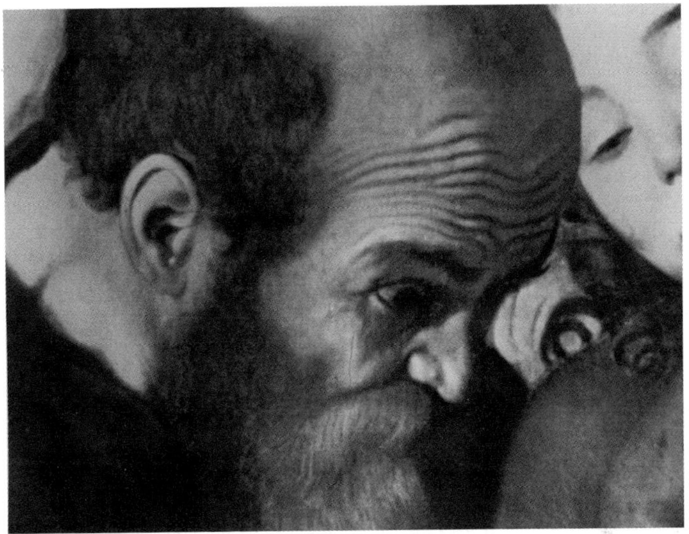

resolved within the reception of his work; it is this conflict, in part, through an emphasis on the viewer's response and a dialectical approach, that makes his art modern.

Many writers from the seventeenth century until the present have asserted that Caravaggio presents unvarnished reality in his paintings, the reality of his studio models that focuses exclusively on the here and now, on that which is seen. The scenes he presents as factual in his art, as real, are actually imaginative historical and biblical reconstructions disguised to look as real as possible, even if they include appearances of Christ or angels. His paintings do not present unmediated reality, but are based on an ideological position, one that asserts the limitation of humanity's ability to imagine that which lies beyond material existence. This position can be misconstrued as anti-religious. It is likely that Caravaggio was aware of the possible negative interpretation of his art,

37 Detail of head of St Matthew, from Caravaggio, *Inspiration of St Matthew*, 1602, oil on canvas (destroyed; illus. 36).

and capitalized on it so as to create controversy that would further his career and his fame. He was not devious to the point of slyly *authorizing* negative attitudes towards religion to lurk beneath the surface of his imagery, but he may have intended in a clever way to permit negative religious ideas to be *suggested* in order to create tension and to challenge the beholder to confront his paintings and engage deeply with them.

Some scholars have called attention to Caravaggio's ambiguity.[2] When they use that term they usually mean 'indeterminacy', in the sense that one cannot work out exactly what Caravaggio's pictures signify because of the way they are constructed or the uncertain manner in which the protagonists interact. The word I have been using here, 'oppositional', indicates a conflicted sacred content because his paintings may be read positively or negatively from a religious point of view. Caravaggio's pictures, in my opinion, are more oppositional than they are indeterminate because, in the end, positive religious meanings prevail in his paintings. Even so, many have detected negative religious meanings in his works, for example Giulio Mancini in the seventeenth century, or some present-day scholars.[3]

Caravaggio's novelty in the *Calling* (see illus. 18), in which Matthew questions Christ, entailed oppositional aspects from a religious point of view, expressed neatly in the positive summoning of Christ and the problematic resistance by Matthew. The psychological power and expressive force of the painting depend on this oppositional tension. The claim that the bearded man in the *Calling* cannot be Matthew because he does not immediately follow Christ, as the Bible requires, may be rejected. Instead, it seems that here Caravaggio adopts an Augustinian approach where we see God's mysterious grace (represented in the pointing Christ at the right) working on the will of Matthew before he rises to follow him. The saint's quizzical reaction to Christ's call is an example of human incomprehension that is overcome by grace. The light that floods Matthew's face is suggestive more of the beginning of conversion than of any emotion the tax-collector's gaze might reveal. In a moment Matthew will find the attraction of Christ irresistible, and this divine power is what the Augustinians would emphasize.[4]

This stress on the hesitation of Matthew and the working of grace on his mind may be connected to the Molinist struggle between Dominicans and Jesuits over the relative merits of predestination and free will, subjects that were debated in the very years in which Caravaggio was at work in the Contarelli chapel.[5] Although Caravaggio most probably had no detailed knowledge of this debate, he may have been aware in general terms of the competing powers of grace and freedom in the process of conversion. During the earlier discussions concerning grace at the Council of Trent, a few substantial theologians took the Augustinian position that in the process of receiving justifying grace, humankind's will remained passive, not actively cooperating with God. Even if Caravaggio has preferred to stress Matthew's free will in showing him puzzling over Christ rather than demonstrating his faith, the money-gatherer looks towards the Lord with a neutral, benign and perhaps even receptive expression, showing his interest in him rather than rejection (see illus. 29). Matthew has turned his legs, visible under the table, in the direction of Christ, a gesture that is perhaps the first indication of his willingness to follow (see illus. 18). Christ's feet, which are difficult to make out at the bottom of the picture, show that he has already turned to walk away. His exit to the right signals his certainty that his call will be effective and that Matthew's will is about to be turned to good account. Through the operation of grace the oppositional aspects of this painting are transcended by a higher understanding. In the gesture of Caravaggio's Matthew, the usual piety suffers in the service of realistic emotion, but in the end a positive religious expression prevails.[6]

Caravaggio may have intended to make his pictures ambiguous, in part to be audacious and to appeal to a new kind of art market. But a deeper religious impulse lies behind his ambivalence. One way of looking at Caravaggio's paintings is to focus negatively on the gulf between humanity and divinity, as seen in his protagonists' incomprehension of things sacred; but from another point of view, the same pictures reveal astonished humans at the moment when they recognize spiritual truth. Instead of focusing on his protagonists' ignorance of divine things, one may stress instead their sudden comprehension, as in the *Supper at Emmaus* (see illus. 45) and *Doubting Thomas* (see illus. 28). In the first *Inspiration of St Matthew* (see illus. 36, 37), the saint may strike the viewer as an illiterate peasant, incapable of reading his Gospel, much less writing it. But in noticing his eyes, wide open in amazement, one realizes the painting's positive religious message: Matthew has a sudden revelation in reading and understanding the words the angel writes as it guides his hand. He grasps in a flash the deep significance of the forty generations listed at the beginning of his own Gospel, namely, their legitimization of Christ as the Messiah.[7]

The very difficulty protagonists such as Matthew have in recognizing the divine underlines the deeper significance of their sudden revelations. Humans' hard-won apprehension of the celestial world points to the great obstacles they have overcome in transcending their limited understanding in order to gain spiritual insight. Early Christian fathers such as St John Chrysostom had discussed the humble, lower-class origins of the Apostles and the divine intervention that was necessary for them to write their Gospels.[8] Caravaggio clearly shows Matthew's poverty, and he frames the angel's intervention as active, setting the stage for the saint's sudden comprehension of the text before him. This picture was intended through the humble Apostle to appeal to the masses of the poor, but after its rejection it ended up in the collection of Vincenzo Giustiniani, the influential supporter of Caravaggio's career, who offered to buy the work for his private gallery because he seems to have appreciated its strangeness, adventurousness and even seditiousness.[9] The painting thus appealed equally to simple churchgoers and to sophisticated collectors, exemplifying another oppositional characteristic of Caravaggio's art.

There is no painting that Caravaggio made with only a negative religious meaning; where a negative connotation seems to prevail, the problem may lie in the faulty reception of the picture by viewers, as in the instance of the artist's hostile seventeenth-century detractors. In the case of his *Death of the Virgin* (see illus. 26) – for which Giustiniani had helped him to gain the commission and secured a high price in his contract with the patron, Laerzio Cherubini – Caravaggio was in the end criticized for representing the Virgin as uncompromisingly commonplace. To the priests of Santa Maria della Scala, who read the painting negatively, the quotidian world of the work seemed sharply removed from the heavenly one they envisioned. To them, the Virgin's depiction as a cadaver was fatal to the success of the work. But for those able to perceive it, the grieving Apostles gathered around the Virgin show genuine human feeling at her loss, and the red curtain at the top of the painting in fact alludes to her transport to heaven. The viewer who perceives the painting in this way may choose to set aside the negative view that focuses on the Virgin's dead body, and attend to this alternative conception, one that is more positive in religious terms. The artist created tension in his viewers' reception of the painting, so much so that the interpretive problems could not have been easily resolved. Many argued that he failed to emphasize the sacred content or refused to grant his works divine purpose.

The idea of positive and negative religious attitudes is supported by the play of oppositional themes in late sixteenth-century preaching. Such antipodal themes are found in the homilies of Cornelio Musso, Bishop of Bitonto and a renowned orator who revived the patristic model of the homily. He was prominent at the Council of Trent, particularly for his position on justification. He saw existence as constituted of paired opposites, 'hate and love, fear and hope, joy and sadness; punishment and reward, vituperation and praise, merit and demerit, salvation and damnation'.[10] Such antinomies are derived from the ideas of St Augustine, whose Christian message was founded simultaneously on hope and punishment, love and fear. For Musso, Christ comes both to redeem and to judge. Caravaggio thought deeply about structuring his canvases through oppositions that were important to him: the contrast of secular and sacred, human and divine.

After the *Calling* and *Martyrdom*, *bravi* disappeared from Caravaggio's pictures, to be replaced by peasants and roughly dressed, barefoot holy figures. For the Augustinian Church in Rome, Sant' Agostino, he made the *Madonna di Loreto* (illus. 38), with kneeling peasants praying before the Madonna and Child. Giovanni Baglione and Bellori both criticized this painting because of the exposed legs and muddy feet of the male pilgrim and the soiled and torn cap of the old woman, both of whom kneel before the Virgin and Child. Baglione claimed that 'because of this pettiness in the details of a grand painting the public [*popolani*] made a great fuss [*schiamazzo*] over it.'[11] The perception of such impropriety demonstrates sensitivity among viewers to indecorous details in a painting near an altar. Such a picture, so people thought, should stress the divinity of the scene. Furthermore, Caravaggio's painting could have been construed to imply that only simple pilgrims believed in the miraculous transport of the Virgin's house from the Holy Lands to Loreto. In fact, Caravaggio's patron for this canvas, Ermete Cavalletti, had made a pilgrimage to Loreto in 1602, where, according to tradition, the pilgrims entering the shrine had bare feet and wore torn clothing to display their humility.[12] Moreover, Caravaggio apparently travelled to Loreto to see the Holy House for himself. It turns out that in his painting, perceived to be indecorous in Rome, he had actually been faithful in a positive sense to the pilgrimage practices in Loreto. The details that had been subject to criticism were in fact supported by ritual.[13] But it was the artist's choice to emphasize not merely bare, but dirty, legs and feet, as well as thoroughly soiled clothing, clearly indicating his pilgrim pair to be unwashed peasants.

Caravaggio's paintings have unusual, disturbing and ambiguous approaches to religious imagery and meaning. The positive and negative interpretations possible in his religious paintings – their oppositional potential – are built into the canvases by the artist himself, for many reasons: to represent humanity's difficulty in comprehending the divine realm; to reinforce the power of his new realism through the plain, frank and sometimes enigmatic comportment of his protagonists; to encourage the participation of the observer in actively interpreting his works; and to instigate controversy and consequently make his mark in the Roman art world. Caravaggio's art is modern because of this contradictory, ambiguous approach, where positive and negative meanings are both potentially present and where the viewer's act of interpretation is an essential part of the reception of his paintings. In a way that is quite modern, the thoughtful viewer of his works is called upon to resolve their positive and negative meanings while confronting his complex imagery.

38 Caravaggio, *Madonna di Loreto*, 1603–5, oil on canvas.

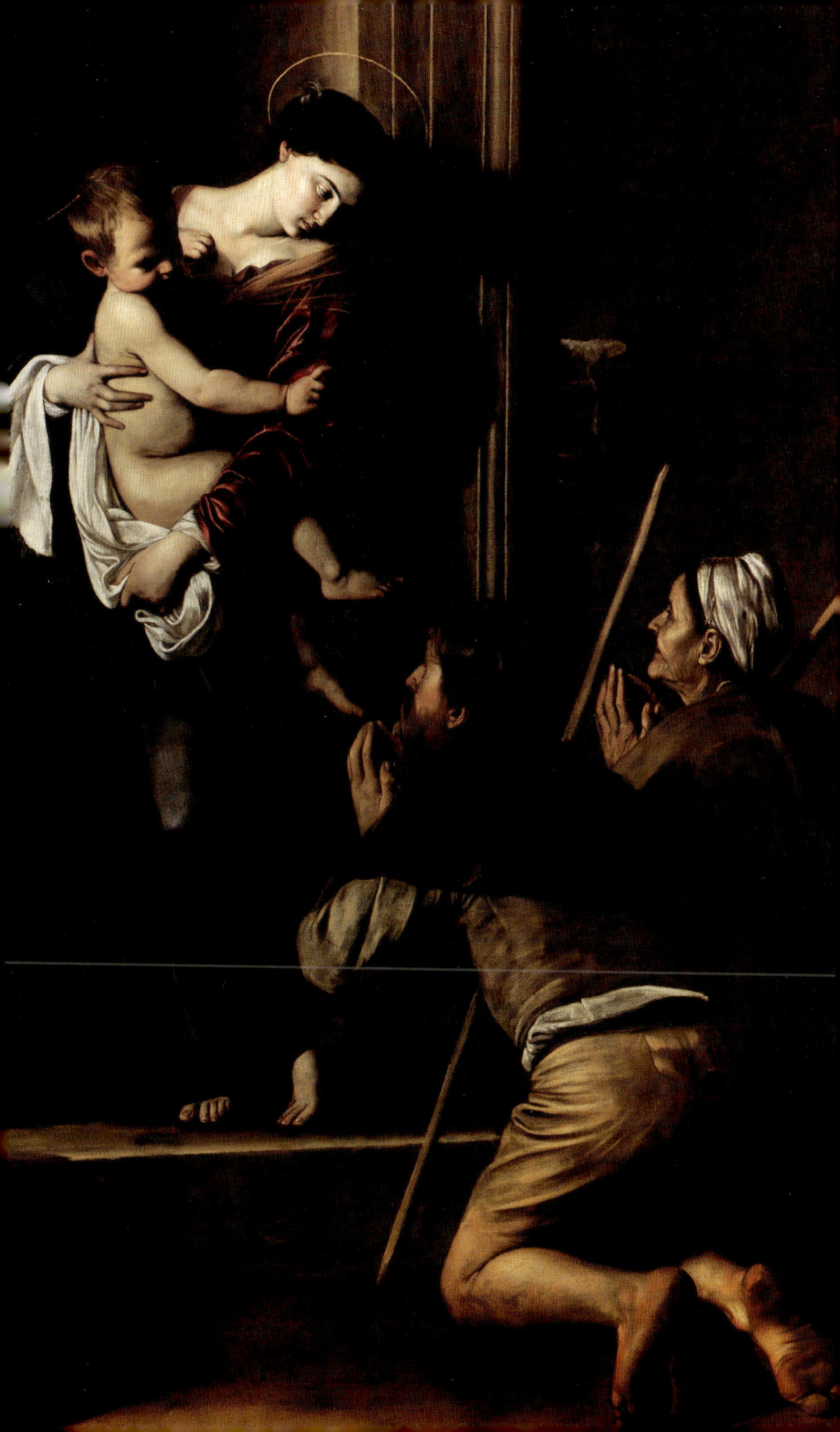

EIGHT

The Social Embedded in the Religious

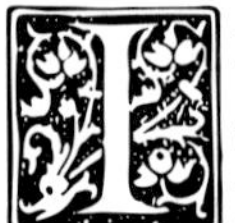IN HIS *Vite*, Giovanni Pietro Bellori displays an attitude that is hostile to Caravaggio, although he grants that the painter advanced his chosen art through realism, which previously had not been much in fashion. Bellori concludes that the best elements of art eluded Caravaggio, who insisted on representing 'cose vili' (sordid things).[1] This pronouncement is usually characterized by art historians as the kind of caustic reaction one might expect from an arch-classicist who had a strong distaste for Caravaggio's brand of unvarnished realism. But Bellori's remark contains an important critical insight about the artist's work, centring on what is nominally construed as a stylistic matter but is more essentially one of class.

Caravaggio was a major force in the creation of a new taste in art for common or 'low-life' themes. More than that, he seems to have been aware of the advantages of creating paintings with the potential for conflicting interpretation, and to have known that such oppositional readings require a dynamic audience response that takes place in the public sphere. He was conscious of the social aspect of his modern viewpoint, with its emphasis on eroding the barrier between decorous, large-scale history painting and a genre approach featuring poor protagonists. He intentionally created provocative art that incorporated, if not 'sordid things', at least gritty, common figures with an ambiguous expressiveness marked by a decidedly novel subjectivity of presentation. His realistic style, with its lack of artifice, was conceptually congruent with the inclusion in his pictures of socially marginal 'low-life' types.[2] He saw the need to renew religious painting through a deeply expressive and thoughtful reconsideration of traditional approaches, and to expose more openly and candidly the relationship of the religious and social spheres in a culture in which the two were inseparably linked. Caravaggio set out on purpose to bypass conventional art institutions, such as the staid Accademia di San Luca in Rome, even though he seems to have joined this particular institution himself, apparently for the status it imparted, but was never part of its inner circle.[3] He ignored entrenched, conservative critical voices by appealing directly to people of all social classes within the public spaces of churches. It is for these reasons, in part, that Caravaggio may be considered a modern painter.

When Caravaggio painted the lower classes, including cardsharps and fortune tellers, in his early pictures, such images invited a critical interpretation of the marginalized poor and rogues like the dangerous, unscrupulous *bravi* (swordsmen). He derived his low-life types from sixteenth-century northern European engravings of gamblers, while his *bravi* were based on characters from Italian theatre, including the *commedia dell'arte*.[4] Caravaggio thus did not merely find his ragged proletarians in the streets, as Bellori claimed, but also in popular visual sources and theatrical conventions.[5] He combined his common models, who appear in his Roman and Neapolitan paintings, with his knowledge of types as seen in prints, adding another layer of richness to his art. Caravaggio allowed the irreverent, questionable content of genre painting to influence his dissident expressiveness in religious painting.

It was in his first public commission for the *Calling* and *Martyrdom of St Matthew* (see illus. 18, 31) that Caravaggio adapted street types to monumental religious scenes. The half-length figures of cheats and victims in *Cardsharps* (see illus. 9) and *Gypsy Fortune Teller* (see illus. 7) reappeared, barely transformed, in the *bravi* surrounding Matthew, eroding the boundaries between low and high art, the profane and the sacred. As he continued to paint religious pictures, he treated the poor sympathetically. The lowly were now transformed into peasant worshippers (*Madonna di Loreto*, see illus. 38; *Madonna of the Rosary*, see illus. 39); rustic Apostles (*Inspiration of St Matthew*, see illus. 36; *Crucifixion of St Peter*, see illus. 49; *Doubting Thomas*, see illus. 28); poor disciples and innkeepers (*Supper at Emmaus*, see illus. 45); and grooms (*Conversion of St Paul*, see illus. 20). In the *Madonna di Loreto* and *Madonna of the Rosary*, Caravaggio showed peasants as pious family members; in the former picture perhaps as an elderly mother with her adult barefoot son; in the latter as mother and child and three kneeling men, two with bare feet, in the simple garb of pilgrims. He depicted a wealthy gentleman wearing a neck ruffle in his *Madonna of the Rosary*, at the far left – probably the picture's donor – thus revealing his egalitarian approach to religion, with rich and poor shown together and equal under God. In these pictures Caravaggio presented the underprivileged as good people, avoiding the categories of the suspect poor who had bad reputations or those who chafed the authorities in Rome (like the artist himself), such as beggars, thieves, street performers, ruffians and the *bravi* who had appeared earlier in his *Calling* and *Martyrdom*. Mirroring the populism of Neri's Oratory and similar institutions within his culture, he emphasizes in his art, from a class perspective, a rejection of courtly elegance in favour of proletarian simplicity. His eschewing of artificiality is linked with the positive images of poverty in his art.

Bellori admired Caravaggio's early secular paintings for their lifelike quality, but was deeply critical when the artist began to introduce genre or low-life elements into his religious pictures, such as the boy on the left in the *Calling*, drawing coins to himself (see illus. 29). Many were at first enthusiastic in their response to his new kind of religious picture, but before long conservative authorities in both religion and art were airing their disapproval. In depicting in his *Calling* secular and suspect boys – including the one who appears to be stealing coins – Caravaggio violated the Counter-Reformation prohibition against religious pictures including objects or characters that do not belong, 'disproportionate' things such as 'gypsies counting money' (mentioned by Cardinal Gabriele Paleotti in his treatise of 1582 on sacred images).[6] The *bravi* in religious scenes such as Caravaggio's *Calling* were ambiguous in meaning and potentially dangerous: the boy with the sword might even be ready to threaten Christ if necessary in order to protect his master. Soon the *bravi* would be replaced in Caravaggio's pictures by the lowly devout: peasants with religious feeling. They brought with them their torn shirts and dirty feet, marks of the truth of nature and truth to life, but also the potential for censure.

Caravaggio's modernity grows not from the social sphere directly (as nineteenth-century Parisian art does in the interpretations of Marxist critics, for example), but from the religious domain that encompassed the social. Religion, including institutions such as Roman confraternities and congregations dedicated to helping the poor, was the only collective means to relieve the deleterious effects of poverty. The presence of Church institutions such as confraternities indicates that the leaders of the Counter-Reformation steered a careful course between popularizing, democratic tendencies and traditional Church paternalism. In addition to embracing the poor and socially marginal, Caravaggio's paintings in the Contarelli chapel touch upon larger international political concerns. In a number of ways, ties to France are introduced. For example, Henry IV's conversion to Catholicism, in which Cardinal Del Monte played a role, is alluded to indirectly in the *Calling* (see illus. 18). The painting emphasizes the theme of conversion in San Luigi dei Francesi, the French national church in Rome and the centre of the city's ceremonies celebrating the monarch's embrace of Catholicism.[7]

By bringing the poor – with all the freight of their reality, their tattered clothes, bare, unclean feet and lack of comprehension – into sacred dramas, Caravaggio revealed another aspect of his modernity. He disregarded wilfully the notion that only ideal, noble figures, typically based on antique formal precedents, were worthy of inclusion in religious paintings, or, at the lower end of the social scale, clean, attractive peasants, as in the paintings of Federico Barocci. Or, perhaps more accurately, in 1599 in the Contarelli chapel Caravaggio began his career as a painter of monumental religious canvases with what he knew and had painted before: a common humanity. He adapted his earlier art to the new task. In fact, he had not painted tattered clothing before his *Supper at Emmaus* of 1601 (see illus. 45), either in his genre or religious works. The hole in the coat of the disciple on the left in this painting is the earliest example (bringing with it a visual pun of the elbow piercing the surface of the canvas). His first underling or servant in a religious painting was the maid in the *Judith Beheading Holofernes* of 1598–9 (see illus. 17), followed by the innkeeper in the *Supper at Emmaus* and the two executioners in the *Crucifixion of St Peter* (see illus. 49).

Earlier artists had represented the poor, but Caravaggio's realist style brought out the details of poverty as never before: his saints and worshippers alike have dirty fingernails and soiled feet. In painting such details as these, he was not merely mindlessly and naively copying nature, as Bellori later thought, but establishing a visual rhetoric of poverty that presents a humble humanity facing religious mysteries of which it has only partial understanding. This point serves to counter the arguments of Caravaggio's contemporaries that he merely profaned sacred meaning through his realism. To his lowly approach he added another layer of richness by frequently quoting previous art, in particular Michelangelo. His paintings were thus simultaneously sophisticated and simple; they appealed to the poor and the wealthy alike.

The common appearance of Caravaggio's figures marks them not only as poor but ignorant. In his *Madonna of the Rosary* (illus. 39), five earnest, ordinary worshippers kneel before St Dominic and the Virgin, all reaching for a rosary, a devotional aid particularly favoured by the poor. This picture has been interpreted by some as undermining genuine religious expression by presenting an ironic depiction of the manipulation of the poor masses by the Catholic Church.[8] In Caravaggio's own time, Giordano Bruno strongly criticized Christianity in this way, because he saw it used by the powerful as a tool for social control. He asserted that by raising false hopes for personal salvation, rulers were able to manipulate the behaviour of their subjects.[9] Whether Caravaggio intended to criticize the Church in this painting is unclear, but he was certainly aware that in Rome the exasperated Pope faced the perennial problem of dealing with the poor, by turns through charity and banishment. A large number of religious confraternities, congregations and societies, such as the Oratorians, specialized in helping the poor, and Caravaggio had connections with these through his patrons and commissions. He took to heart in his paintings both the idea of Christian solace for the poor and the ideal of saintly poverty. His attraction to the poor and their importance in his paintings suggests affinities with later artists such as Gustave Courbet and Honoré Daumier, although in the society in which Caravaggio found himself, the direct confrontation of political powers by an educated class within the public sphere over the subject of poverty was not yet possible.

In the first *Inspiration of St Matthew* (see illus. 36, 37), Matthew is represented on a social level as poor and on a religious level as ignorant of divine mysteries. Caravaggio negotiates richly antinomic strategies in this work as he

39 Caravaggio, *Madonna of the Rosary*, 1605–6, oil on canvas.

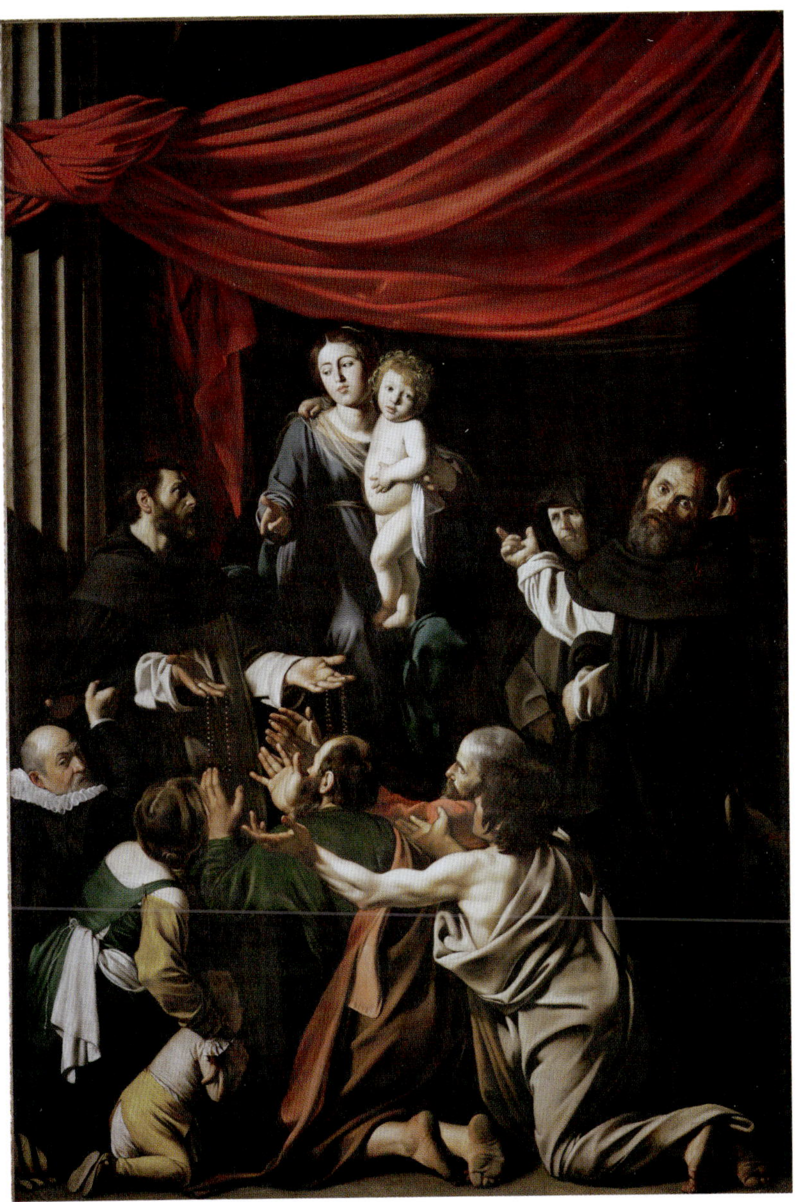

addresses the problems, seemingly contrary yet entwined, of poverty and ignorance along with dawning religious comprehension, within a framing of sacred signs that can be perceived as either negative or positive. The saint's poverty can be read negatively, as showing a lack of proper respect and decorum, or positively, in that his simplicity prepares him for divine understanding. One could cite the writings of both Caravaggio's religious contemporaries and historical authorities including the early Christian Church Fathers to gain theological validation for the common or 'low' imagery in his paintings, but the question still remains of whether his contemporaries conceived of such justifications when they looked at his canvases.

In his *Death of the Virgin* (see illus. 26), Caravaggio depicts Mary simultaneously as an uncompromisingly ordinary human in social terms and, to his critics, as one cut off from the divine world in religious terms. The church for which this altarpiece was painted, Santa Maria della Scala, was supported by the Casa Pia, a charity dedicated to the reform of 'fallen' women or those in danger of becoming so. Thus Giulio Mancini's description of the Virgin in this painting as looking like a prostitute seems to conflate the purpose of the church with the painted image. The picture's removal from the church in 1607, six years after it was commissioned, seems to have been a result of the decreasing influence of the Casa Pia that accompanied the simultaneously growing power of the conservative Carmelite fathers at the church. In his painting Caravaggio shows the Virgin's bodily decomposition, which especially violated the Carmelites' devotion to the principle of saintly incorruptibility.[10] The painting's rejection may also be indicative of a diminishing interest in the Rome of Paul V in representing the saints as poor.[11]

On a personal level, Caravaggio aspired to activate in his life a modern sense of expanded autonomy within a repressive social system that hardly ever authorized such change. He had a keen critical awareness of class differences, and he saw a way to refashion himself by reaching for class status and privilege at the same time that he represented contentious social and religious forces in his art. He lived at a time when freedom was limited and when, in spite of strict class boundaries and social hierarchy, a modicum of social mobility was available to individuals, like himself, of limited means who possessed extraordinary talent, drive and a new vision for art. A distinguished painter in Caravaggio's day could exercise prerogatives unimaginable to people who remained in the low social classes. But his ambition had its negative side, as well. While the artist's own experience of destitution in Rome in the mid-1590s suggests his disposition to empathize with the poor, by 1600 his ambition had propelled him to rise above his social station, acting like a knight (before he really became one), carrying a sword and knives illegally and, as is confirmed in his police record, bullying others in order to assert and protect his rights. A parallel may be drawn between his own experience of the polarizing forces of poverty and ambition and the conflict between lowly and divine impulses in his first large-scale religious paintings in the Contarelli chapel, works that gave him the fame and notoriety he sought.

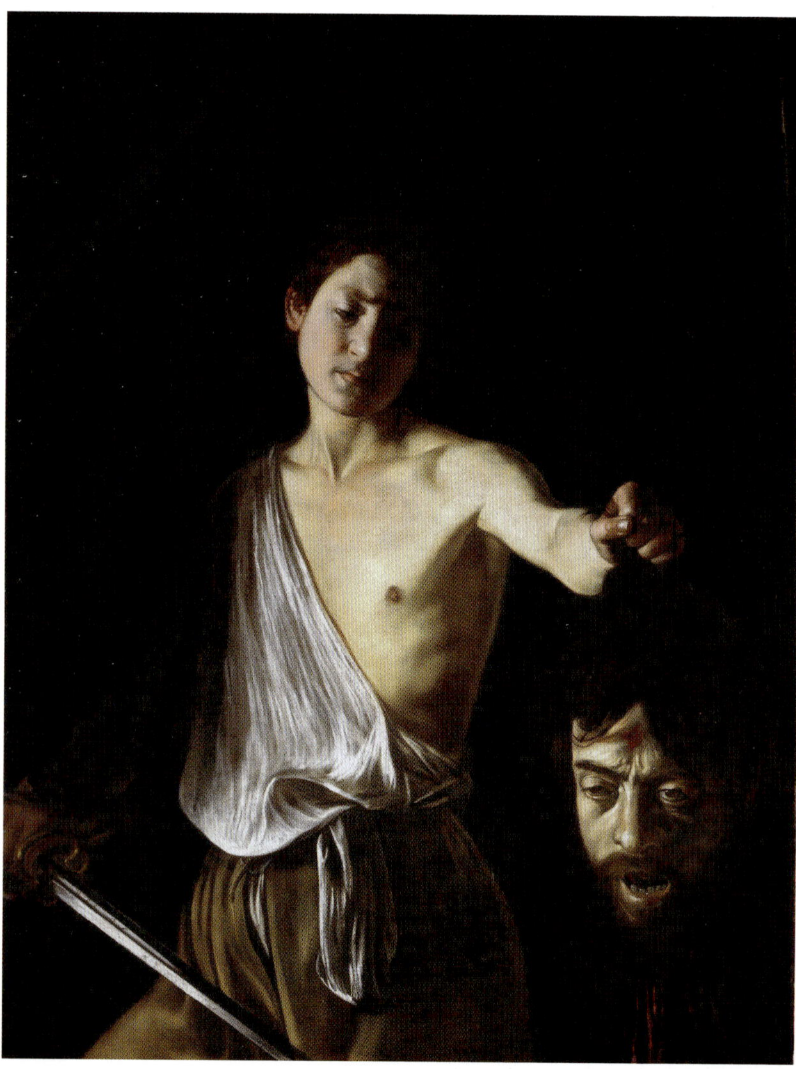

NINE

The Created Personas of the Self-portraits

IN THE SELF-PORTRAITS embedded in his narrative religious paintings, Caravaggio creates artificial personas or guises that establish a perverse self-image and create a dissident expressiveness. He presents himself in problematic ways through at least five self-portraits in his religious works. These portraits cannot be read naively as a guide to or reflection of his personality; a better way to approach them is to ask why he presented himself in his pictures through role-playing, and why he chose to create in the self-portraits a largely negative persona. The portraits are artful contrivances that are both self-reflexive and self-reflective, the former because their insertion into his pictures gives them the quality of rhetorical self-fashionings in which he becomes a poseur; the latter because of their implicit self-criticism. These self-images point to Caravaggio's status as a sinner and a proud man, an approach that is supported by the details of his violent life. His self-representations are simultaneously ironic and serious. On one level they may be interpreted as self-conscious images presenting the artist as one whose pride and actions demonstrate his failure as a Christian; on another, they may be seen as the representation of a sinful humanity in general. His use of self-portraits in

40 Caravaggio, *David with the Head of Goliath*, 1609–10, oil on canvas.

this way is both novel and, through a complex expression of self-awareness, modern.[1]

Previously, artists had typically included self-portraits in their paintings without guile, as records of their appearance, as in Raphael's *School of Athens* (1509–11), in which the master appears discreetly at one side of the fresco as a bystander, lacking any role in the narrative. Caravaggio's self-portraits, on the other hand, are singularly unflattering and may be interpreted as positioning him negatively within the stories of his paintings. In his *David with the Head of Goliath* (illus. 40), for example, he depicted himself as the evil Goliath. If the initials on David's sword in this painting read as 'H-AS O. S.', and stand for *humilitas occidit superbiam* (humility kills pride), then Caravaggio, who identified himself as the monstrous Goliath, admitted to his own pride.[2] Caravaggio may have created this painting in part as a meditative assessment of his murder of Ranuccio Tomassoni on a Roman street in 1606, a crime prompted by the artist's pride, which led him to a duel.[3] In this painting Caravaggio represents himself as damned, as the embodiment of evil. Through his gruesome self-portrait as the severed head of Goliath he reveals his failure as a Christian, having committed a mortal sin. The young David, Caravaggio's 'slayer', shows a pensive mixture of compassion and regret. With evident calculation, the artist actively and self-consciously manipulates his persona by forming his own mythology, emphasizing his arrogance, pride, depravity and narcissism.[4] In a strangely contemplative way, he carries over his pride from his life into his art.

Caravaggio's perverse self-representations played into the hands of his detractors, among them Giovanni Baglione,

Giovanni Pietro Bellori and his other early biographers. Even if new historical discoveries have tended to confirm the factual statements of his biographers regarding events in his life and commissions for paintings, their interpretations of his personality and judgements of his art were heavily biased. Their view of Caravaggio as a malevolent man, for example, was bolstered by a physiognomic interpretation of his unattractive face, unkempt appearance and tattered clothes. In his life of Caravaggio, Bellori made a pointed connection between the artist's unattractive features and his similarly dark art and troubled personality:

> Caravaggio's style corresponded to his physiognomy and appearance; he had a dark complexion and dark eyes, and his eyebrows and his hair were black; this colouring was naturally reflected in his paintings . . . he retreated to the dark style that is connected to his disturbed and contentious temperament.[5]

The literature connecting Caravaggio's supposedly flawed personality and features to his equally faulty art reflects the physiognomic theories put forward by Giovanni Battista della Porta in his contemporary *De humana physiognomonia*.[6]

One must ask why Caravaggio chose to represent himself in this negative light. The psychopathological theory that he did so because he murdered a man cannot be adequate, because the artist depicted himself as a troubled man in his *Martyrdom of St Matthew* (see illus. 31, 41), a painting he made several years before killing Tomassoni. Clues to his purposeful portrayal of himself as unpleasant may be found in his early biographies, even if they were written by those prejudiced against him. Baglione, Bellori, Giulio Mancini, Joachim von Sandrart, Francesco Susinno and others describe him as haughty, belligerent, quarrelsome, disdainful of others, short-tempered, disturbed, eccentric, barbaric, brutal and tormented.[7] Even if such characterizations of the artist's personality were carried over in an unauthorized manner by his critics to evaluate his paintings negatively, these destructive traits in Caravaggio's behaviour are partly confirmed by historical evidence independent of his biased biographers, such as his police record. Caravaggio was a thoughtful, reflective artist who approached the task of making religious paintings with deep insight, but he was nevertheless unable to suppress his tremendous pride, and simultaneously, perhaps because of that, found it useful to promote himself through self-representation as an offensive man.

If Caravaggio conflated his pride and his wayward image, his justification for doing so was his great achievement in the art of painting. His pride was undoubtedly connected with his hot temper. Recent research has demonstrated that some of his street brawls took the form of vendettas against those who had criticized his paintings, including his murderous attack on Tomassoni, whose family seems to have been friendly with his rival in painting, Baglioni.[8] Looking back from the perspective of the early seventeenth century to the time when he had arrived in Rome virtually penniless, he was aware of his outsider status as a man who had risen from poor beginnings to prove himself through revolutionizing art. He saw himself as a loner and his art as unique, and on that basis he fashioned the self-image that comes across in his paintings.

A self-portrait appears in one of the first major public religious paintings Caravaggio made in Rome, his *Martyrdom of St Matthew* (illus. 41, see illus. 31). Here, the artist depicts himself near the centre of the background as a man who, once he spies Matthew's assailant, decides to flee. Unlike the figures near him, who are well dressed, he wears only a shirt, shoes and light tan hose that is gathered in front, and seems to have thrown a cloak quickly over his shoulders. His state of partial undress suggests that he must be a neophyte awaiting baptism,

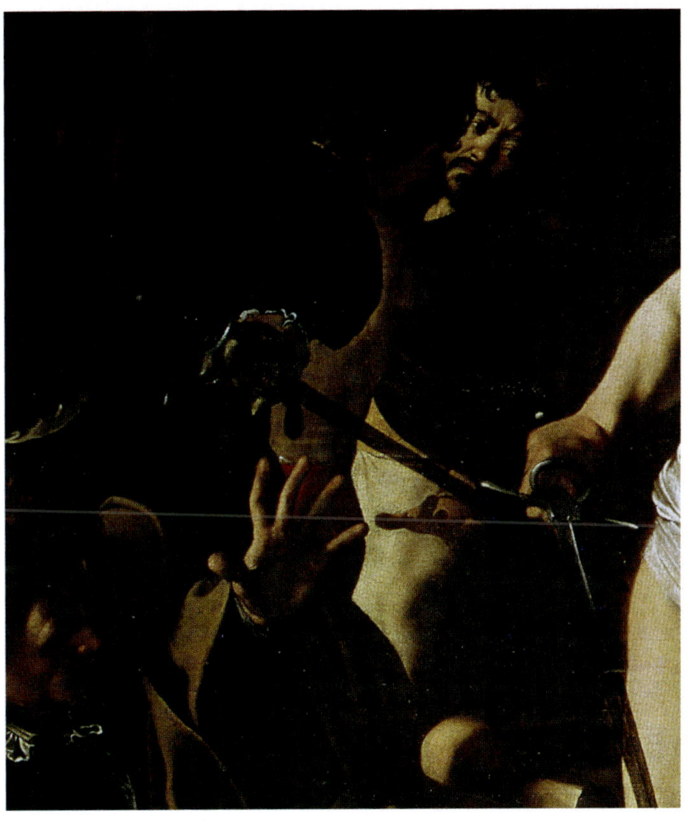

41 Detail of self-portrait of the artist, from Caravaggio, *Martyrdom of St Matthew*, 1599–1600, oil on canvas (illus. 31).

as are the three partly nude men at the bottom of the painting, seated above a baptismal pool.[9] He therefore represents
himself as unbaptized. His flight from the execution of the
saint implies cowardice, and his escape suggests that he will
remain unbaptized.[10] Caravaggio's eyes do not fall directly
on the executioner; rather, he seems to overlook him as he
glances in the direction of the palm held by the angel or the
altar boy fleeing at the right, thus introducing ambiguity into
the narrative.[11] In his flight, with the scowl on his face and the
wave of his hand, he veers towards sin and evil rather than
redemption and good, and so by displaying himself in this
manner he brings a negative valence to his artistic expression
and self-image.

Caravaggio represented himself with a problematic
relation to Christianity in other paintings. In his *Taking of Christ*
(illus. 42) he portrays himself at the right, holding a lamp. One
might expect him to try to catch a glimpse of Christ's reaction
as he is seized, but the artist's gaze is instead clearly directed
towards the lamp that he holds. This unusual glance can
be explained both negatively and positively. He includes his
self-portrait among those who capture Christ, as the one who
holds the lamp to facilitate the Lord's arrest – a problematical
self-image indeed.[12] But the lamp towards which he directs
his gaze may be understood allegorically as the light of Christ
that shines forth as a sign of universal salvation, initiated by
the sacrifice that is set in motion by his capture, the scene
depicted in this painting.[13] Another view of this painting is
that by holding the lamp in the dark Caravaggio points to
his own particular kind of picture-making, emphasizing his
tenebrism.[14] Such ambiguity through possible, conflicting

meanings is characteristic of Caravaggio's art as a whole, and both his contemporaries and modern commentators have been caught in the web of these disparate readings.

Another self-portrait appears in the *Resurrection of Lazarus* (see illus. 62), immediately behind Christ's raised arm, where Caravaggio looks to the left. He seems to have inserted himself here in the role of a sinner. His hands are clasped as if in prayer, suggesting that he is in need of redemption (he had by this time killed Tomassoni).[15] Caravaggio depicts himself a little behind Christ looking towards the light, a symbolic idea that is reinforced by another way of seeing the painting, in which his face confronts the Lord's directly, as he hopes for the grace of salvation.

The final self-portrait is behind the dying saint in the *Martyrdom of St Ursula* (see illus. 66). Here, Caravaggio repeats his self-representation from the *Taking of Christ*, but with a different emphasis. In this, probably his last painting, his visage is starker, and pasty; his eyes are no longer alert, as they were in the *Taking*, but glazed and beginning to close. His mouth has fallen open, as if lethargy prevents him from shutting it properly. His self-image is more pessimistic, desperate even, and he looks towards the light with a sense of hopelessness, as if he is lost to the light of salvation. In this painting Caravaggio looks off into space, shifting his gaze from the main subject of the painting, the shooting of St Ursula.[16] But it is significant that he represents himself looking towards the light, for him a spiritual substance as important as any human figure in his art.

All five paintings discussed here compromise normative Christian interpretations as far as the artist's representation

overleaf: 42 Caravaggio, *Taking of Christ*, 1602, oil on canvas.

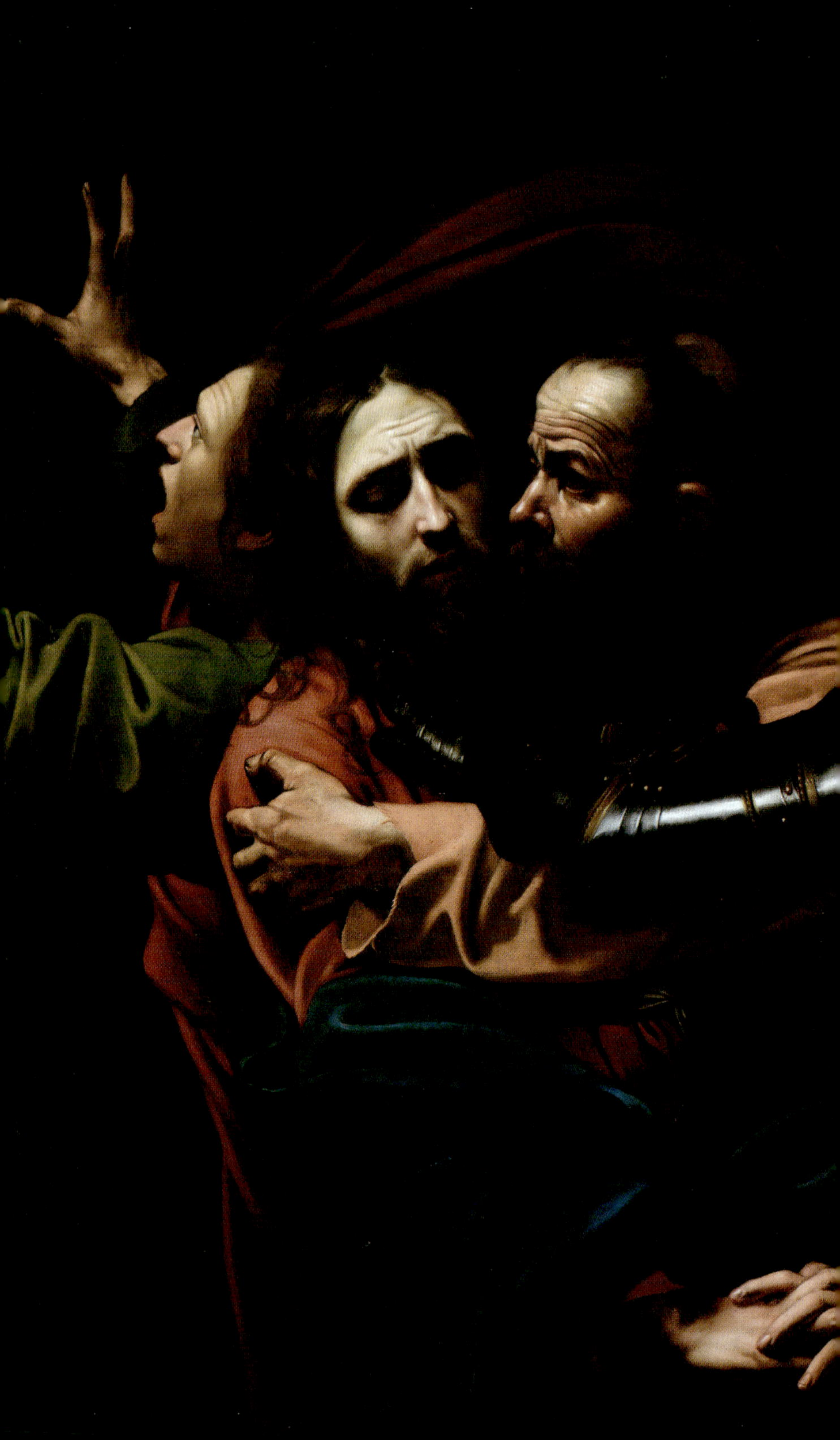

of himself is concerned, since the positive religious elements are countered by troubling aspects. The theme running through all these paintings is Caravaggio's use of a negative self-representation to depict his own failure as a Christian. It is highly likely that he perceived that the root of this failure lay in his own pride. These paintings depict his inability to come to terms with Christian doctrine, in particular its focus on humility. In looking at the five paintings analysed here as a group, one may conclude that Caravaggio is positing his own malfunction as a Christian for the very reason that he is a proud man.

Caravaggio was perhaps the first painter to present his self-image as an aspect of his modernity, because of his unprecedented depth, richness and introspection in self-representation. No other artist had inserted a series of self-portraits with such complex meanings into religious narratives. In showing himself in his own paintings as an arrogant man either rejecting or in need of Christian salvation, Caravaggio played into the hands of his seventeenth-century critics. He represents himself as perverse and a sinner. His motivations for doing so were different from those of his contemporary detractors in their biographies. They saw him as an evil man who produced bad art; he saw himself as a flawed but proud man who produced exceptional art.

TEN

Scepticism, Eroticism, Irony, Wit

ARAVAGGIO'S UNRULY reputation grew from his hot temper and sword-fighting in the streets, but also from his groundbreaking approach to painting, which tested the limits of what was acceptable in religious representation. In its links with scepticism and its display of eroticism, irony and wit, his art went beyond being merely disruptive. These aspects of his art engaged the viewer in a rich visual and intellectual dialogue that encouraged the pursuit of deeper and more complex meanings than was customary, as well as new kinds of meaning that simply had not existed before in art. Caravaggio was a daring painter who risked failure, had no shortage of maligners willing to criticize him, and endured repeated rejection of his works.

The speculations of contemporary sceptical philosophers have rich analogies with the representation of humankind's ignorance in his murky paintings. Scepticism became a powerful force in Europe following the publication in the 1560s of the works of the ancient Pyrrhonist philosopher Sextus Empiricus. In common with the sceptical writings of the philosophers Michel de Montaigne (1533–1592) and Francisco Sanches (c. 1550–1623), Caravaggio's art fostered a deep uncertainty and a new questioning attitude in the wake of the discarding of the old cosmic and religious verities. His art mirrors the sceptical view that humanity has a limited ability to understand the larger divine world that lies beyond human experience. His tenebrous spatial settings and doubting protagonists suggest affinities with the kind of Catholic scepticism that was espoused by Montaigne and others, in response to a rapidly changing conception of the world.

In their opposition of light and dark, which points to a limited human comprehension of God and his cosmos, Caravaggio's works fall in line with the ideas of Montaigne, who believed that people can accept only what God chooses to reveal.[1] Likewise, Caravaggio's art parallels the writings of Sanches, who held that while some knowledge may be obtained through divine revelation, the apprehension we pursue through our own efforts can only be imperfect. Sanches maintained that even though our eyes take in things, we do not truly understand them, but are blind in the midst of light.[2] The agreement between Caravaggio's art and this sceptical trend is shown in his perplexed mortals when they unexpectedly encounter divine figures such as Christ or angels. In the *Doubting Thomas* (illus. 28), the disciple adheres to the sceptical premise that one should trust only what one can verify through the senses of sight and touch. Even after penetrating Christ's wound, Thomas and his companions exhibit only surprise, showing as yet no sign of faith. Caravaggio's paintings connote the loss of old certainties through his protagonists' position close to the picture plane, within the empirical reality close at hand. The closeness of his art to the beliefs of Sanches and Montaigne reveals a modern outlook on religion.

Caravaggio has often been accused of encouraging ambiguity by creating religious paintings that seem too secular, in some cases too erotic. He displayed divine beauty in his angels through eroticism, making no distinction between celestial splendour and sensuality. In the *Martyrdom of St Matthew* (see illus. 31), for example, a nubile angel leans over a cloud, exposing its backside. In the first *Inspiration of St Matthew* (see illus. 36), a sensuous angel invades the personal space of the saint: what was one to make of this seductive seraph? In this painting, a clever, ironic contrast centres on Matthew's humble appearance and the charming, androgynous angel. As he comes face to face with divinity, Matthew is heavy, square and earthbound, while the angel is alluring, lithe and curving in form. One of the angel's hands is placed delicately at its neck, while the other gracefully guides the massive hand of the saint in writing. The angel's eyelids are half-closed as it mouths the words of the Gospel on heavy, rounded lips. The saint's attention is fixed on the words on the page, and he is unaware of – or at least inattentive to – either the sybaritic touch of the angel's hand or its soft breath that must caress his face. Is Caravaggio here sacralizing the sensual, that is, using eroticism as a metaphor for divinity, or sensualizing the sacred to the point of offending the Church? Particularly in the case of his rejected religious pictures such as this one, which were unmoored from their sacred settings and moved to private collections, such ambiguity could work to enrich and playfully confuse the fixed boundaries of genre.

The angel implies that heavenly beauty can be understood by mortal observers only by means of a physical, earthly kind of attractiveness, through worldly metaphor. Caravaggio made his angels seem true to worldly experience, whereas other artists tried to elevate them to otherworldly perfection. Caravaggio's angels seem to belong to the earth more than to heaven, and even if they come down from celestial heights, man never rises to them. Ippolito Falcone, a Theatine seminarian and author from Syracuse, wrote in 1668 that when Caravaggio was asked to paint angels in the empty upper half of his *Burial of St Lucy* (see illus. 58), he responded that because he had never seen them, he did not know how to portray them.[3] Falcone's comments are clearly an exaggeration, since the artist did paint angels, but the writer gets at the essential truth that Caravaggio's seraphs seem more sensually boyish than divine.

From the beginning, the painter had made erotic angels similar to the one in the first *Inspiration*, starting with the voluptuous seraph seen from the back in the early *Rest on the Flight into Egypt* (see illus. 14) of about 1595–6. After he left Rome in 1606, Caravaggio no longer painted naked angels; his later ones are more conventionally draped. Perhaps this situation indicates that in southern Italy he did not find the same kind of sophisticated patron who had appreciated his witty angels in Rome. The more conservative religious tradition in the south may have forced him to rethink the way he depicted angels, since his later ones are marked by a higher level of propriety.

In the first *Inspiration* (see illus. 36, 37), Caravaggio elected to highlight Matthew's underlying spiritual and mental struggle with a humorous treatment. Through depicting playful interaction with the angel, the artist lays bare the humanity of the struggling Apostle, who elicits in the viewer an empathic response engendered by irony, resonating more deeply than a conventionally serious approach. In this painting in particular, Caravaggio seems to veil the underlying seriousness of religious content, which ends with Matthew's comprehension of the text before him, with what seems on the surface to be an almost irreligious irony. The artist trumps the saint's ignorant appearance, a problematic aspect of the picture, through giving him wide-open eyes set in an expression of astonishment, indicating Matthew's sudden insight into Christ's role as Messiah.[4] But this aspect of the painting's meaning, so important for its proper understanding, went unnoticed or was ignored. The picture was, after all, intended as an altarpiece, and tradition required that such a work be decorous and worthy of respect and reverence. While Caravaggio's crude Matthew makes a point about the simplicity and poverty of the Apostles and the divine source of the Gospels, it was not considered an image worthy of promoting intercession with God.[5] One has only to look at Caravaggio's second version of the *Inspiration* (see illus. 35), and see the alterations he made to create a more conventional altarpiece, to realize that the appearance of both angel and saint in the first version gave the Church authorities pause, and that their tolerance for irony was small.

In highlighting Caravaggio's transgressions against Church norms, we may turn to a painting based on his first *Inspiration*, made by Lucio Massari in about 1610 (illus. 43).[6] In Massari's version, all the unseemly aspects of Caravaggio's have been deleted: Matthew's foot (no longer dirty) is held back, not projected towards the picture plane and the viewer; a decidedly less erotic angel does not touch the saint; Matthew

writes without the physical intervention of the angel; and he does not look like an illiterate peasant. Massari's 'cleaned-up' version, like Caravaggio's own second attempt, makes clear in visual terms what exactly the offending aspects of the first version were, and what he failed to provide. Massari's painting

43 Lucio Massari, *Inspiration of St Matthew*, c. 1610, oil on canvas.

offers visual evidence that is valuable in supplementing the text-based tradition of Giovanni Pietro Bellori and other writers, such as Giovanni Andrea Gilio, who (like Gabriele Paleotti) wrote a Counter-Reformation treatise on decorum in religious art.[7] A telling difference between Caravaggio's and Massari's versions is that the latter is not nearly so interesting to look at and think about, even in religious terms.

Two of the visual sources for Caravaggio's first *Inspiration* – Raphael's *Jupiter and Cupid* (1517) from the Villa Farnesina and Agostino Veneziano's engraving of the *Inspiration of St Matthew* (1518; illus. 44) – give further insight into the mixing of secular and sacred in an ironic manner.[8] Raphael's fresco has a humorous element in the way Jupiter pinches Cupid's cheeks; by contrast, Veneziano's idealized, classicized Matthew lacks any sense of wit. Through a calculated strategy of ironic play, Caravaggio subverted classical models such as these in the process of quoting them in his depiction of Matthew. Like Caravaggio, both Raphael and Veneziano show a seated figure with crossed legs, one of which projects towards the viewer, but with suitable classical restraint. Caravaggio violated the norms of borrowing from works like these in his ironic treatment of Matthew's exposed leg and dirty foot, which accost the observer in his first *Inspiration*. The irony consists in a humorous inversion of classical art and the rules of decorum by imitating in a 'false' way. That is, Caravaggio distorts and debases his models from the viewpoint of his classical and conservative contemporaries by taking from these prototypes what was considered unworthy of imitation. He could do this because religious works were now beginning to be considered in a new, profane way, in the context of private collections, changes in marketing conditions for paintings and widening strategies for gaining attention, which Caravaggio himself developed. In response to the conservative treatises on rules for making art, he created a novel kind of painting under these new conditions.[9] In his 'serious play', Caravaggio responds to

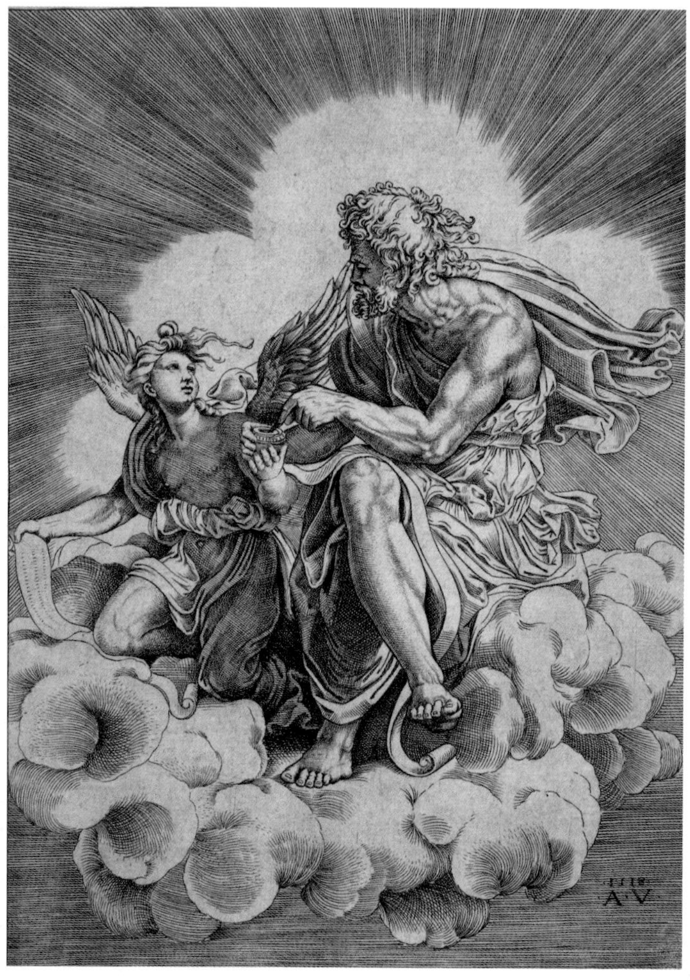

44 Agostino Veneziano after Raphael, *Inspiration of St Matthew*, 1518, engraving.

pictorial conventions by borrowing from his predecessors, and considers the sacred contexts of his religious works; but he also thinks of their status as art objects in a modern way, by undermining and distorting tradition as well as drawing upon it.

What Caravaggio may not have considered sufficiently is that his ironic treatment and uncompromising realism – notwithstanding their underlying purpose of emphasizing the simplicity of his peasant saint in the first *Inspiration* – had not only the potential, but were highly likely, to be misconstrued. He must have been aware that he was stretching the limits of religious acceptability in some of his paintings, a point that was made a little later by critics such as Giulio Mancini and Giovanni Baglione. Caravaggio did not intend to be consciously anti-religious, but he did want to be audacious. As part of an overall strategy of emphasizing the distance between humanity and divinity, he depicted human reactions to the divine in a way that seemed irreligious to some, but which seemed genuine to him. His irony, which was often understood negatively, did not help with the reception of his pictures. Even so, he must have been delighted by the controversy, the 'buzz', that his pictures created, as mentioned by Baglione, who in his life of Caravaggio has Federico Zuccaro say of the Contarelli chapel paintings: 'What is all the fuss about?' ('Che rumore è questo?').[10] Caravaggio must have been interested in stirring up controversy through his paintings, and in working their imagery to ensure their animated reception.

It is strange that behind Caravaggio's images of divine epiphanies there lurks a certain irony. His Apostles and disciples experience revelations not at some remove in time or place from holy figures such as Christ or angels, but in their immediate presence, so that recognition of their divinity should have been immediate and obvious to them, as it is to the viewer of the pictures. It might be asked why in the *Doubting Thomas* (see illus. 28) the Apostle thought it necessary to insert his finger so far into Christ's wound, or why in the first *Supper at Emmaus* (illus. 45) the Lord had to bless the meal before his followers were able to recognize him, even if he did appear to them 'in another form' (Mark 16:12). Caravaggio constructs his paintings of sudden revelation in such a way that the viewer is privy to the in-joke that the Apostles seem thick-headed in their inability to catch Christ's divinity sooner, as the observer has already done. Such a reading of these pictures is positive from a religious point of view, but at the expense of the seriousness and gravity that are expected of sacred paintings. Even within positive readings of Caravaggio's works, therefore, an irony that is aesthetic as much as it is religious is detected.

This special type of irony is another reason why so much of the criticism of Caravaggio's paintings by his contemporaries was negative. Positive readings of his pictures in his own time are rare; his art was reviled by almost everyone who wrote about him because he was not taken seriously as a religious painter by the *literati* of the art world, even if he exerted an enormous influence on the painters of his time. Today, the reaction to him could not be more different. He is now usually understood as an artist who thought deeply about religious expression in painting.

In these pictures Caravaggio underlines his protagonists' discovery of Christ's divinity in a most remarkable way, with

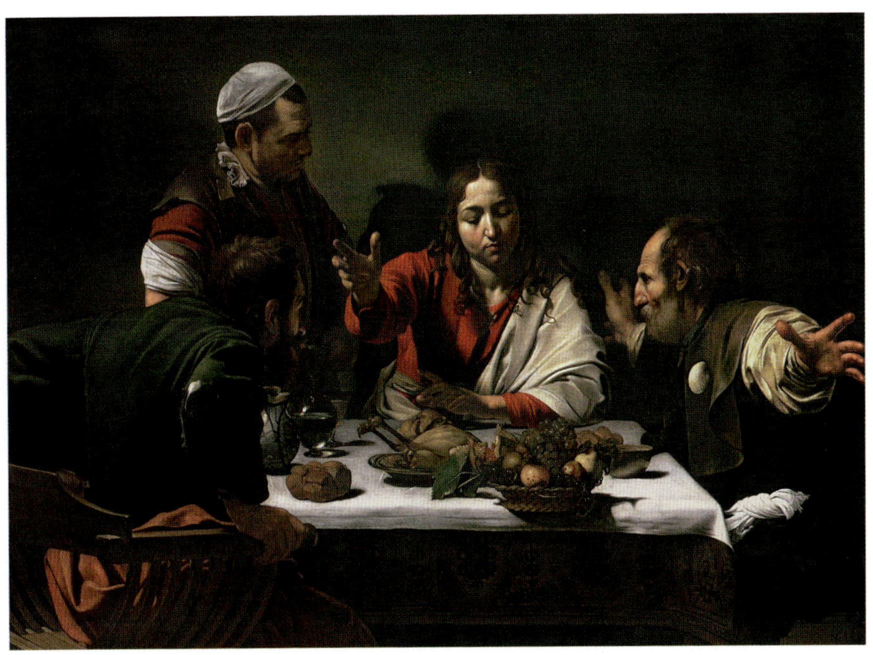

wry wit rather than with the ennobling idealization of form favoured by other artists. The search for Christ's spiritual nature in *Doubting Thomas* is reduced to a crude physical act, all the more so because of the artist's forthright realism. Like comic actors, the trio of disciples leans in unison towards the finger that penetrates Christ's cut flesh, focusing their three pairs of eyes on the wound with great attentiveness. In the London *Supper at Emmaus* (illus. 45), Christ's divinity is communicated in his gesture of blessing, and his knowing concentration on this act, in the presence of two astonished disciples who seem ready to bolt out of their chairs in a startled moment of recognition. The position of Christ's hands and his beardless state are taken from Michelangelo's *Last*

45 Caravaggio, *Supper at Emmaus*, 1601, oil on canvas.

Judgment, but his hands hover over a greasy chicken and decaying fruit instead of the saved and damned souls (how many of the artist's contemporary viewers would have noticed that the grapes and other fruit in the basket at the near edge of the table contain religious symbolism, or that the shadow of the basket creates the shape of a fish, an emblem for Christ?). In these paintings, as in the *Inspiration*, divinity is recognized through the surprise of a sudden revelation that finally ends ignorance. In the *Calling* (see illus. 18, 29), Matthew's ignorance is also an important theme, for, dressed in fine clothes and surrounded by his suspect cronies, he does not yet fully realize that he is about to become an Apostle. He seems already to sense Christ's divinity, however, and in all these paintings, man's dependence on God's grace in order to comprehend the divine is implicit.

Darkness and Light

OST ARTISTS BEFORE Caravaggio depicted a bright, daylit world where light is favoured over dark. Caravaggio proposed a startling new approach in which near total blackness is the unnatural but normal condition, relieved by a piercing, mysterious light that seems to be of simultaneously natural and divine origin. In his mature art, which is dominated by religious subjects, a theology of light and dark is implied in which darkness seems to indicate the lower order of the human world. His murky backgrounds metaphorically suggest an earthly zone removed from a theological heaven beyond human experience. The artist's black backgrounds do not deny religious meaning but rather symbolize humanity's weak understanding of God and his divine realm, which, far from being an irreligious concept, was an idea accepted by many churchmen. This view was famously expressed by St Paul in 1 Corinthians 13:12: 'For now we see through a glass, darkly; but then face to face.' Caravaggio's light must struggle against the darkness so that its very presence seems miraculous, for, strong as the illumination is in his pictures, it never achieves victory over the darkness.[1]

The theme of the world as a naturally dark place was revived in a neo-medieval manner in countless sermons, tracts and religious poems in this Counter-Reformation period, and Caravaggio's *tenebroso* style seems consonant with such works.[2] His tenebrism has its profound analogies with the oppositions of the divine and mundane. His intense illumination, often searing through the darkness in scenes of conversion, is like the light described by St Paul: 'For God . . . commanded the light to shine out of the darkness . . . to give . . . knowledge of [his] glory' (2 Corinthians 4:6). The dark world of humanity may be associated with evil, and Christ with light: 'I am the light of the world: he that followeth me shall not walk in darkness, but shall have the light of life' (John 8:12). In the process of seeking salvation, Christians commonly used metaphors of dark and light, for example those associated with St Ignatius of Loyola's *Spiritual Exercises*. The exercitant underwent an extended period of prayer and penance in a darkened room to find the light of God. In this context, then, darkness may have a positive value, in that it is penitential.

In the Contarelli chapel paintings, Caravaggio developed for the first time the rich sense that his light, emanating from a single source, is at once ordinary and divine. His light here seems to be of solar origin, but it must be recalled that in his time both churchmen and natural philosophers (whom we would call scientists) thought of the light of the sun as simultaneously physical and spiritual. In a new antipodal conception, Caravaggio's realistic art embraces a light that seems concurrently earthly and spiritual, and which cannot be described as conventionally natural.

In Caravaggio's *Calling of St Matthew* (see illus. 18), we see a preternaturally strong light invading the world of the painting from an outside source that cannot be defined in ordinary terms. The light behaves normally as it cuts through the darkness of what looks like a Roman street, but at the same time it reinforces, mysteriously and with a powerful divinity, the authority of Christ's call. A diagonal shaft of light raking across the back wall suddenly gives way to shadow; precisely at the point where the line separates light from dark it bisects Christ's halo (illus. 46). Just below this line, Christ's head and hand are picked out in *chiaroscuro*, shown partly in strong illumination and partly in deep shadow, adding mystery to his presence. Christ's hand is exactly parallel to the light, and just below it. The Lord's beckoning gesture and the streaming light act with a mutual, reciprocal and insistent force. The light comes from behind Christ, implying that he is responsible for it and that it accompanies him. As in almost all Caravaggio's paintings, here too the artist refuses to reveal the source of his light, but its close connection to Christ imbues it with divine meaning. The overwhelming intensity of the light against the blackness of the spatial setting suggests the presence of God, not in the physical space of the painting nor in a discrete heaven above it, but ineffably and everywhere, in a manner that recalls Giordano Bruno's concept of the deity. Bruno posited God's immanence in the world and yet his transcendence to it.[3] He saw God as infinite and unknowable, existing as pure, unfathomable essence.

In another picture painted at about the same time as the *Calling*, Caravaggio's *Conversion of St Paul* (see illus. 20), strong illumination falls on Paul, entering the picture at the upper right, where it is seen against the blackness as barely visible shafts of light from above. In this painting the light must be

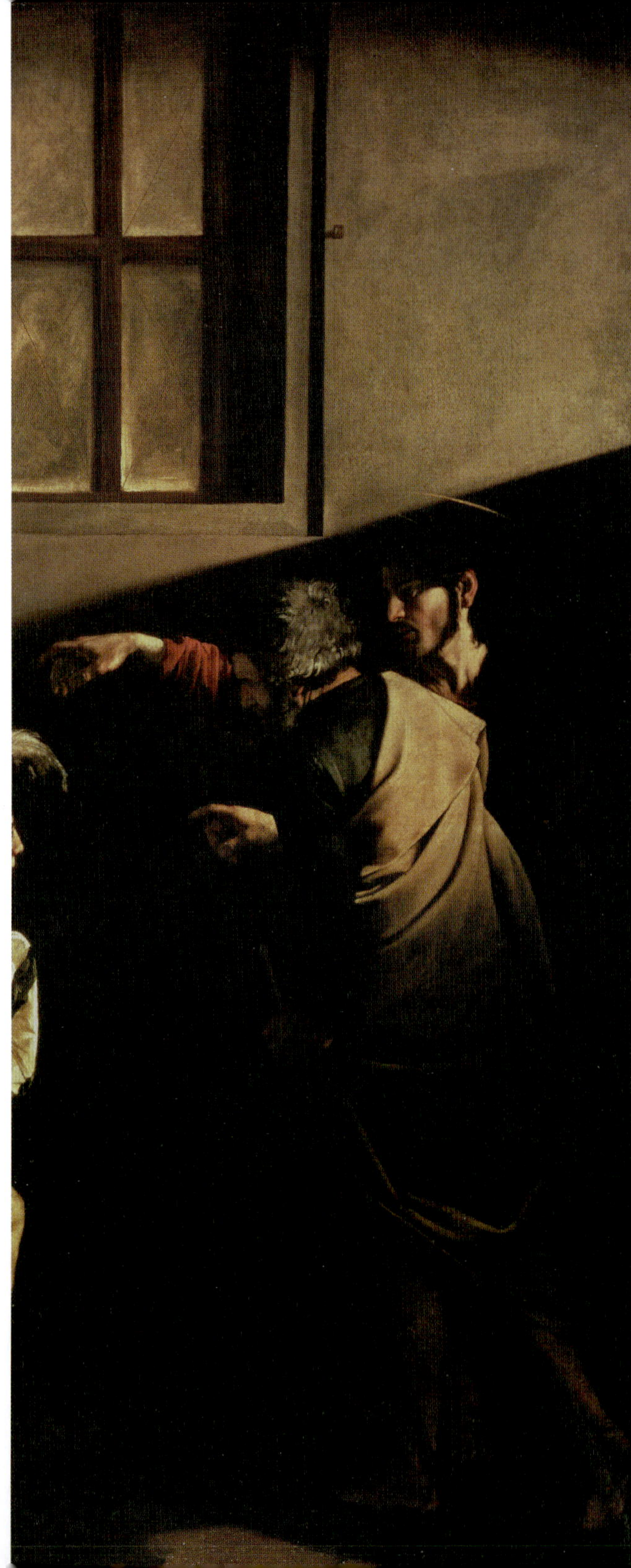

wholly spiritual, since the Acts of the Apostles (26:13) tells us that the divine light of Paul's conversion outshone the sun. But in the *Calling*, the light may be defined in solar terms as both entirely natural and completely spiritual.

It is in 1600, in his *Calling*, that Caravaggio first articulates the synthetic and unifying nature of his light, which has an unseen divine source beyond the picture frame but which is equally part of the natural world and can be taken for sunlight. Caravaggio's approach here goes beyond that of previous religious painters in suggesting the simultaneously natural and divine origin of light. In the *Calling*, the extreme contrast calls special attention to the light; the particular way it interacts with Christ also denotes this dual function. In his earlier paintings, he did not always use light in a religious context, and when he did he usually avoided asserting its simultaneous spiritual and earthly effect: he sometimes used separate light sources to represent nature and divinity. For example, he had depicted strong illumination in his *Ecstasy of St Francis* (see illus. 15) in about 1595–6, but the light falling on the saint and angel is *only* divine, since it miraculously appears before the dawn, which is represented by a separate muted and natural light in the background. Likewise, in his early *Rest on the Flight into Egypt* (see illus. 14), we see mixed sources of light, where bright light of uncertain origin falls on the foreground group set in front of the less intense light of a distant evening sky. In the *Calling*, by contrast, light is *both* divine *and* natural simultaneously, and comes from a single source. The artist's *Entombment of Christ* (illus. 47) shows an intense divine light overpowering the ambient light of evening. His Mary, with raised arms, looks directly into this miraculous light,

46 Detail of Christ and St Peter, from Caravaggio, *Calling of St Matthew*, 1600, oil on canvas (illus. 18).

the source of which is outside the painting and unseen by the viewer. Caravaggio thus modifies the highly tangible realism of his scenes with an unworldly light of mysterious origin.

Striking analogies are apparent between Caravaggio's conception of light and those of the natural philosophers of his period: Bernardino Telesio, Francesco Patrizi, Tommaso Campanella, Giordano Bruno and Galileo Galilei. For them, as for Caravaggio, light was simultaneously natural and divine. They discussed light in both physical and spiritual terms, even though they claimed to study nature in itself.[4] In their investigations of light, the natural philosophers saw a confluence of matter and divinity, partly because this substance (or essence) remained a mystery to them. Caravaggio's conception of light, which grew from the same cultural climate, is essentially congruent with their thought.

For the sixteenth-century natural philosopher Telesio, heaven – and especially the sun and its light – represents the principle of heat. Cold is represented in inert matter, the earth and darkness.[5] Matter is passive and colourless; for Telesio, this means matter is black.[6] Whiteness and light, called the 'non-physical face' or 'species' of warmth by Telesio, actively work against the darkening effect of matter.[7] A parallel is discernible here with Caravaggio, who articulates a strong light intruding on the dark matter of the earth. His darkness can seem terrifying, as if at any moment the light may be extinguished, returning the earth to the blackness of inert matter, cut off from spiritual radiance.

Caravaggio is famous for stressing the close, empirical study of nature through observation, but his light reveals unexpected connections with the idealistic, Platonic strain

47 Caravaggio, *Entombment of Christ*, 1602–4, oil on canvas.

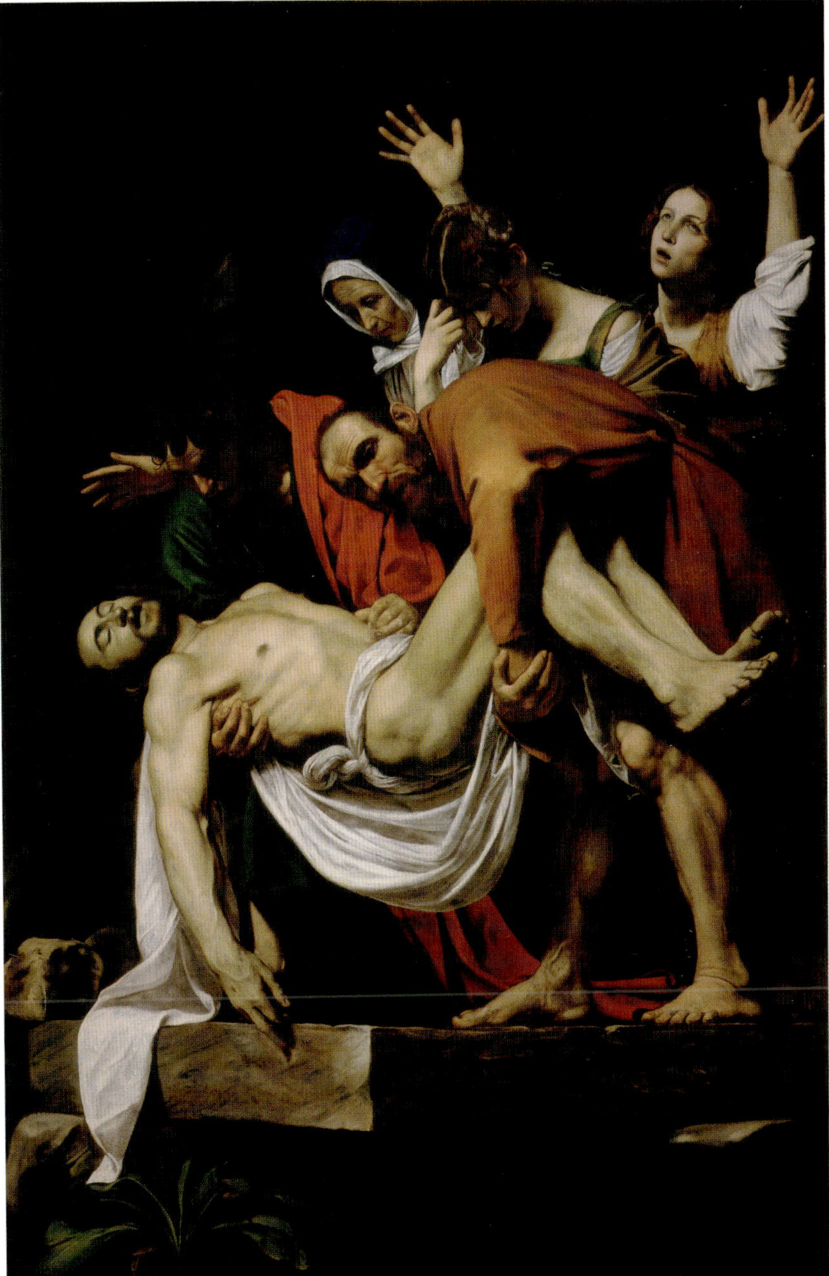

of Renaissance thought. His mystical light has its analogies with the ideas of Neoplatonic and Christian writers as diverse in time and place as the contemporary natural philosopher Francesco Patrizi (discussed below) and St Augustine. In the decade before Caravaggio's birth, the art theorist Giovanni Andrea Gilio wrote in his *Due Dialoghi* (1564) that light signifies mental illumination ('la illuminazione de la mente') and the expulsion of ignorance-shadows ('le tenebre').[8] In this allegorical approach he anticipates Bruno. Caravaggio's paintings reveal correspondences with such metaphorical ideas on light: for example, in the way divine light overpowers earthly shadow and nourishes Paul's inner transformation in the *Conversion of St Paul* (see illus. 20).

Perhaps the most interesting natural philosopher to compare with Caravaggio on the subject of light is the Platonist Francesco Patrizi. According to Patrizi, who accepted a chair in Platonic philosophy at the Sapienza in Rome about a year before Caravaggio arrived in the city, God created space before anything else, then filled it with light, the most beautiful, efficacious thing. In his *Nova de universis philosophia* (1591), Patrizi makes the whole universe depend on the principle of light. Like Telesio, he envisions light as both divine and natural substance, part of both the incorporeal and the physical worlds. Patrizi considers light as occupying an intermediate place between the purely intelligible and the purely sensory, that is, between divine, incorporeal things and physical reality.[9] He sees light as the closest analogy to God in the physical world.[10] Sunlight is both corporeal and incorporeal, finite and infinite, depending on how it is viewed. Light is not strictly physical, but closely related to divinity. Thus, for Patrizi, visible light from the sun is an incorporeal and spiritual entity, but it has become physical and sensible by existing in space.[11] Patrizi states that God is everywhere – in that all things are the emanation from him – yet nowhere, since his incorporeal character precludes a definite location.[12] Similarly, Bruno asserts that God is immanent in everything in nature, while at the same time he alone exists in a pure essence outside the explicated universe, transcendent and unfathomable.[13] For Patrizi, space is the place for both material and incorporeal bodies, except for God, who does not require space in order to exist. God conceals himself from us, and the only way we can know him is through his lights, but feebly.[14] God can be grasped only indirectly for both Patrizi and Caravaggio, through light.

Extraordinarily, we find the realist Caravaggio consistent in his approach to light with the ideas of a Platonist. Although through his realism Caravaggio was averse to Platonism, he seems intuitively to have understood light in Patrizi's sense, as simultaneously physical and spiritual. For Campanella, too, light is the source of both sensible and divine knowledge.[15] Caravaggio's intense light searing through the blackness has an almost palpable quality as it defines and shapes bodies into three-dimensional volumes. In this aspect, his light seems to belong to this earth. But this same light attends his images of calling and conversion. The light, divine in this aspect as it accompanies Christ and reinforces his purpose, aids him as he brings illumination to unsuspecting humans. For both Patrizi and Caravaggio, light mediates between God and the material world.

Patrizi states that the maximum visible light is that of the sun; the minimum is the opposite of light, the blackness of the earth or opacity. Earth is permanently black and the source of all darkness, just as the sun is the cause of light's diffusion and whiteness. He upheld the traditional Neoplatonic view that the earth is dark because it is furthest from the light of God, which exists in the empyrean. He envisions the earth in the centre of the universe, but it is not therefore privileged; rather, because it is at the centre it is distant from God and shrouded in darkness. Blackness is associated with the earth, subject to corruption, and whiteness with the sun and God. This theory combines metaphysical and ethical dimensions with physical ones.

In both Patrizi's philosophy and Caravaggio's paintings, the pure light of God is mixed on earth with corruptible shadow, because we perceive higher things poorly. In Caravaggio's paintings, God's light of grace invades man's venal world only selectively, as a sign from a higher realm. In suggesting through his obscure settings that the earth is furthest from God and his light, Caravaggio shows his agreement with Patrizi. In the *Calling of St Matthew* (see illus. 18), Christ and the light behind him invade the murky setting, which represents the darkness of humanity's world. In spite of his view that humankind and the earth are distant from God, Patrizi was optimistic in conceiving the world as touched by divinity; its preservation is assured by the goodness of God, since all lower things participate in the higher ones.[16] This idea corresponds roughly to Caravaggio's representation of humanity participating in divine things by means of God's miraculous light, and his offer through the grace of Christ – God in human form – of conversion or enlightenment.

In his *Trattato dell'arte della pittura* of 1584, Giovanni Paolo Lomazzo was the first writer to include a lengthy discussion of the symbolic nature of light in an art treatise. In describing the metaphysics of light, he, like Patrizi, borrows heavily from the Neoplatonic tradition of Ficino. Lomazzo says that light is brightest near God, becomes duller at mid-range, and furthest from its divine source is truly dark ('molto oscuro').[17] This view of light applies to Caravaggio, whose intense and focused light is not accompanied by the general diffusion of light in the bright blue sky of daytime. His light is a beam of brightness emanating from an invisible source and penetrating the general darkness. An essential feature of his paintings is that his light seems to invade a space of almost impenetrable blackness. His light radiates from the solar source that is at once part of nature and the supplier of illumination imbued with sacred meaning. Even as Caravaggio's light seems simultaneously natural and divine, his obscure settings are unnatural, as Giulio Mancini noted, symbolically denoting the dark world of humanity.[18]

Caravaggio probably achieved his studio lighting effects by aiming strong sunlight at his subject, either directly through a window or skylight, or by means of mirrors. Both Giovanni Pietro Bellori and Joachim von Sandrart wrote that Caravaggio worked in a dark room with a single source of light from above.[19] In 1605 his landlady complained that he had damaged the ceiling of his rented house; perhaps he had knocked a hole in the ceiling to let in sunlight.[20] Greater artfulness, however, than a brute act such as that was required of him to make the light in his paintings seem divine. To many seventeenth-century commentators, Caravaggio used *tenebroso* lighting merely as a startling technique devised to garner attention for himself; they hardly imagined that his light had theological or cosmological significance. An exception is a poem by Marzio Milesi on the subject of Caravaggio's *Calling of St Matthew*, written shortly after the painting was unveiled in 1600. Milesi, who found genuine religious feeling in Caravaggio's canvases, associates the strong light coming from behind Christ with Christ himself: 'And Jesus, who so shines/ that he attracts the eyes and minds of the beholders/ to contemplate him, seems to make blessed/ the spirits of the mortals.'[21]

Giordano Bruno's ideas on light are useful when analysing Caravaggio's paintings because both men think of the sun allegorically as a source of divine light that relieves the natural darkness of the earth. Bruno sees the divine presence as pure light, but believes the light that reaches us is confused and mixed with darkness. He places the sun, that most potent of all natural religious symbols, at the centre of our solar system and imagines it as standing for a divinity that all men can see and whose spiritual light reaches all humanity. For Bruno, who maintained that humans are able only partially to see beyond the shadows of ideas to the pure idea and union with God, the world is not entirely dark or evil in its shadow state, but is lit by the sun, that powerful symbol of the deity.[22] These ideas are consonant with Caravaggio's light. Like Bruno, Caravaggio thinks of humankind as in the shadow of light.[23]

Bruno and Caravaggio cannot conceive of nature without understanding its relationship to divinity, and both associate shadow with human ignorance and light with God. But they have important differences. For Bruno, on a moral and religious plane, the homogeneity of the infinite universe involves the omnipresence of good. The evil that we believe we discern is an illusion brought about by only partial understanding; a total sight of the universe would eliminate the shadows from it.[24] By contrast, in Caravaggio's paintings, light and shade represent a struggle of the individual mind to face the tragic side of life and to search desperately for faith. According to him, humanity's doubt is part of religious experience.

While light–dark contrasts remain strong in many of the paintings of Caravaggio's late period, the cues that would indicate an otherworldly source for the light are not always as clear as they were earlier. For example, the second version of *Supper at Emmaus* of 1606 (illus. 48) has an entirely uniform dark background, lacking a diagonal shaft of light dividing a back wall into brightness and shadow. Christ has no halo, so the artist precludes the possibility of a subtle and symbolic interaction of an implied shadow-nimbus and wall light (as in his first *Supper at Emmaus*, illus. 45). The light in the second *Supper* could be regarded as both divine and ordinary, but such an impression is less certain than with the *Calling*. In the Contarelli *Calling* and Caravaggio's other religious paintings, the observer of the pictures recognizes the light as having at once a mysterious divine source and a seeming naturalness, but the protagonists within the canvases do not always seem to be aware of its spiritual import.

Caravaggio's light clearly has its analogy with divinity, but his darkness does not necessarily mean the same thing in every painting, or at least to every viewer. The blackness in his *Madonna di Loreto* (see illus. 38), for example, has been

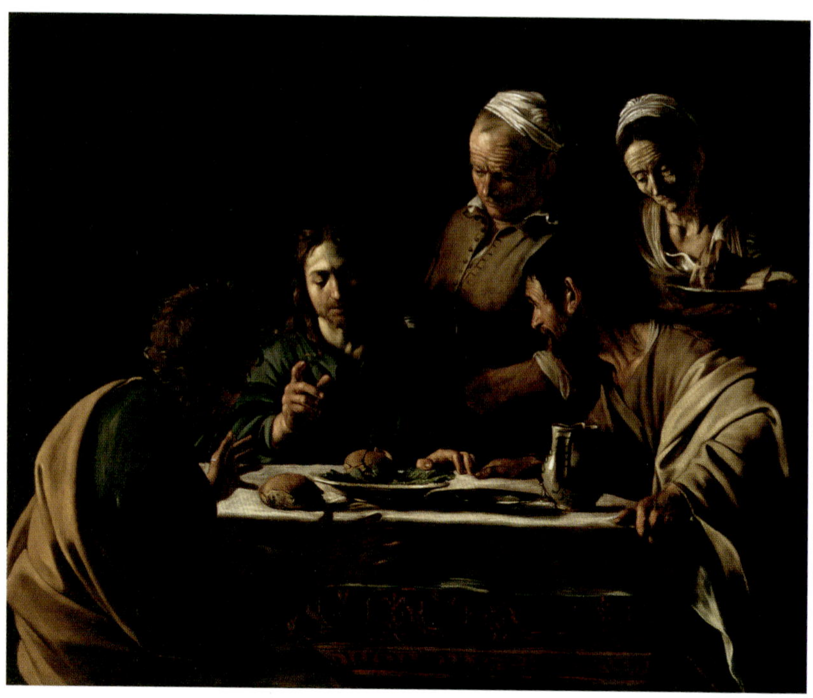

called spiritual, sacred, penitential and mystical.[25] These points may be valid, because darkness is multivalent and its interpretation depends on how the painting is viewed, how the subject is handled expressively by the artist, and how the darkness and light work together to create the overall effect. But blackness in Caravaggio's art can indicate the dark world of humanity similar to the conception of the theologians and natural philosophers of his time. In spite of his mysterious light, conservative religious authorities concerned with maintaining respectability in art were sceptical of Caravaggio, whom they perceived as introducing too much naturalism into religious painting.

48 Caravaggio, *Supper at Emmaus*, 1606, oil on canvas.

TWELVE

The Science of Art

WHILE CARAVAGGIO exhibits an empiricist's preoccupation with the particularity of things, simultaneously through his dark backgrounds and strong light his canvases signify humanity's relation to the divine world that exists beyond the physical senses. His novel treatment of space presents a dramatic contrast of near total blackness breached by preternaturally intense light that may be apprehended through the Christian metaphor of dark symbolizing the human world and light signifying salvation. His tenebrism may also be understood in relation to ideas about the physical heavens, the world system as it was conceived by both theologians and natural philosophers of his period. The contrast between light and dark in his canvases serves as a religious analogue of the scientific debates in his time over the structure of the cosmos.

The painter's umbral backgrounds denote a scepticism about the comprehensibility of the heavens; they betoken the limits of human knowledge, the inability to know what lies beyond immediate sensory experience. As in the spatial conceptions of the contemporary natural philosophers, in Caravaggio's paintings space seems unknowable and immeasurable. Unlike Leon Battista Alberti, who in the fifteenth century had established a geometric method of spatial construction for painting, Caravaggio creates a largely intuitive space that is a mysterious, black void. He was working at a time when the box-like space of Alberti was usually discarded in favour of more subjective approaches to spatial construction. The Mannerists of the early sixteenth century had already ignored Albertian perspective, and by the time of his *Last Judgment* (1534–41) Michelangelo had replaced space articulated by geometric projection with space defined by the human figure. In the seventeenth century, spurred on by scientific advances, artists such as Andrea Pozzo developed more elaborate geometric spatial systems, particularly for use in the complex projections required for ceiling paintings. In Caravaggio's time, intuitive and scientific conceptions of space existed side by side in painting, with an emphasis on the former.

In the wake of Nicolaus Copernicus's *De revolutionibus orbium coelestium* (1543), the natural philosophers were proposing new cosmic systems to replace the traditional Aristotelian-Ptolemaic scheme further developed by St Thomas Aquinas, of a finite world enclosed within a theological heaven. It is clear that by 1600 the traditional Aristotelians and Thomists were being seriously challenged by a younger generation of natural philosophers. They proposed novel conceptions of the universe that brought into question the location of the theological heaven and God's special place in it. In Caravaggio's time, many unfamiliar, competing and contradictory theories were promoted about the heavens, variously calling for an earth- or sun-centred system, some finite and others infinite. Giordano Bruno, Bernardino Telesio, Francesco Patrizi,

Thomas Digges and William Gilbert all proposed an infinite universe, but each in a different way, some with theological heavens, others with physical ones, and some with the two congruent. For example, in 1576 Digges proposed arranging the planetary orbs around the sun, in the new Copernican order, and replacing the traditional finite, fixed shell of stars with an infinite starry domain that also served as the court of God and the habitat of the elect and angels.[1] Needless to say, in Rome this scheme was viewed as heretical, as was the more radical theory of Bruno, that the physical universe was uniform and infinite with no fixed centre and no place left for the Christian heaven.

Caravaggio's shadowy paintings imply an anxiety about the world and humankind's place within it. In his canvases space is left unexplained, and everything is lost in a sea of blackness beyond the immediate foreground of well-lit protagonists. The Christian heaven never appears at the top of his canvases, a lack that in part reflects the feeling among those of Caravaggio's generation that the new science had made God and the traditional celestial empyrean appear strangely remote.

Caravaggio's study of the natural world has a triple significance. First, even if his religious paintings are carefully staged tableaux depicting biblical events in a novel and self-conscious style, he paints the things of the world beautifully, with all the insistence of a true empiricist. In spite of his works' complexity of construction and meaning, the objects and surfaces he paints – shiny satin or matt wool clothing, the skin and underlying muscles and bones of the human body – show the effect of his naturalist's eye and careful observation, which reveal the same new dedication to nature, the same sense of discovery, as is found in the work of his contemporaries studying in such fields as anatomy, botany and astronomy.

Secondly, Caravaggio's light reflects metaphysical thought. His intense and piercing light has qualities that go beyond the observation of nature, and a double significance that matches the investigations of both the scientific and the metaphysical sides of the natural philosophy of his day: it seems at once natural and divine. While the same claim could be made for the work of earlier religious artists, Caravaggio is more insistent in stressing the earthly/divine duality of his light by means of his *tenebroso* technique, in which he deliberately sets a symbolic, unnatural blackness of space and earth against an intense, searing light.

Third, Caravaggio's art shows the limitations of human knowledge, through murky spatial settings that stand as metaphors for human ignorance of the divine world or the theological heavens, the world beyond our immediate perception. Both sacred writers and natural philosophers used darkness to describe humanity's isolation from God. These same issues found in Caravaggio's paintings – the positive, practical, new investigation of nature and, simultaneously, the metaphysical qualities of natural phenomena and the limits of human apprehension – largely shaped the concerns of the natural philosophers of his time.

As a member of Cardinal Del Monte's household in Rome, Caravaggio may have been aware, however indirectly, of the debates about the world system. The cardinal pursued scientific interests, as did his brother Guidobaldo, a mathematician, natural philosopher and astronomer. Guidobaldo was a strong supporter of the young Galileo Galilei, who visited the home of the cardinal in Rome and received his help in gaining Medici patronage. The cardinal himself experimented with new medicines in his own alchemical laboratory at the Casino Ludovisi, where he had Caravaggio paint a ceiling representing the celestial sphere containing the earth, sun and moon traversed by the signs of the zodiac, along with the pagan gods Jupiter, Neptune and Pluto.[2] It was also while he was a member of the cardinal's household that Caravaggio developed his famous *tenebroso* technique. His obscure backgrounds do not depict either literally or metaphorically any cosmological system, but they do suggest an apprehensiveness about humankind's place in a universe that was, with respect to the theories then being disputed, unfamiliar and unknown.

Caravaggio's exclusion of God the Father and his radiant heaven from his paintings was sometimes questioned by his Church patrons.[3] This sceptical position on the part of the artist was congruent with people's reactions to the natural philosophers, who in their debates about the nature of universal space made God seem remote and difficult to comprehend, and his place within their competing schemes unclear.[4] Caravaggio's canvases bear out the view of the philosophers that the natural world can be construed only against the background of implied, largely invisible spiritual forces. In his works' problematic presentation of space, in their dark uncertainty, in their implication of an immanent yet transcendent God and in their light, both divine and earthly, they conform to the views of the natural philosophers of his time. The effect of the great variety of world systems as proposed by the natural philosophers was to create confusion, as expressed in John Donne's words: 'A new Philosophy calls all in doubt.'[5] This sceptical trend is reinforced even by the normally optimistic Bruno, who ultimately rejected notions of mental ascent to a higher metaphysical or divine plane. In his *Eroici furori* (1585), he speaks of the 'deficiency of the human sight and apprehensive potency towards things divine'.[6] The uncertainty of the design of the world system resulting from the new cosmological debates may be reflected in Caravaggio's tenebrism, which has spiritual and metaphysical implications that go well beyond the simple idea of 'cellar lighting'.

Caravaggio's obscure backgrounds cannot be associated with any particular cosmic scheme. His imagery, while resolutely omitting any representation of a theological heaven, otherwise generally remains fixed within the Christian tradition. Although Bruno was confident in his belief that a good and wise God had created a beneficial, infinite universe, Caravaggio was more ambiguous in his religious expression, and given to a more tragic outlook. Bruno could be critical, too, rejecting the notion of the earth as privileged, fixed and central, and destroying the Aristotelian distinction between terrestrial and celestial regions. Such radical cosmological ideas are paralleled in the uncertainty, emptiness and scepticism found in Caravaggio's space.

Caravaggio did not yet live in an age dominated by the values of the new science called the 'scientific revolution'. Much of the important work of Johannes Kepler, Galileo and William Harvey was not begun until 1605 or later, by which time Caravaggio's art had already reached its mature stage. The natural philosophers of the later sixteenth century (and much of the seventeenth) studied nature by making simple observations, but many were also drawn to alchemy, astrology, metaphysical speculation and natural magic. Well into the seventeenth century and beyond, men we think of as scientists, even Isaac Newton himself, were captivated by hermeticism. Often no sharp distinction was made between the two scientific cultures, old and new, but an amalgam was created of both at once. The natural philosophers link their study of nature with spiritual concerns. Telesio, for example, assures his reader that he will engage only in the most rigorous discussion of nature based on careful observation. But not far into his text he is already explaining God's divine role in the creation and functioning of natural phenomena.[7] He claimed that heat – most importantly here its manifestation as light – was created by God and directed by him in its effects.[8] The physical and sacred aspects of things are seen as interwoven in both the writings of the natural philosophers and the paintings of Caravaggio.

In their speculations about the heavens, the natural philosophers begin with the premise that God is unknowable, but then quickly proceed to find ways in which they can define him and demonstrate how he organized the universe in both its physical and its metaphysical aspects. Something like this is also true of Caravaggio: he stresses humankind's bewilderment in the face of divinity, but, in the end, the protagonists of his paintings gain spiritual insight. For both Caravaggio and the philosophers, it is impossible to separate the physical and the spiritual realms, in spite of their claims to follow only nature. Many connections exist between Caravaggio's art and the philosophical movements of the late sixteenth century. Stoicism is reflected in the artist's use of humble and impoverished figures, as in his first *Inspiration of St Matthew* (see illus. 36); scepticism in his emphasis on man's limited knowledge of the divine, as in his *Calling of St Matthew* (see illus. 18); atomism in the materialistic aspect of his naturalism; natural philosophy in his study of nature; and even Platonism in the mystical aspect of his light.

Caravaggio's art does not reflect the confident view of the humanists of the fifteenth and early sixteenth centuries that human beings are in harmony with God and the splendid natural order he created. Rather, his works assert the pessimistic outlook of the late sixteenth century, when the Church was under attack and when the Council of Trent underscored the sinful nature of humankind. The void in Caravaggio's paintings is not Bruno's optimistically conceived infinite physical space, but a psychological darkness that reveals the inadequacy of human beings to fathom divine mysteries.

This mysterious side of Caravaggio's art is balanced by his intense study of nature through observation. In such investigation, and in his practice of painting directly from live models without making preliminary drawings, his art has close ties with the new empirical sciences. His empirical approach emphasized the evidence of the senses and resulted in a verisimilitude that was praised by his seventeenth-century biographers, such as Joachim von Sandrart in his *Teutsche Academie*.[9] Caravaggio's works reveal similarities with the genuinely empirical side of the natural philosophy of his day. His paintings are grounded in the observation of nature, as is Galileo's science, and one of his canvases has even been linked, on a metaphorical level, to Galileo's new approach to mechanics. The physical actions of the three men lifting the saint's

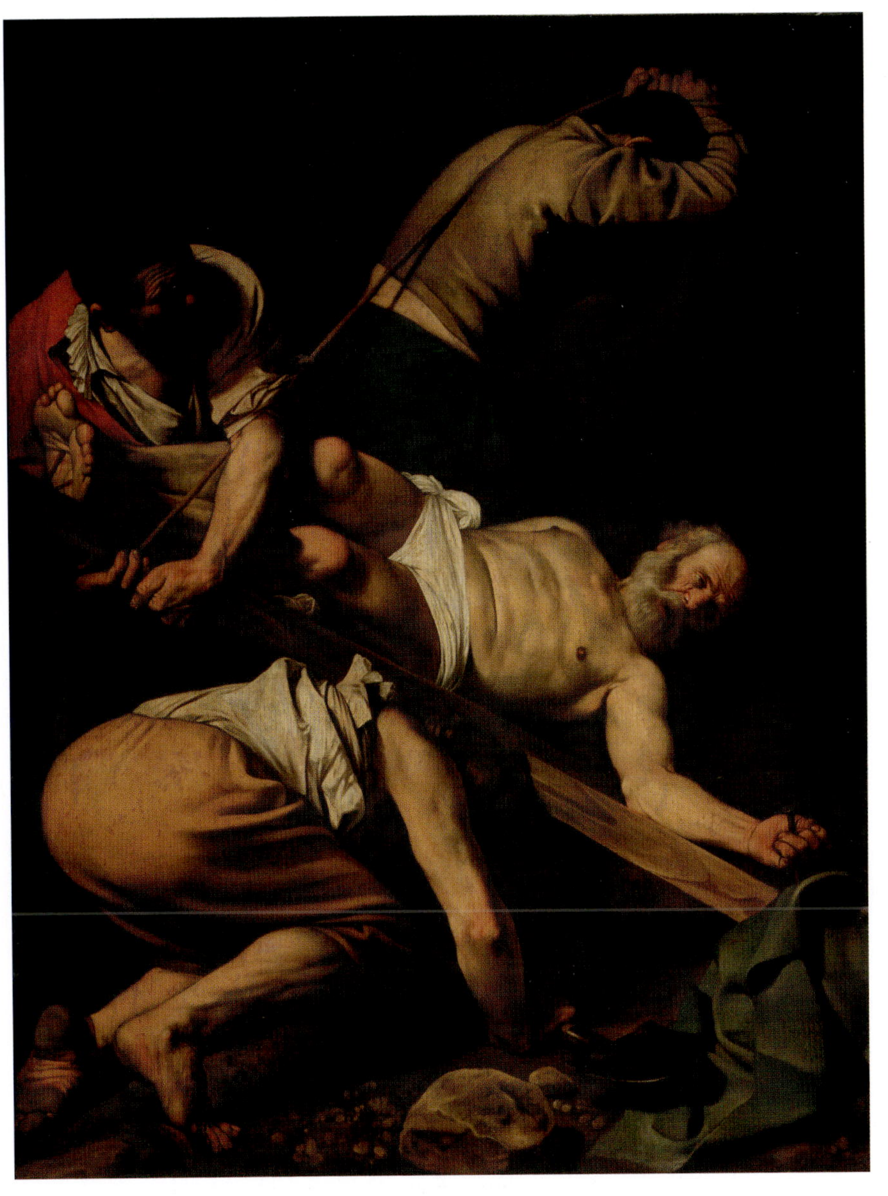

49 Caravaggio, *Crucifixion of St Peter*, 1600–1601, oil on canvas.

cross with rope, hand and back in Caravaggio's *Crucifixion of St Peter* (illus. 49) have been compared to Galileo's *On Motion* of 1590.[10] Caravaggio shows a gritty new emphasis in painting on weight and force, a resistance to gravity, as his trio struggles, each in a different way, to lift the weight of the cross.[11]

Galileo remained largely silent on the subject of faith; for him science was of a different dimension from religion. But this separation of the methods of science and faith did not mean that Galileo rejected religion or even God's role as architect of the universe. He conceived of God as the creator of the world, who 'brought forth [its] structural design from within himself, whereas [humanity,] despite strenuous efforts, scarcely perceives the plan embodied in [its] struc- ture'.[12] But in his pursuit of scientific truth, particularly in his Copernicanism, Galileo fell foul of religious authorities, just as Caravaggio did when his sense of artistic truth seemed to vio- late their beliefs. In their great innovations, both the painter and the scientist are protagonists of a culture of dissent.[13]

Caravaggio's exceptional ability to depict the real world on a painted surface may demonstrate his interest in Giovanni Battista della Porta's description of the marvels of crafts- manship and technology in his *Magiae naturalis* of 1558 and its many subsequent editions. Della Porta worked with illusion- istic devices such as concave mirrors, lenses and the camera obscura. It is likely that Caravaggio used mirrors as pictorial aids in painting his pictures: in 1599 he had been lent a large mirror to paint his *Narcissus*, and before that, he showed a convex mirror in his *Conversion of the Magdalen* (illus. 50). He probably used a mirror to compose his figures and to gauge the effects of three-dimensional reality in two dimensions.[14]

Giovanni Baglione described Caravaggio painting with a mirror, and when in 1605 his landlady seized his belongings for non-payment of rent for the house he leased on the Vico San Biagio, among them was a 'speccio a scudo' (a shield-shaped mirror) and a larger flat mirror.[15]

Because of his scientific interests, Del Monte may have aided Caravaggio in the use of optical instruments. It is unlikely that Caravaggio used a camera obscura, which can produce a virtual image of an external scene, or a parabolic mirror, which can similarly capture and project an image from nature, since they provided only a dim, fuzzy image that effectively eliminated detail; furthermore, the latter had a very limited focal area.[16] In any case, Caravaggio's religious works do not merely transcribe the visual data that he found in the studio, but required his powers of invention. He seems also to have used mirrors to direct the sunlight, constantly on the move, that entered through his studio window. But even if he used mirrors, he manipulated what he saw: in *Boy Bitten by a Lizard* (illus. 51) the reflection from the window is on the wrong side of the glass vase, on the right, while the subject is lit from the left. Furthermore, through the metaphorical, polemical and ironic elements of his art, not to mention the figural and spatial distortion, he explored expressive realms beyond the capacity of a merely literal naturalism or a dependence on technical devices.

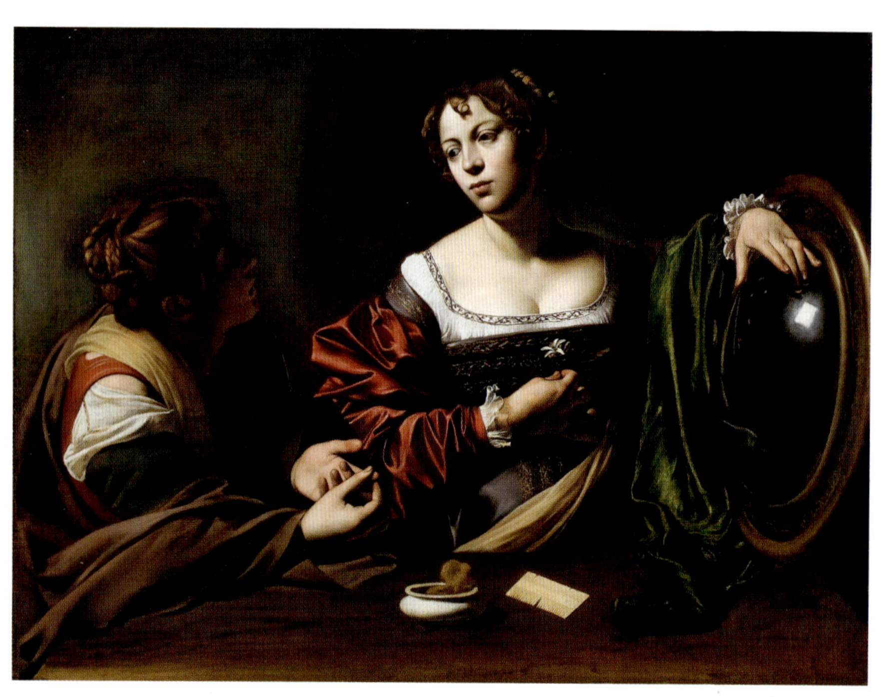

50 Caravaggio, *Conversion of the Magdalen*, c. 1598–9, oil on canvas.

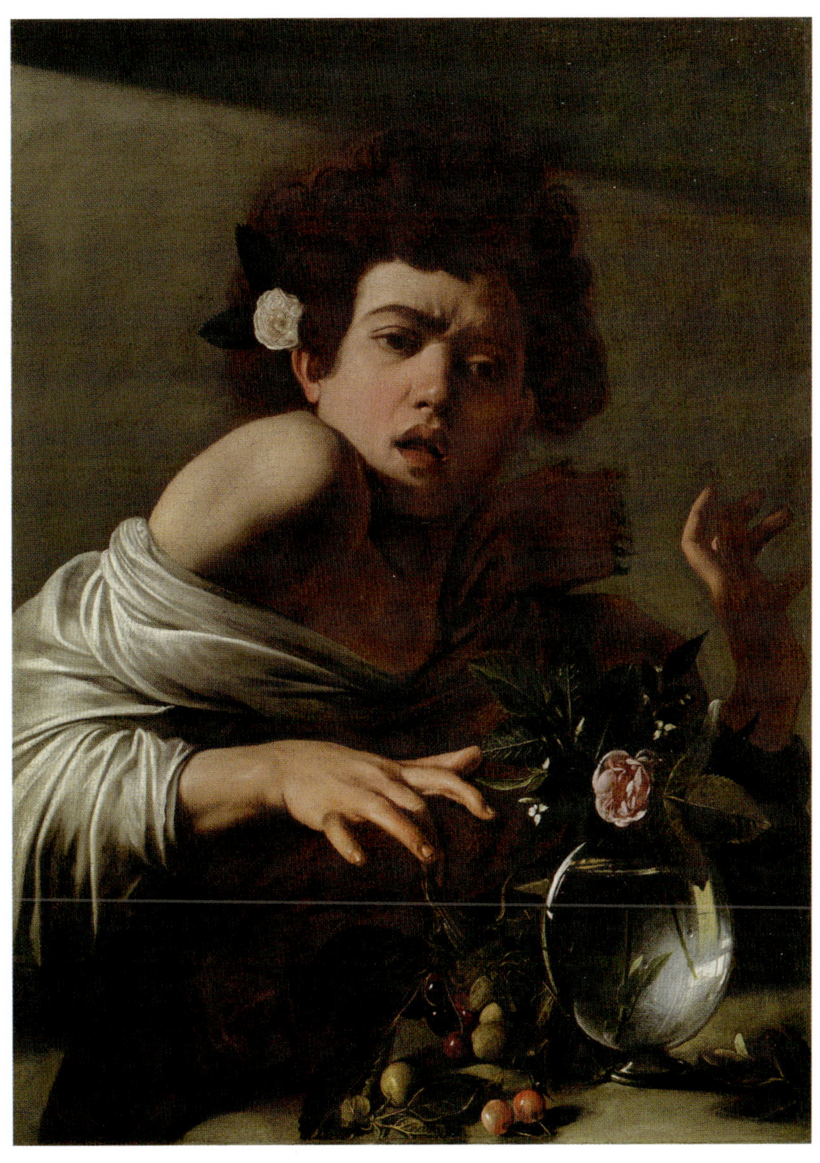

51 Caravaggio, *Boy Bitten by a Lizard*, c. 1596–7, oil on canvas.

THIRTEEN

The Religious Orders

NY ATTEMPT TO TIE Caravaggio's religious expression narrowly to one or another of the religious orders, societies or personalities (Jesuit, Oratorian, Franciscan, Borromean, and so on) presents difficulties. His art has the closest affinity with Augustinianism, but not exclusively so. Augustinian influence is more decisive in the *Calling of St Matthew* (see illus. 18) and in a number of his other paintings than that of the Roman Oratory or the Jesuits, and more pervasive in his work than the Franciscan impulse promulgated by some scholars. Caravaggio may have developed a special relationship with Augustinianism in his personal life, since he had committed a murder and was dependent on God's grace, an aspect that Augustinian theology emphasizes.[1] Nevertheless, Franciscan influence has been found in the *Ecstasy of St Francis* (see illus. 15) and *Taking of Christ* (see illus. 42), the latter painted for Ciriaco Mattei, who, with his brother the cardinal Girolamo, was devoted to St Francis. As with the artist's other patrons who had particular religious practices and affiliations, the brothers may have discussed with Caravaggio devotional subjects that were important to them and that they wished to see reflected in the paintings he made for them. In the *Taking of Christ*, the

Lord exhibits self-denial in accepting his arrest, an act that reflects a particular form of Franciscan severity and spirituality during the Counter-Reformation.[2]

Franciscanism, however, with its piety and simplicity, is only one perceptible strain in Caravaggio's art, and hardly accounts for the theological implications of his more daring, troublesome paintings. A Jesuit influence has been detected in his vivid depictions of events as called for in the *Spiritual Exercises* of Ignatius Loyola.[3] However, Caravaggio's settings are often minimal, hardly conforming to the 'composition of place' required by the *Exercises*; in this way, his paintings are different in character from those sponsored by the Jesuits, such as the fresco cycle of lurid and didactic martyrdoms in the church of Santo Stefano Rotondo in Rome, which include elaborate settings (see illus. 22). Besides, he was never patronized by the Jesuits.

The influence of the Roman Oratorians on Caravaggio's humble saints and peasants has been seen as decisive by some, especially as expressed through the down-to-earth simplicity of the order's founder, St Filippo Neri.[4] Cardinal Del Monte had links with the pauperist religious faction in Rome, including the Roman Oratory, and Caravaggio's protectors, the Colonna family, were closely connected with Neri's inner circle.[5] But Neri, whom Caravaggio never met, especially admired the paintings of Federico Barocci. Neri's successor, Cardinal Cesare Baronio, preferred the pictures of Cristoforo Roncalli, who painted pietistic, decorative images. Moreover, the Oratorians limited their humility to their social programmes and to their vows of poverty. In their religious images, they expected Christ and the saints to be depicted with dignity and respect. Those works by Caravaggio deemed indecorous – his images of dirty saints and peasants – would have offended the Oratorians as much as any other group within the Church.[6] On the other hand, it may be that the Oratorians would have responded positively to the saint in the first *Inspiration of St Matthew* (see illus. 36, 37), where in his ignorance, bowed head and bare legs Matthew could have been interpreted not as coarse or indecorous but as a humble follower of 'naked Christ'.[7] When it came to his *Entombment of Christ* (see illus. 47), painted for the Oratorian church of Santa Maria in Vallicella, the artist ensured that his canvas was free of any controversial imagery.[8]

The hallmarks of Caravaggio's art include the immediacy and reality of his religious scenes, his protagonists' close, personal contact with Christ and the reception of grace through conversion. These aspects are typically Augustinian. Three of his major Roman paintings had been commissioned in churches of the Augustinian Order: the *Madonna di Loreto* (see illus. 38) for Sant' Agostino and the *Conversion of St Paul* (see illus. 20) and the *Crucifixion of St Peter* (see illus. 19, 49) for Santa Maria del Popolo. In several of his paintings, Caravaggio follows the Augustinian position that grace descends on humans irrespective of their own participation. He indicates the dependence of his protagonists on undeserved grace by their unpreparedness (*Calling of St Matthew*, see illus. 18) or their astonishment at Christ's divinity (*Supper at Emmaus*, see illus. 45).[9]

Sixteenth-century Catholic reformers such as Juan de Valdés and Pietro Martire Vermigli believed with St Augustine that humankind is predestined for heaven by God.[10] Caravaggio's

Calling of St Matthew supports the doctrine of predestination. In this work, Matthew's utter surprise and lack of 'good works' are expressed by the way he stops counting money and turns towards Christ, but hesitates to follow (see illus. 18, 29). The Augustinian content of the *Calling* reflects Caravaggio's own conception of Matthew's indecisiveness more than it does the addendum to the contract of 1591 that he inherited from Giuseppe Cesari, which specified that the saint should rise and follow Christ.[11] The fathers of the French church of San Luigi dei Francesi may well have approved of the Augustinian implications of the fact that the painting's imagery focused on conversion. This concept is a quintessentially Augustinian idea, reflected in these priests' special dedication to the conversion of Jews.[12] The *Martyrdom of St Matthew* (see illus. 31) also departs from Cesari's contract addendum of 1591 that Caravaggio was supposed to follow in 1599, because he added a scene of adult baptism at the bottom of his canvas.[13]

The *Martyrdom* thus stresses two important ideals of Counter-Reformation Rome: the conversion of peoples in foreign lands (according to the *Golden Legend*, a thirteenth-century collection of hagiographies by Jacobus de Voragine, Matthew was in Ethiopia to convert pagans) and martyrdom in the service of the Church. In Contarelli's original commission of 1565 to Girolamo Muziano, a prominent Roman artist, the central painting of the vaulted ceiling was to represent St Matthew baptizing the king and queen of Ethiopia.[14] Although this subject was eventually abandoned, Caravaggio borrowed the idea by including a scene of baptism in his *Martyrdom*. He thus makes the same point about the conversion and baptism of foreigners. Caravaggio's pattern of patronage, therefore, as well as his personal inclination, supports the Augustinian imagery we find in these works.[15]

The subject of Matthew's execution reflected current interest in the heroic deaths of early Christian saints and martyrs, newly investigated through the discovery of paleo-Christian catacombs in Rome in the late sixteenth century and recorded in Antonio Bosio's *Roma sotterranea* of 1632. Parallels were drawn with current Catholic priests, who likewise fell victim to persecution at the hands of the Protestants in the northern countries during the religious wars and in the New World and Asia, where Catholicism was making inroads. Cardinal Baronio, Procurator General of the Roman Oratory and Church historian, reflected the common feeling of the contemporary clergy when he stated with envy that he would be honoured to die the death of those just men.[16] In his *Discorso intorno alle immagini sacre e profane* of 1592, Cardinal Gabriele Paleotti wrote that artists should not hesitate to paint the torments of the Christians in all their horror, to glorify through art the courage of its martyrs.[17] The scenes of torture and persecution in the Roman church of Santo Stefano Rotondo (see illus. 22) were intended to inspire priests and other Catholics to be prepared to die for their faith. These frescoes were commissioned by Pope Gregory XIII, who had strong ties with the Jesuits. Caravaggio's canvas depicting Matthew's martyrdom, too, would serve as a model for modern evangelists across the globe.

Muziano never painted anything in the Contarelli chapel, and when Giuseppe Cesari eventually took over and frescoed the ceiling in 1592–3, his subject was *St Matthew Resurrecting the Daughter of the King of Ethiopia* (illus. 52).[18] At this point

mature than is normal in Madonna pictures, and the obvious décolletage of the Virgin. Caravaggio's works were likewise rejected because of a lack of decorum or for technical reasons, but not for theological infractions on the part of the artist. The instructions that Caravaggio was intended to follow in creating his paintings for the Contarelli chapel were more detailed than most, but in the end the artist departed from them significantly. In light of this relative artistic freedom, aside from the need for propriety and a basic knowledge of the subject to be represented, it is understandable how Caravaggio might have chosen without constraint to emphasize Augustinian values and more generally to experiment with novel ways of presenting the stories in his pictures.

FOURTEEN

The Reception of Caravaggio's Art

CARAVAGGIO fundamentally altered the practice and perception of painting; his works rely more than much previous art on the actively engaged viewer to interpret their ambiguities and novelties. By presenting ambiguous narratives he motivates the observer confronted with his canvases to ask questions. Some of his key works, such as his *Calling of St Matthew*, first *Inspiration of St Matthew* and *Death of the Virgin*, assault and bewilder the viewer, with narratives that present reality devoid of the traditional sixteenth-century visual rhetorical signals that would provide keys to interpretation. Caravaggio's critics began a debate in his own time over the negative or positive religious meanings of his paintings, and that debate continues today, although in a more sophisticated form.

The negative extreme, where Caravaggio was seen as irreverent in his religious expression, was taken by many early writers on his art, including Giulio Mancini, Giovanni Baglione, Francesco Scannelli and Giovanni Pietro Bellori, who emphasized the coarseness and vulgarity of his figures and gave reasons why his paintings were not conducive to piety.[1] The middle course was represented by Cardinal Ottavio Paravicino, who wrote to a friend that Caravaggio's paintings were somewhere between the sacred and the profane.[2] On the positive side, supporting a serious religious impulse, was the jurist Marzio Milesi, whose verses praise the sacred and devotional content of Caravaggio's works.[3] In modern criticism, some scholars have stated a strong case against a conventional religious approach in Caravaggio's paintings.[4] They see in his figures man's incapacity to fathom divine mysteries, and they view his scenes as devoid of eschatological significance, where death is final and salvation impossible. Others see Caravaggio as embracing a positive, traditional religious attitude.[5]

The letter on Caravaggio's art written by Paravicino in 1603 tells us much about the critical insight of sharp-eyed connoisseurs of Caravaggio's paintings and the fluidity of meaning that they perceived in his religious works. The letter describes an imaginary Caravaggio speculating that he might paint for a sophisticated cleric with broad learning 'some painting that would have been in that middle area, between the sacred, and the profane'. The very fact that Paravicino put these words into his fictive Caravaggio's mouth makes it clear that the cardinal was aware of a potentially wide scope for meaning in art. His comments suggest that the painter himself was quite conscious of crafting pictures to suit the taste of particular patrons who were in a position to appreciate ambiguous meanings and a certain openness of interpretation.[6]

The rejection and revision of his Roman works for churches have become part of the Caravaggio legend. By 1602 the artist had made changes to all five of his major religious paintings to date in public settings: the *Calling*, *Martyrdom* and *Inspiration of St Matthew*, from the Contarelli chapel (see illus. 18, 31, 36, 37, 41, 46); and then the *Conversion of St Paul* and, according to Baglione, the *Crucifixion of St Peter* as well, both in the Cerasi chapel of Santa Maria del Popolo (see illus. 19, 20, 49).[7] Later, his *Madonna dei Palafrenieri* (see illus. 53) and *Death of the Virgin* (see illus. 26) were rejected.

The changes made to his pictures may have been based in part on Caravaggio's own revisions, particularly in the *Calling* and *Martyrdom*. Bellori claims that the first *Inspiration* (see illus. 36) was rejected by the priests of San Luigi because of its indecorous and too realistic treatment of the saint's crossed legs and exposed feet.[8] At first glance, the saint may seem to be an illiterate peasant, violating the guidelines set down by Cardinal Gabriele Paleotti in his *Discorso intorno alle immagini sacre e profane* of 1582, in which he warns the painter not to depict a saint in a way that inspires no devotion, and states that such holy figures should look intelligent.[9] Art historians have proposed competing explanations for the rejection of his pictures variously on documentary, technical and stylistic grounds, the artist's personality or the influence of religious institutions or cultural practices. The first *Inspiration* was most probably rejected for indecorousness; in any case, the painter's works present problems arising from his foundational ideas on religious expression in art. He clearly thought deeply, if unconventionally, about the religious content of his works, and their reception was sometimes problematic, as the remarks of Baglione, Bellori and others demonstrate.

In recent years documentary evidence has come to light and new theories have been proposed to suggest that his canvases were rejected not because they were indecorous but for mundane, practical reasons, or repainted by the artist himself because of stylistic or conceptual problems. The first *Inspiration* may have been replaced, it has been argued, because it was the wrong size for its intended space. The repainting of the *Conversion of St Paul* (see illus. 20) meant for the Cerasi chapel may have been the artist's decision, or it and its lost companion, the first version of the *Crucifixion of St Peter* (see illus. 19, 49), may have been redone because of the liturgical need to reverse the positions of the paintings in the chapel. Some have suggested that his *Madonna dei Palafrenieri* (see illus. 53) was not rejected by the Palafrenieri (papal grooms) for indecency, but rather that the picture lost its place in St Peter's because of a dispute over the rights of the papal grooms to their altar in that church.[10] But even after this dispute was resolved in early May 1606, the Palafrenieri continued to claim that they did not want Caravaggio's picture; by June 1606 it had been sold to Scipione Borghese for 100 *scudi*. Technical reasons such as these for the replacement of his paintings were not mentioned in the early sources on Caravaggio, which instead made it clear that his works were viewed by many as too secular or indecorous.

One notices strong differences in the reactions to Caravaggio's art, on the one hand by his patrons and supporters, who were enthusiastic in purchasing his works and in providing him with unflagging support when he was in trouble with the law, and on the other by his early biographers, who were unsparing in their withering criticism. When his biographers state that private collectors immediately sought his works after they were rejected by churches, they tacitly acknowledge the emergence of a new kind of art market, promoted by patrons both secular and religious, and grounded in aesthetic appreciation by cognoscenti. Such knowledgeable collectors must have been aware of the controversial nature of Caravaggio's art, and may have been struck by the ambiguous nature of its religious content. The fact that his rejected works were so coveted by collectors, including those within the religious community, indicates that some readily accommodated the ambiguity of their sacred imagery.

Caravaggio's admirers noticed his strangeness; indeed, it may be that his perceived eccentricity was an aspect of his appeal, and that it was partly because of his unconventionality that he was thought able to reinvent religious painting. Two of his supporters wrote about this strangeness: in one case his patron, Cardinal Del Monte, was quoted in a letter written in 1605 by the ambassador of the duke of Modena as saying that the artist had a 'most eccentric brain' ('uno cervello stravagantissimo').[11] Del Monte made this remark when the ambassador asked him to persuade the artist to send the duke a picture he owed him; the cardinal's response was that he could not promise success. Del Monte mentioned in the same sentence that Caravaggio had been sought out by Prince Marcantonio Doria of Genoa to paint a loggia for him, and that, even though the prince offered him 6,000 *scudi*, the artist did not want to accept the commission. The implication is that a normal artist would have jumped at the chance. In this case, Caravaggio probably declined because he lacked the desire to paint in fresco.

The other document is a notebook entry made by Nicolao di Giacomo in 1609, in which he records that he commissioned Caravaggio to depict 'four stories of the Passion of Christ to be made at the whim [*capriccio*] of the painter, of which he finished one that shows Christ carrying the cross . . .

it turned out really a very beautiful work . . . this painter . . .
has a crazy brain [*cervello stravolto*].'¹² This document is important in the first instance because it makes clear that patrons
wanted works by Caravaggio in which the artist was free to
paint in whatever way he wished, through his *capriccio*. They
valued his novelty, then, and would prefer to see what he came
up with rather than lay down detailed instructions for him
to follow. Secondly, this note seems to connect Caravaggio's
novelty in art with his troubled brain. His contemporaries
may have thought that it was the artist's very strangeness that
in part gave rise to his *invenzioni*.

These two reports written by patrons who knew
Caravaggio directly may be augmented by the statement of
one of his first biographers, Giulio Mancini, who also knew
him and described him as eccentric: 'One cannot deny that
Caravaggio was a very odd [*stravagantissimo*] person.'¹³ Later
in the century, Filippo Baldinucci repeated the idea that
Caravaggio had a 'very strange mind'.¹⁴ Even if he had a
reputation for oddity, in his innovative approach to sacred
art Caravaggio created a modern audience of appreciative
private patrons. He developed a fresh relationship with them
in which artistic freedom and novelty were prized, and laid
the foundation for a new, independent market for religious
artworks. This new market was based on commissions by
private patrons for religious pictures and on the resale to such
patrons of his works rejected by churches.

Earlier, Caravaggio's secular works of the mid- to late
1590s had been sought after by the new audience in Rome
of private collectors. There can be little doubt that the artist's
familiarity with and appeal to that market carried over into

his conception of his first large-scale religious canvases. His personal history as a secular painter had a profound effect on the revolution he created in religious art. His new conception in religious pictures of emphasizing the mundane, human world came about in part as his response to private patronage with its taste for secular images. Simultaneously, these religious canvases reflect contemporary debates that brought new emphasis to topics such as grace and free will, subjects that are treated in his narratives.

The ambiguity of Caravaggio's paintings and their new presentation of religious ideas may have been calculated to have special appeal to cultivated patrons and collectors such as the Mattei brothers and Vincenzo Giustiniani, who commissioned religious pictures from him and acquired the works that had been rejected by churches. Such patrons were shaping new kinds of taste in art around 1600, in which novelty and sophistication were prized as much as new ways of thinking about religious expression in art. Some of his sophisticated contemporary viewers, including such artists and poets as Peter Paul Rubens and Giambattista Marino, responded positively to his refreshing insights into religious meaning. After the *Death of the Virgin* (see illus. 26) was rejected by the Carmelite church of Santa Maria della Scala, in a famous example of Caravaggio's alleged impropriety, it was put up for sale. On the advice of Rubens, the Duke of Mantua purchased the work through his agent in Rome, Giovanni Magno. Pressure was exerted by artists in Rome to have the picture put on public display before it was removed to Mantua, and it was exhibited before the Roman people in April 1607. The excitement the picture generated among the artists and general populace of Rome indicates that its rejection by a church had no bearing on its being admired in a non-religious context.

In 1603–6 Caravaggio's public commissions became less numerous, partly because he made altarpieces that many found offensive. His depiction of Apostles, saints and worshippers alike as poor disturbed many viewers, in particular the religious authorities who made decisions on which painters to employ to decorate churches. Caravaggio had been influenced by the 'low church' of his youth in northern Italy, including Archbishop Carlo Borromeo's work there with the poor. But towards the end of the Roman phase of his career, with the election of Paul V Borghese in 1605, the Catholic Church was moving away from the austerity of Borromeo and the severe Counter-Reform imagery of Caravaggio's pictures. Borromeo's belief that churchmen should embrace humility and model themselves on Christ's poor disciples was falling out of fashion.

The Church now wanted to create an aura of power and authority, and increasingly the poor were regulated and controlled. Clearly committed to the Christian poor, Caravaggio completed his *Madonna di Loreto* (see illus. 38) in about 1605, depicting two lowly pilgrims; and, indeed, his dedication to the underprivileged was affirmed and remained unchanged to the end of his career. He received only three commissions for altarpieces in Roman churches between 1603 and 1606. He had hopes of receiving more papal commissions with the election of Paul V – through the recommendation of the new pope's nephew Cardinal Scipione Borghese he was able to paint the pontiff's portrait and received a commission from

St Peter's for the *Madonna dei Palafrenieri* – but the supposed indecency of the latter picture and its subsequent rejection threw Caravaggio into a state of despair. When Scipione Borghese bought the rejected *Madonna* it became secularized, purchased by the connoisseur in him, not the cardinal.

After this, in Rome Caravaggio's works were admired in private, but he was no longer at the centre of the world of religious painting. His increasing isolation was partly because of a desire for more accessible and optimistic imagery in sacred art. He found that more graceful works by younger painters who were inclined towards classicism, such as Guido Reni, were now preferred. When he completed his *Death of the Virgin* in 1606, he showed his unwillingness to compromise, since the proletarian Mary looked scandalously dead. Once more he was reduced to anguish when this work was rejected. His declining fortune was also caused by his notoriety for violent behaviour and his police record, which grew alarmingly during these years. As a result of his escalating marginalization in the Roman art world, he was becoming increasingly irritable and picking fights with his enemies, including those whom he saw as threatening his artistic reputation.

Such feelings came to a head on 28 May 1606, when his proud and irascible nature led to a serious crime: on the Via della Scrofa with some of his supporters, Caravaggio seems to have gone out looking for a fight with his old rival, Ranuccio Tomassoni. Reports from the next several days claiming that the duel began because of an argument over a tennis match wager were inaccurate. Witnesses' accounts indicate that the tennis story was a ruse to cover the fact of the duel, an illegal activity.[15] In the swordfight that ensued, Caravaggio killed

53 Caravaggio, *Madonna dei Palafrenieri*, 1605–6, oil on canvas.

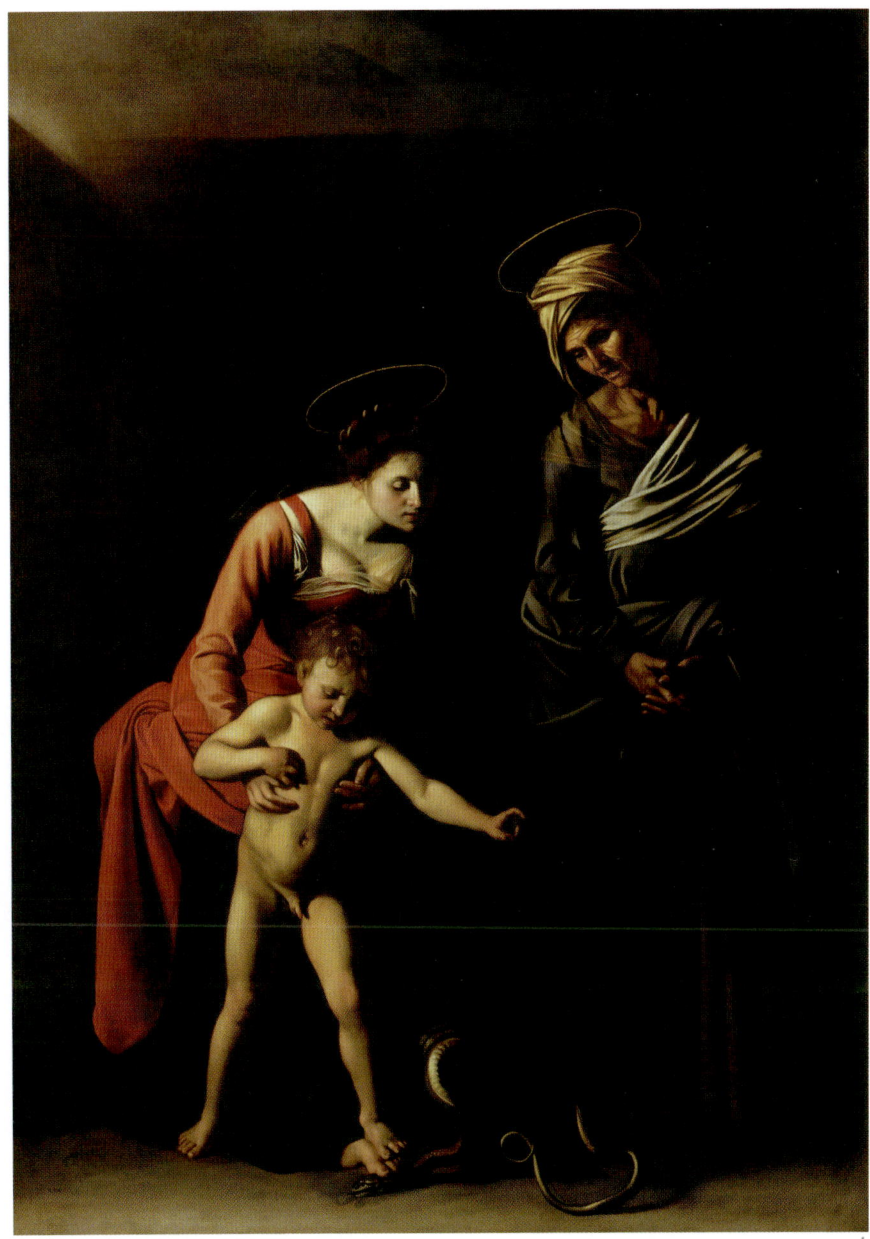

Tomassoni. As a result of this life-changing event, the artist fled to the mountains southeast of Rome, and then to Naples and elsewhere in the south, never to return to the city that made him famous.

Later, towards the end of the century, Bellori founded his dislike of Caravaggio's art on ideals of classicism that had hardened into entrenched dogma only after the artist's death. The famous critic condemned Caravaggio on the basis of an academic aesthetic that had first appeared in about 1600 in the classical style of the painter Annibale Carracci, Caravaggio's contemporary, and in the theoretical ideas of the papal diplomat and writer Giovanni Battista Agucchi as early as 1615.[16] Bellori thought of Caravaggio as a rebellious outsider who emphasized 'filth and deformity' in his paintings, at a time when the poor were viewed with even greater suspicion than when the artist was alive.[17] Caravaggio was hemmed in by hostile critics and by artists with temperaments and styles very different from his own, and one way of looking at his art suggests that it became outmoded as the seventeenth century wore on.

Caravaggio's canvases thus reflected a cultural moment that had long faded by the time of many of his critical biographers. It has been argued that his paintings have more in common with late sixteenth- than with seventeenth-century art and culture. His depictions of martyrdom, for example, are said to be rooted in the gruesome late sixteenth-century frescoes at Santo Stefano Rotondo (see illus. 22) and to be conceived within the mindset of the Counter-Reformation, which emphasized saintly sacrifice.[18] Even if such pictures focusing on religious suffering continued to be made during the more confident age of the so-called Church Triumphant, there is some truth in this assertion. Caravaggio's art necessarily grew from sixteenth-century precedents, but this fact does not prevent us from discerning in his paintings elements that we now recognize as modern, or from finding qualities in his work that appear more consistently in later periods of art.

Fortunately, one of the side effects of Caravaggio's move to southern Italy in 1606 was his discovery that there the pauperist strain of Counter-Reformation piety, to which he was so drawn, was particularly strong. The fate of his *Seven Works of Mercy* (see illus. 60) of 1607, painted in Naples, demonstrates his success in the south. By 1613 several offers of 2,000 *scudi* or more, six times the original fee, had been made to purchase this picture, but the Confraternity of the Pio Monte, which had commissioned it, turned down all offers.[19]

The influence of Caravaggio's innovative dark style continued to spread long after his death, in the art of the Italians Carlo Saraceni, Bartolomeo Manfredi and Artemisia Gentileschi; the Dutchmen Hendrick ter Brugghen, Gerrit van Honthorst, Dirck van Baburen and Rembrandt van Rijn; the Frenchmen Simon Vouet, Valentin de Boulogne and Georges de La Tour; and the Spaniards Francisco Ribalta, Jusepe de Ribera, Diego Velázquez and others. Their work is inconceivable without his example, even if in Rome the wild enthusiasm for his art by the younger painters eventually gave way to classicism and the High Baroque.

During much of the eighteenth century and the first half of the nineteenth, Caravaggio's reputation declined, even if nineteenth-century painters such as Gustave Courbet embraced a proletarian approach to art that was reminiscent of his own. Renewed interest in Caravaggio accompanied the rise of modern art in the twentieth century that introduced radical new styles conditioned by complexity, ambiguity, contradiction and the response of the viewer. The art historian Roberto Longhi was especially important in bringing Caravaggio to the attention of the public and raising his critical fortune among twentieth-century scholars.[20] It is not so much Caravaggio's realistic style that has influenced today's art, although examples may be found, particularly in photography and cinema, but rather his paintings' ambiguities and antinomies, qualities that are essential to the conception of modernity.

FIFTEEN

Life in Southern Italy, 1606–10

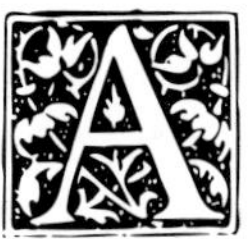FTER HE KILLED Ranuccio Tomassoni, Caravaggio fled to the mountains southeast of Rome, to Zagarolo or Palestrina, finding protection under the Colonna family and all the while continuing to paint. He then moved to Naples, where he led a kind of double life. Since his reputation as the pre-eminent painter of Rome had preceded him, he was venerated by the Neapolitan art community and served as an exemplar for local artists, many of whom adopted his style. He was now adjusting his approach to painting, making it less controversial; it was only when he reinvented his art in southern Italy that church commissions once again became numerous. Simultaneously, however, he was a fugitive under death sentence and lived in constant fear that he would be forced to return to Rome to face justice. That he found it difficult to reconcile these two sides of his life is indicated by his behaviour, which seemed increasingly strange to people around him, and by his ceaseless movement from place to place.

Because of his fame, Caravaggio had no difficulty in securing important public commissions in Naples. His works there included the *Seven Works of Mercy* (see illus. 60), *Crucifixion of St Andrew* (illus. 54) and *Flagellation of Christ* (illus. 55). Through

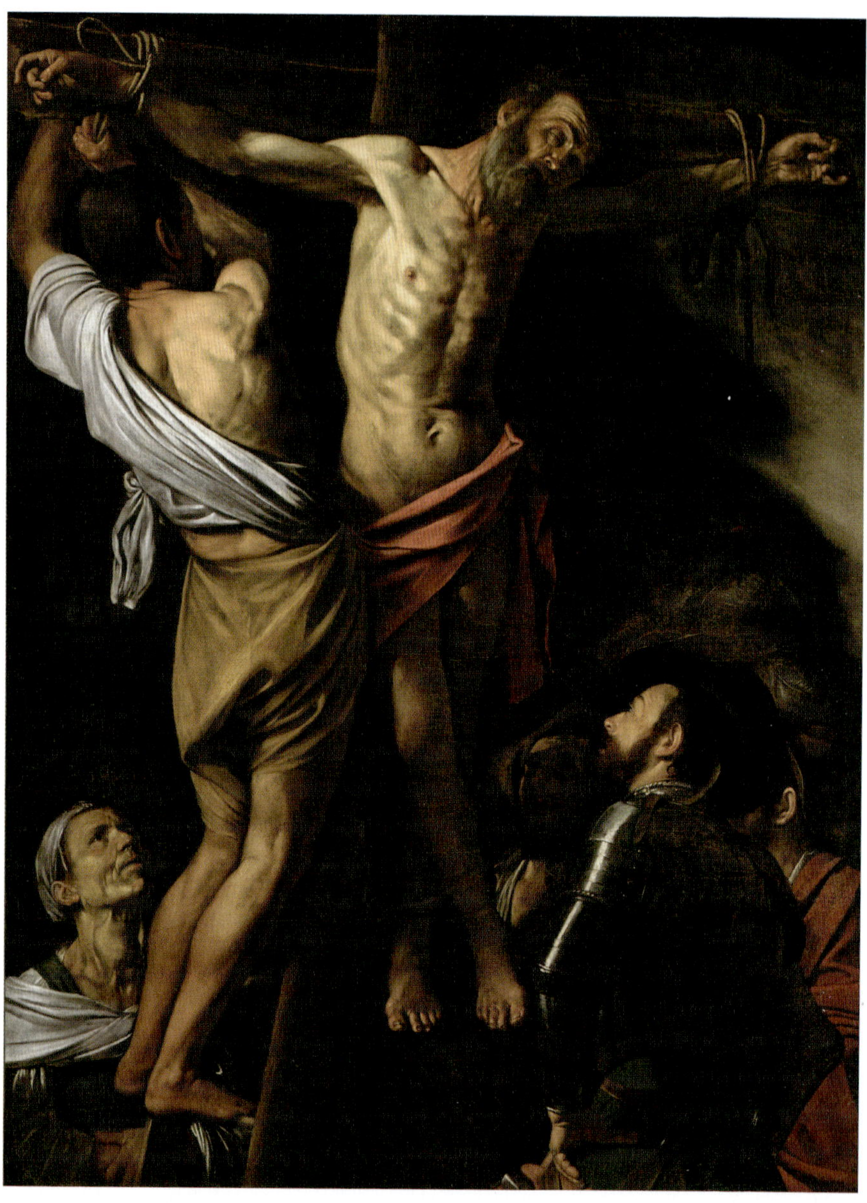

54 Caravaggio, *Crucifixion of St Andrew*, 1607, oil on canvas.

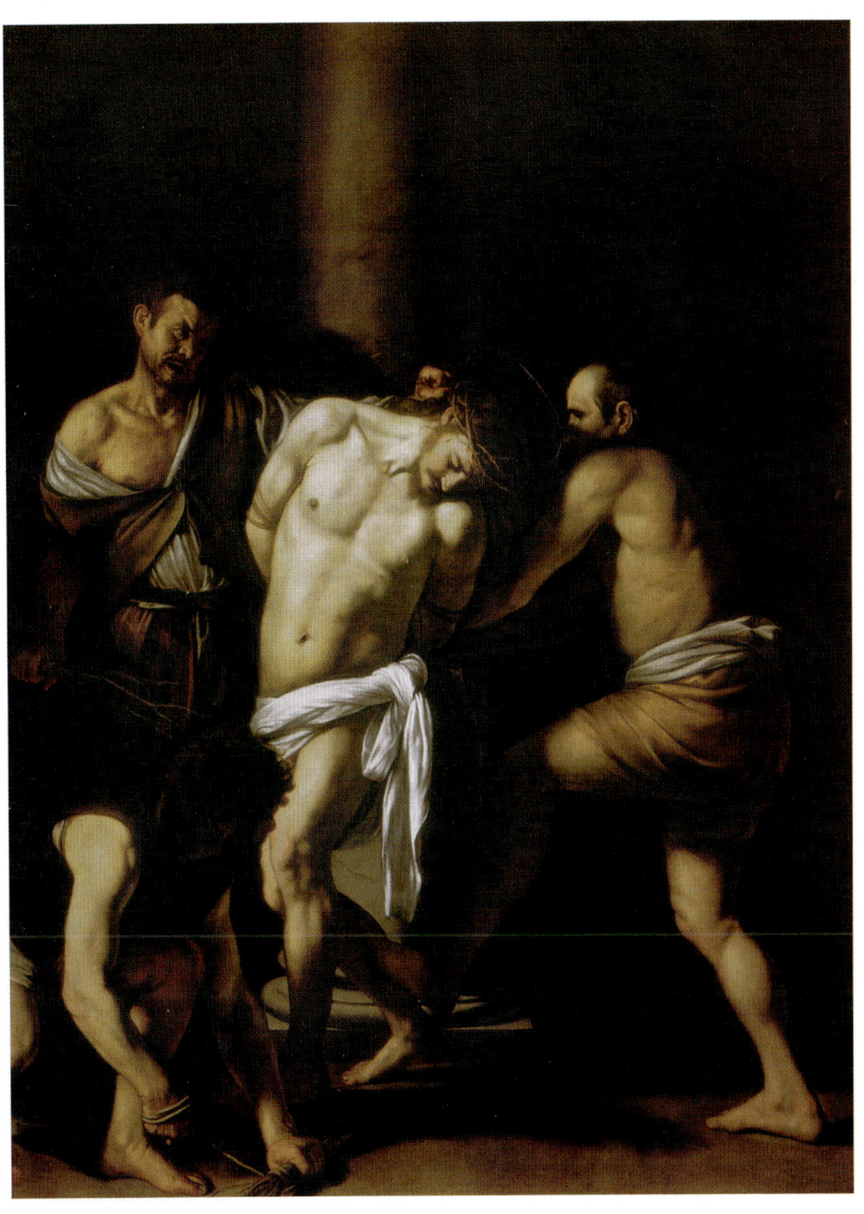

55 Caravaggio, *Flagellation of Christ*, 1607, oil on canvas.

the example of these works he attracted the attention of such local painters as Giovanni Battista Caracciolo and Louis Finson, who became devoted followers. Within a few years many other artists there also fell under his spell; he thus changed the course of Neapolitan art. In spite of his great success in Naples, in July 1607 he left for Malta. He may have been drawn to this island fortress by the prospect of attaining a knighthood, perhaps hoping that it might offer a route to a papal pardon. Meanwhile, his fame endured in Rome, where painters and the public alike flocked to see his *Death of the Virgin* (see illus. 26) when it was exhibited at the Accademia di San Luca.

Once in Malta he made portraits of Alof de Wignacourt, the Grand Master of the Knights of the Order of St John. As a result of these paintings – one of which survives, a striking image of Wignacourt in armour accompanied by a page (illus. 56) – Caravaggio was invited to join the knights, realizing a lifelong ambition. He won his Cross of Malta after an appeal to Pope Paul v by Wignacourt, who in his bull of reception compared Caravaggio on the island of Malta to the ancient Greek painter Apelles, famously extolled by his fellow citizens of the island of Kos.[1] The Pope had given his approval through a special authorization, in spite of the artist's killing of Tomassoni. Caravaggio was made an honorary knight (*per grazia*) of the *Ordine di Obbedienza*, a status granted to those who could not prove they were of noble rank.

Caravaggio then made his largest painting, *The Beheading of St John the Baptist* (see illus. 61), for the oratory of the cathedral in Valletta. Wignacourt was so pleased with this work that he awarded the painter a gold chain and two slaves, among

56 Caravaggio, *Alof de Wignacourt*, 1607–8, oil on canvas.

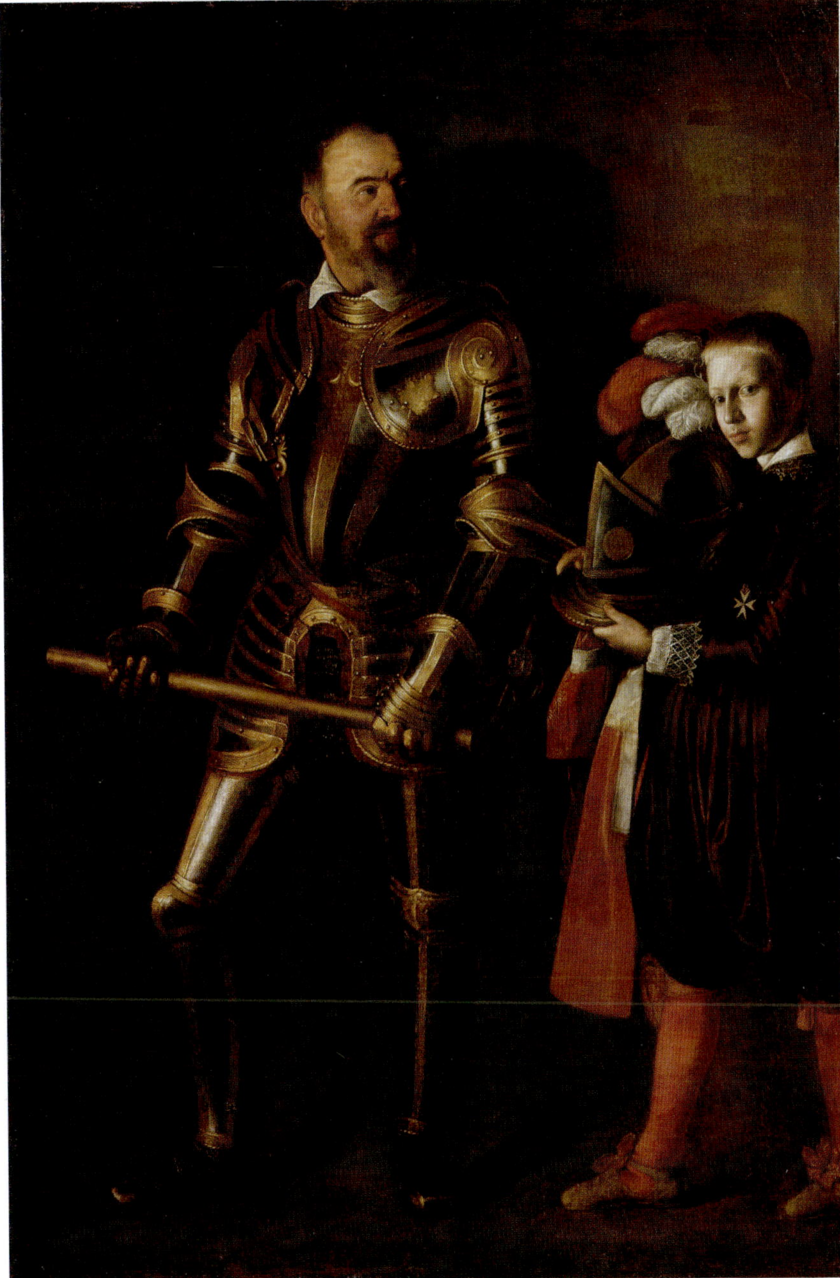

other gifts. This period of adulation was short-lived, however. In August 1608 Caravaggio attacked and seriously injured a Knight of Justice, Fra Giovanni Rodomonte Roero.[2] The painter thus lost the support of the Order. He was thrown into prison in an underground cell at the Castel Sant'Angelo, but managed an incredible escape, apparently using a rope to scale the walls. Somehow he was able to sail out of the harbour undetected and leave for Syracuse. His escape was so remarkable and his passage to Syracuse so uneventful that he must have had the help of fellow knights, perhaps even Wignacourt himself. After his escape was discovered, the knights expelled him from the Order of St John, with a statute reading that Caravaggio was 'deprived of his habit, and expelled and thrust forth like a rotten and fetid limb'.[3]

Caravaggio arrived in Syracuse to great adulation. He was greeted warmly by the artists, literary lights and Senate of the city as the most outstanding living artist, and found himself exceedingly handsomely rewarded for his artistic commissions there. For the church of Santa Lucia al Sepolcro, dedicated to the city's patron saint, he was commissioned by the Senate to paint an altarpiece, the *Burial of St Lucy* (see illus. 58). In spite of all the praise, though, he was becoming more and more unhinged. Anxiety filled his mind; he lived in fear of attack by the Knights of Malta or by deputies of Roman law. Francesco Susinno describes in his biography how the artist went to bed fully dressed with his dagger at the ready.[4] He was intolerant of the least criticism, restless and impatient, and thought mad by some who crossed his path.

Despite his success in Syracuse, he felt driven to move on, and left for Messina, arriving there in late 1608 or early 1609.

Messina was larger than Syracuse, and offered more opportunity for commissions. The wealthy Giovanni Battista de' Lazzari commissioned Caravaggio to make a painting for the high altar of the church of the Padri Crociferi. Susinno claims, perhaps fancifully, that the artist was given free rein to invent the subject. For the resulting impressive *Resurrection of Lazarus* (see illus. 62), according to Susinno, Caravaggio received the substantial fee of 1,000 *scudi*, about six times what he had realized from his public Roman commissions eight or nine years earlier.[5] Following the painting's warm reception, he was offered another 1,000 *scudi* to paint the principal altarpiece for the Capuchin church of Santa Maria la Concezione. For this church he produced his *Adoration of the Shepherds* (see illus. 64), in a suitably modest and lowly style reflecting Capuchin humility. This painting was also well received, but in spite of these great achievements the artist moved again, this time to Palermo.

There, for the Oratory of St Lawrence, Caravaggio painted the *Nativity with SS Lawrence and Francis* (see illus. 65), perhaps his most conventional altarpiece. He did not remain long in Palermo, for by October 1609 he was back in Naples. His great success in Sicily, where he had been welcomed as a celebrity and paid handsomely, contrasted with his fearful personal state, in which he constantly felt threatened with capture or death. People were suspicious of his aberrant behaviour. Giovanni Baglione says that he returned to Naples because his enemies were chasing him. Apparently Caravaggio was right in thinking so, for on 24 October 1609 he was so seriously wounded in the face at the Osteria del Cerriglio that he was said to be unrecognizable. The man behind this attack, as both Baglione and new research strongly imply, was Giovanni Rodomonte Roero, the Knight of Justice whom Caravaggio had assaulted in Malta.[6] In spite of this setback and his constant fear, between October and July in Naples Caravaggio produced a large number of works, including *Salome Receiving the Head of John the Baptist* (see illus. 67) and the *Martyrdom of St Ursula* (see illus. 66).

Meanwhile, in Rome, powerful allies – the Colonna, the Doria, Cardinal Ferdinando Gonzaga and Scipione Borghese – were working to obtain Caravaggio's pardon by the Pope. In July 1610, assured that his pardon was certain and with a safe conduct from Gonzaga, he decided to make his way back to that city.[7] But when he arrived at Palo, near Rome, the captain of the fortress there put him in prison for two days, having apparently arrested him in error, thinking he was another man.[8] In the meantime, the *felucca* with all his belongings travelled further up the coast towards Port' Ercole. He was furious: on the boat were a number of paintings he intended to give to Scipione Borghese in appreciation for helping him return to Rome. He set out on foot towards Port' Ercole, some 100 km distant, through marshy terrain infested with mosquitoes, in the heat of mid-July.

When Caravaggio finally arrived at Port' Ercole, perhaps having traversed part of the distance by boat, he discovered that the *felucca* had departed; it eventually made its way back to Naples with his paintings and other belongings on board. He became very ill from fever and was put to bed. A few days later he died in this desolate place, not far from Rome. The entire city was awaiting his arrival, and then came word that he had died. A report of 28 July read: 'News has arrived of the death of Michel Angelo Caravaggio, famous painter and most excellent in colouring and imitation of nature, following his illness at Port' Ercole.' Three days later another report said: 'Michel Angel da Caravaggio, famous painter, is dead at Port' Ercole while travelling from Naples to Rome thanks to the grace of his Holiness in revoking the warrant for murder.'[9] A letter written to Scipione Borghese on 29 July 1610 by Deodato Gentile, Bishop of Caserta, gives an accurate report of Caravaggio's death.[10] After he died, he was extolled by many as a great artist.

Certainly, we would like to know more about Caravaggio's personality. As it is, more than 400 years after his life ended, we are left only with documents spare in information and sometimes prejudiced in interpretation, and with our own inference and psychoanalysis at a distance. Perhaps he believed that his ancestors really were noble, and conceivably one of the reasons he worked so hard as a painter was to garner the respect he thought he merited. His reputation as the best artist in Rome was not simply based on his invention of a new kind of *tenebroso* realism with striking expression in his figures. More importantly, he revealed an honesty and verity in their miens, and, as he matured as an artist, produced a deep expressiveness unequalled by any other artist until Rembrandt, and a sense of the truth of reality not matched until Gustave Courbet.

Caravaggio had a fine sense of his own importance, and also, conceivably, of his own ability to understand the complexity and depth of the human psyche and to translate that into paint. He was convinced that no other artist could do this as well as he did, and, perhaps, like Leonardo da Vinci, he looked down on others because he perceived that he was superior in his own understanding and achievements. In spite of his high opinion of his own art, according to his early biographers he abstained from praising himself openly, but loudly and publicly disparaged the works of other painters.[11] He was preoccupied with his own privilege and status, so much so that when subjected to criticism he reacted violently. Having let his temper get the better of him when he killed Ranuccio Tomassoni in Rome, his career as the most respected artist of his time came to an end there. He went to extraordinary lengths to obtain a knighthood, but then by fighting a brother knight ruined his chances to retain respect within the Order of St John. Perhaps one of the reasons why he moved from place to place so often in southern Italy was not only to avoid his pursuers, imagined or real, but to receive ever fresh accolades, something he seemed to require.

One conundrum that is hard to crack is why, if he was so concerned with his noble status and high birth, Caravaggio sided with the poor in his paintings. Many examples exist of his sympathetic treatment of the humble: the plebeian kneeling couple in the *Madonna di Loreto* (see illus. 38); the humble saint in the first *Inspiration of St Matthew* (see illus. 36); the lowly Apostles in the *Doubting Thomas* (see illus. 28); the huddled group at the bottom of the *Madonna of the Rosary* (see illus. 39); the prominent workmen in the *Burial of St Lucy* (see illus. 58); the simple herdsmen in the *Adoration of the Shepherds* (see illus. 64) in Messina. Even though he thought of himself as superior to most men through (questionable) noble lineage, he privileged the poor and seemed to identify with them in his paintings. One reason he did so was because charity was an aristocratic activity, and his paintings were directed mainly to wealthy patrons and supporters who encouraged easing the lot of the poor through benefaction. Perhaps also his outlook was influenced by his own experience of near poverty at certain points in his childhood, especially after his parents died, or by his penniless state when he arrived in Rome. He seems also to have been genuinely moved by the concern shown for the poor by Carlo Borromeo and Filippo Neri. Or, at least, he knew how to capitalize in his paintings on the widespread feeling among his well-to-do patrons of their Christian duty to help those in need. Caravaggio's works were more admired by his wealthy and sophisticated collectors than by the poor themselves, who apparently complained about their indecorous treatment in his paintings.[12]

Then there is the matter of his strange behaviour, his 'crazy brain' that even his strongest supporters noticed. His conduct, including street fights and eventually a murder, betrayed a mind more deeply troubled than is indicated merely by his short temper, his pride in his art or his feelings of privilege. His artworks with disturbing features have already been discussed, as have some of the circumstances in which he elicited remarks by his patrons about his strangeness. Beyond that, it is difficult to penetrate his mental state, for it can hardly be fathomed at a distance of more than 400 years, and so it must remain a mystery to us.

SIXTEEN

Reconciliation and Spirituality

I N CARAVAGGIO'S LATE works, the bold, striking and disruptive effects of the paintings from his middle years are more and more replaced by three tendencies. A stronger balance in his compositions emerges, so that his pictures are more structured and symmetrical, as well as having a directness and economy in their realism. Secondly, we see in these late works a deepening of emotional expression that is less flamboyant than before and that reveals a calmer, more meditative spirituality. Finally, the artist's technique changes: he paints his pictures more rapidly, in a rougher, sketchier style, with thinner paint and long, narrow lines of white in the highlights. Now, as he moves quickly from place to place in southern Italy, he often paints from memory, without models.

In spite of increasingly symmetrical compositions and quieter body language in the figures, though, it can hardly be said that Caravaggio's art becomes more conventional, because he builds on his previous innovations to create a more profound expressiveness that defies the ordinary. His late works exhibit fewer of the spectacular effects of his earlier Roman pictures; the reaction of sudden surprise among his protagonists diminishes, along with the effect that an instant in time is captured. At the same time that he tempers his earlier theatrical effects, he tentatively approaches the classical organization seen in the work of other painters of his time, such as Annibale Carracci. Caravaggio also creates deeper, more complex spaces for his protagonists in his larger, multi-figured compositions, with the figures diminishing in size in several zones of space, as also found in the work of other painters. In his largest paintings, the figures occupy less of the picture space, and are often confined to the bottom half of the canvas.

The separation of the human and divine realms still exists in Caravaggio's late works, but perhaps not as emphatically as before. For example, the flying angel in his *Nativity with SS Lawrence and Francis* (see illus. 65) seems to contemplate the Christ Child along with the mortals, in a spiritual accord. But this closeness is largely annulled by the lack of awareness among the human participants of the presence of the angel, who points up towards a heaven that is noteworthy for its absence: we see only darkness. Scepticism in his protagonists' reactions to divine events is no longer so pronounced a characteristic, as a sense of the deeply spiritual emerges. The ambiguity of meaning of his earlier works and their oppositional or dialectical aspects are also less pronounced. Changes of this sort can be seen in the *Nativity with SS Lawrence and Francis*, and in his other nativity painting from these late years, the *Adoration of the Shepherds* (see illus. 64) in Messina. In these works we see only deeply heartfelt devotion among the figures, and none of the disturbing elements of his earlier works, such as questioning protagonists, suggestions of eroticism or indecorousness. But even as Caravaggio's works become increasingly compliant with religious norms and grow deeply expressive, they remain unique.

The artist's second version of the *Supper at Emmaus* (see illus. 48) typifies the changes in his late work. The striking quality of the earlier version (see illus. 45), with its focus on a startling revelation at the moment when the disciples recognize Christ, is replaced by a quieter, more meditative approach. The strong colours and contrasts in value of the first version give way to a more general darkness in the later work. The highlights are now sometimes indicated by streaks of paint, as in the old servant woman, rather than by carefully worked details, as earlier. In this later Milan version the disciple at the right grasps the edge of the table, similar to the earlier London version, in which the man on the left grabs the arm of his chair. But the disciple in the later painting is not readying himself to bolt out of his seat, and seems more reflective in his reaction to Christ's presence. In the later version the disciple at the left merely raises his hands a little in surprise; his higher left hand is mainly in shadow and his right one is entirely. His reaction is therefore not as extreme as that of his earlier counterpart at the right, whose hands are thrown out in sharp perspective, his left one seemingly breaking through the picture plane and projecting dramatically into the viewer's space. Christ's extended hand that blesses the meal in the second version is also less emphatic, and his face is lost in deeper shadow. The meal on the table is less insistent, with neither fowl nor fruit, and more weight is placed on its Eucharistic significance, with a focus on the pitcher of wine and the bread. All the figures seem more introspective, more attentive to the spiritual meaning of Christ's blessing of

57 Caravaggio (copy of lost original), *St Mary Magdalen in Ecstasy*, 1606, oil on canvas.

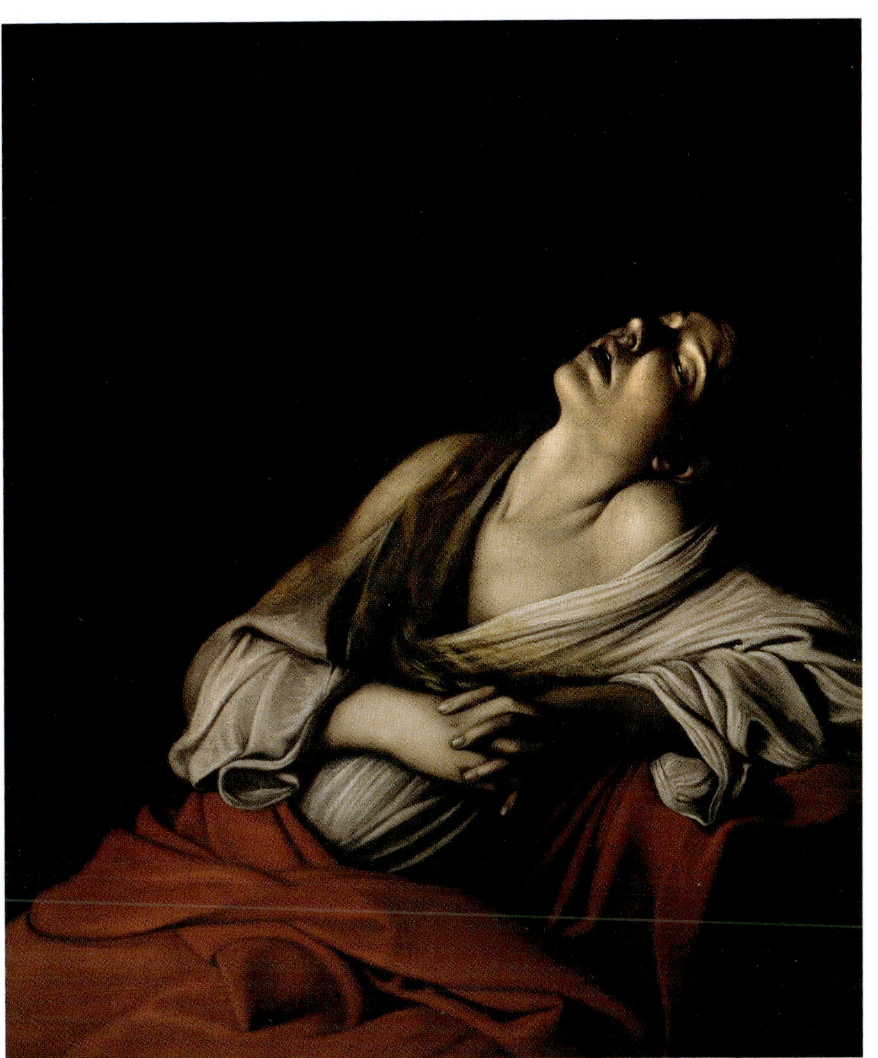

the meal, and show less of a merely physical reaction. These changes show the artist's maturing vision; now he depicts a psychological depth, revealing the participants' thoughts in a way that anticipates Rembrandt.

Caravaggio's *St Mary Magdalen in Ecstasy* (illus. 57; lost, but known through many copies) has a directness, economy and rawness of emotion that are not found in his earlier work. It conveys deep spirituality and feeling through the outward signs of the body. Caravaggio is able to communicate at once intense remorse, sadness and helplessness in the eyes of Mary, largely because of the way he has lit them from below. Her thrown-back head, open mouth and nearly closed eyes convey utter spiritual transport and deep penitence. The latter quality may be autobiographical, since, according to Giulio Mancini and Giovanni Baglione, the painting was made shortly after Caravaggio killed Ranuccio Tomassoni, while he was hiding in the Alban Hills southeast of Rome.[1]

The *Martyrdom of St Ursula* (see illus. 66), which may be Caravaggio's last painting, conveys Ursula's restrained surprise as she becomes aware that the king of the Huns, in the left-hand half of the picture, has just released an arrow and shot her in the chest. The hardness and total lack of feeling of the king as he shoots contrasts with the touching poignancy of Ursula. Her bowed head with its straight nose and chiselled features is classically conceived, at the same time that her restrained expression is both deeply powerful and profoundly sad as she looks down at her breast, which she presses around the arrow. Other parts of the picture, particularly the head of the Hun king, are loosely painted; thus we see three characteristics of Caravaggio's late style exemplified:

muted expression, borrowings from the classical tradition and breadth of handling.

In his large *Burial of St Lucy* (illus. 58), Caravaggio departs from his method in his smaller canvases of painting half-length figures near the picture plane by creating four zones of space in a more ample composition. The two gravediggers at the front of the space are disposed in Caravaggio's new symmetrical manner, their front and back views framing the scene. Immediately behind the gravedigger on the right, in a second zone, stand an officer in armour overseeing the burial and a bishop holding a crosier and blessing the body of St Lucy. Behind the gravediggers and framed by them, in a third zone, lies the dead saint, her head tilted back with her mouth open and her arm stretched out inertly on the ground. Kneeling over her is a single old woman, shown in mourning with her hands held to her face. Behind her, in a fourth space, stands a group of figures, members of the burial party, looking like a classical frieze stretching from left to right. The scale of all these figures as they rapidly diminish in size from front to back seems awkward until we realize that the artist is using forced perspective for emotional effect, to stress the finality of death, with the gravediggers, shovels and earth in front, then the lifeless body of the saint, and finally the mourners in the rear, who, as in the artist's *Death of the Virgin* (see illus. 26), emphasize earthly loss over heavenly glory.

In *St Lucy*, as in his *Beheading of St John the Baptist* (see illus. 61), *Resurrection of Lazarus* (see illus. 62) and *Adoration of the Shepherds* (see illus. 64) from these years, Caravaggio places his relatively small figures in the bottom half of the painting,

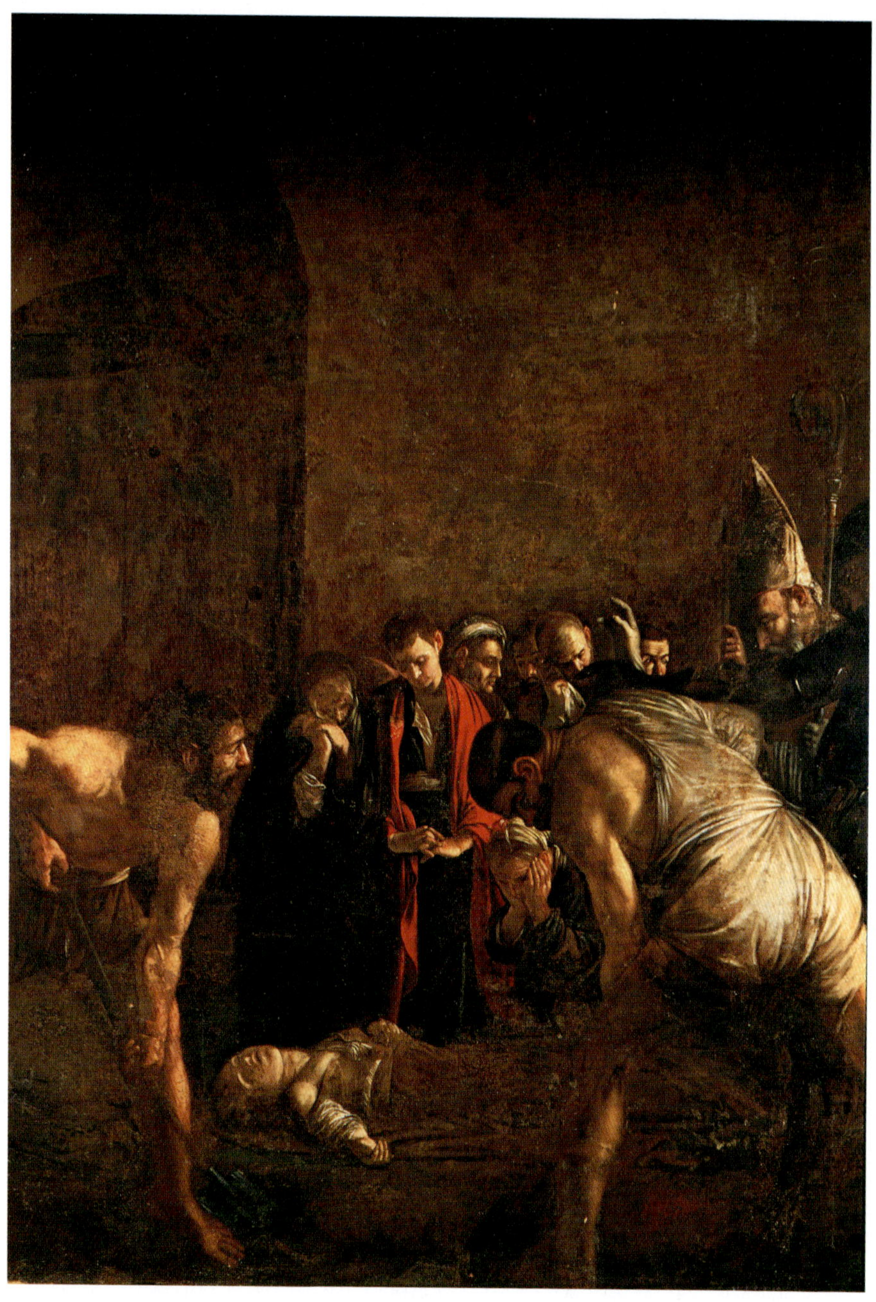

58 Caravaggio, *Burial of St Lucy*, 1608, oil on canvas.

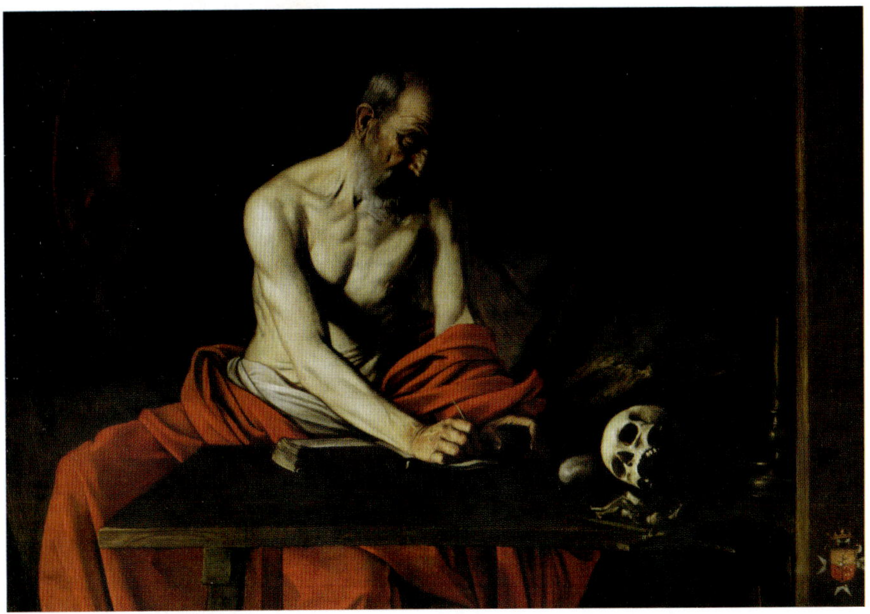

with a largely empty space above. But typical of his earlier works and of the three just mentioned, he shows no heavenly chorus of angels or other holy figures in the upper part of the painting to indicate the saint's destination. He resolutely focuses on the mundane aspect of the subject, in this case, as before, shielding his protagonists from any divine vision that would intrude upon the earthly isolation of humanity. The empty spaces in the top half of his religious scenes must have struck his contemporary observers as strange, perverse and in a way even frightening, since they were used to seeing the heavens overflowing with divine personages in large altar-pieces. Caravaggio seems to use a particular type of visual rhetoric in the blank upper half of religious scenes like this one, corresponding to a figure of speech in verbal rhetoric,

59 Caravaggio, *St Jerome Writing*, 1607–8, oil on canvas.

the enthymeme, where the missing hidden premise in this case is a heaven filled with celestial beings.

As important as his large-scale, multi-figured altarpieces were during the last phase of his career, in the years after 1606 Caravaggio actually painted a considerably higher proportion of relatively small works with half-length figures than during his mature Roman phase (1599–1606). We tend to associate him with this smaller type of painting, depicting partial figures close to the picture plane. The proportion of pictures with full-length figures to ones with half-lengths in his mature Roman phase was about three to one, whereas the ratio in his late period is decidedly less than two to one. Leaving aside the vagaries of commissions for paintings of either type, the half-length picture with few figures or only one allowed Caravaggio in his late career to explore more fully the emotional depth and expressiveness of his subjects. His late works of this smaller type include *David with the Head of Goliath* (see illus. 40), the *Martyrdom of St Ursula* (see illus. 66), *Salome Receiving the Head of John the Baptist* (see illus. 67), the second version of the *Supper at Emmaus* (see illus. 48), *St Mary Magdalen in Ecstasy* (see illus. 57), *St Jerome Writing* (illus. 59) and *Sleeping Cupid* (1608, Florence, Pitti). Arguably these smaller paintings contain some of the most emotionally and powerfully expressive figures of his career, particularly *David*, the *Martyrdom of St Ursula* and *St Mary Magdalen in Ecstasy*.

Unlike Caravaggio's larger pictures from this period, *St Jerome Writing* is a carefully finished work; it emphasizes the Church Doctor's ageing flesh in a penitential theme featuring a stone for self-punishment, and a skull. It was made for the Prior of the Knights of Malta in Naples, Ippolito Malaspina, whose coat of arms appears at the bottom right. This is a pensive picture, showing Jerome lost in thought as he jots down notes at his bedside. By contrast, though small, *Salome Receiving the Head of John the Baptist* was painted quickly, as is revealed in the schematic drapery. The executioner contemplates John's severed head with a feeling of regret, while the old woman meditates on the saint's fate with her hands clasped in prayer. But a grim Salome averts her eyes, unable to look, perhaps because of guilt.

As we have seen, the spectacular, disruptive effects in Caravaggio's pictures that attracted attention around 1600 and made him famous begin to diminish in his later work, as his art matured. But his death at just 38 in 1610 ensured that it would be left to other artists to develop the full implications of the more deeply expressive art of his last years.

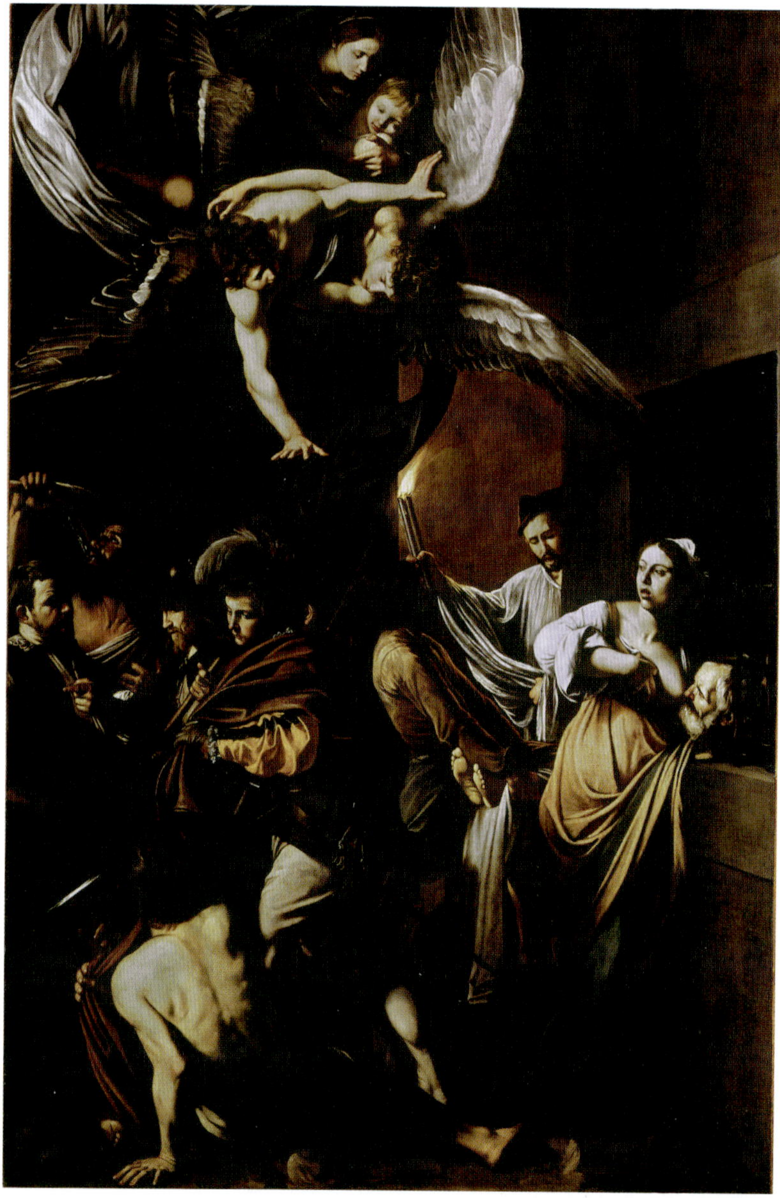

SEVENTEEN

Late Works, 1606–10

IN NAPLES Caravaggio painted his large, complex *Seven Works of Mercy* (illus. 60) for a new charitable institution, the Pio Monte della Misericordia, which had been founded in 1601 to aid the poor and sick. The picture was made to decorate the high altar of the institution's new church. The subject of this altarpiece was rare in Italian art, and when painted at all had usually been divided into separate sections, each showing one scene of mercy. Caravaggio's innovation was to imagine a unified tableau bringing together all the acts of mercy in an outdoor night setting, as if happening on the corner of a narrow Neapolitan street. In a complex grouping of twelve figures he depicts the acts of mercy as described in the Gospel of Matthew (25:34–46): feeding the hungry, giving drink to the thirsty, taking in strangers, clothing the naked, helping the sick and visiting prisoners. By tradition, a seventh act was added to these: burying the dead. Among the figures in Caravaggio's conception are an innkeeper welcoming strangers; St Martin giving his cloak to a partially naked man sitting on the street; the ancient Roman heroine Pero offering her breast to her starving father, Cimon, in prison; and men carrying a corpse by torchlight. Above these figures the Virgin and Christ Child fly, supported

60 Caravaggio, *Seven Works of Mercy*, 1606–7, oil on canvas.

by two angels with enormous wings. The members of this
divine group seem too corporeal, weighty and real-seeming
to remain airborne for very long; indeed they look unstable as
they appear to hurtle down towards the street. Nevertheless,
this large painting is brilliant in its conception and execution,
with a new flickering, luminescent effect in the highlights not
seen in Caravaggio's Roman works.

When he went to Naples, Caravaggio apparently took
with him his *Madonna of the Rosary* (see illus. 39), which he
seems to have painted in Rome. It is not known who commissioned this work, which was undoubtedly intended to be
an altarpiece, or for what location it was painted, but presum-
ably he hoped to sell it to a Dominican church in Naples. It
may have been rejected by a church or congregation, because
in the autumn of 1607 it was put on the art market. If it was
rejected, the cause might have been a combination of the
generally grim demeanour of the saints, the overly didactic
treatment of the subject, the almost parodic representation
of the saints at the right – including the wide-eyed St Peter
Martyr, who looks out towards the viewer, displaying his
attribute of a nasty gash on his head as he points bleakly at
the Virgin and Christ Child – and the too noticeable dirty
feet of the peasants who kneel before St Dominic at the left.
Nevertheless, the barefoot commoners with their cluster of
hands reaching up towards the rosary are moving; in focusing his attention on them, Caravaggio develops the theme of
his *Madonna di Loreto* (see illus. 38). In the *Madonna of the Rosary*
he distances himself from his radical innovations of around
1600, in which he had placed figures in the foreground and
emphasized a dramatic moment. Now he shifts his attention

to the classical art of the High Renaissance, creating a more traditional composition and deeper space for his figures. At the same time, his revised manner reflects the newly emerging classicism embraced by such artists as Annibale Carracci that would lead to the grand Baroque style of Rubens and others. Caravaggio's art is showing signs of becoming more mainstream.

For the de Franchis family in Naples, Caravaggio painted his *Flagellation of Christ* (see illus. 55), which was later placed in their chapel in the church of San Domenico Maggiore. Here, too, he returns to the classicism of the High Renaissance, which is seen both in this painting's symmetrical composition and in Christ's heroic musculature. Caravaggio makes no attempt to hide his source of inspiration: Sebastiano del Piombo's *Flagellation* in San Pietro in Montorio, Rome, of about 1521. The savage expression of the tormentor on the left who grabs the hair of Christ contrasts with the nobility of the latter, who is tight-lipped and stoical in his endurance. Christ leans to his left and balances himself with a movement of his feet that can almost be described as balletic. At the same time that he turns to classicism, Caravaggio applies his paint more broadly and quickly, and these qualities, along with the grim restraint of Christ, mark this painting as characteristic of his late works.

For Don Juan Alonso Pimentel y Herrera, viceroy of Naples, Caravaggio painted his *Crucifixion of St Andrew* (see illus. 54), showing a supernatural occurrence that is hard to represent. After hanging on the cross for three days, St Andrew was to be taken down in response to the demand of the crowd. But the executioner attempting to untie the saint miraculously became frozen, unable to move, in response to Andrew's refusal to be saved. The Roman proconsul who ordered the saint's execution and then his removal from the cross is shown in armour at the bottom right, with his hand on his hip to indicate his perplexity at the surprising event. An old woman with a goitre, a representative of the artist's common humanity, stands at the bottom left, watching the miracle with great intensity.

Caravaggio's first paintings in Malta were portraits of the Grand Master of the Knights of St John, Alof de Wignacourt. His knights had a long and illustrious history: the Order was chivalry's oldest, tracing its origin to the Crusades. In 1565 the knights were attacked by the powerful Sultan Suleiman, but in spite of losing 7,000 defenders, Malta emerged victorious. Wignacourt had taken part in that defence as a young man, and now, many years later, was Grand Master. Of the several versions Caravaggio painted, the single surviving portrait shows Wignacourt in armour, gripping a baton and accompanied by a page holding his helmet (see illus. 56). This portrait is open to different interpretations: the Grand Master, looking off to his left with his head slightly raised, seems proud and confident. But, on the other hand, with his steady glare and the left side of his face lost in deep shadow, Wignacourt looks menacing, like a formidable adversary, clutching his ceremonial baton as if it were a weapon, a truncheon. Both these meanings were undoubtedly intended: he is secure in his benign reign, but would serve as a ruthless opponent if the Turks dared to attack again. His island fortress was firm in its resolve to protect Italy from a southern sea invasion.

Caravaggio then painted for Wignacourt and the Oratory of the Co-Cathedral of St John in Valletta his *Beheading of St John the Baptist* (illus. 61). At over 5 m wide, it is the largest work he ever made. It may have been painted *in situ* in the large oratory on the southwest side of the cathedral.[1] The story of Salome's appeal to her father, Herod, to behead St John the Baptist, a request insisted upon by her jealous mother, Herodias, is told in the Bible (Mark 6:21–9) and elaborated on in the medieval Apocrypha. Caravaggio's version of the scene is very different from what he might have painted only a few years earlier: he declines to show any fancy costumes, and depicts a large prison-yard setting that replaces the earlier dark gloom of his backgrounds. His composition of the principal figures is now classically conceived, with a

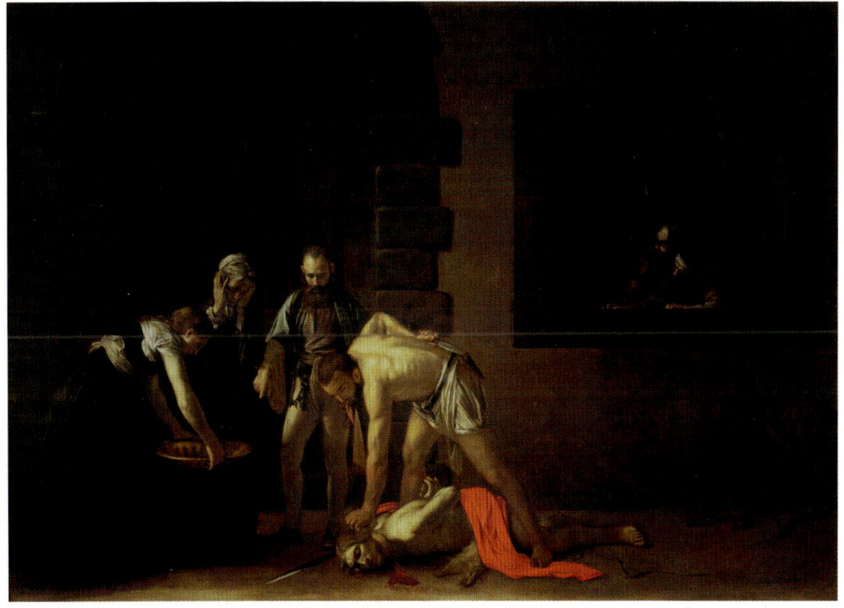

61 Caravaggio, *Beheading of St John the Baptist*, 1608, oil on canvas.

symmetrical arrangement of the four protagonists standing over the body of St John. Furthermore, he balances the entire composition by opposing the five figures on the left with the two prisoners behind the barred window on the right. The figures are viewed from a distance and occupy scarcely more than a quarter of the entire painting, a scheme far different from his earlier works, where half-length protagonists were seen up close, seeming to break through the picture plane and into the viewer's space.

As in the *Flagellation* (see illus. 55) he painted in Naples, here too Caravaggio asserts a new approach that admits classical elements. He gives to John the Baptist a heroic nobility, but the charger held by Salome (meant to receive the head), the sword on the ground, the small knife held behind the executioner's back and intended to finish the job, and above all the neck wound of John and the blood below it on the ground mark the brutality of the scene. Caravaggio signed this work in an unusual way: in the blood he wrote 'f. Michel A.', apparently standing for 'frater Michelangelo' (see illus. 61). The meaning of this signature is antonymous: it marks Caravaggio's pride as a knight and a favourite of Wignacourt, but also recalls his status as one who has murdered through blood (as an honorary knight, it does not imply his duty to protect the Order to the death). In this way, Caravaggio mediates between the harmonious balance of the composition as a whole and the horror of John's murder, punctuated by his signature in blood.

The unforgettable pose of the central figure in Caravaggio's *Resurrection of Lazarus* (illus. 62) has a partial prototype in Giuseppe Cesari's painting of the same subject (illus. 63),

62 Caravaggio, *Resurrection of Lazarus*, 1608–9, oil on canvas.

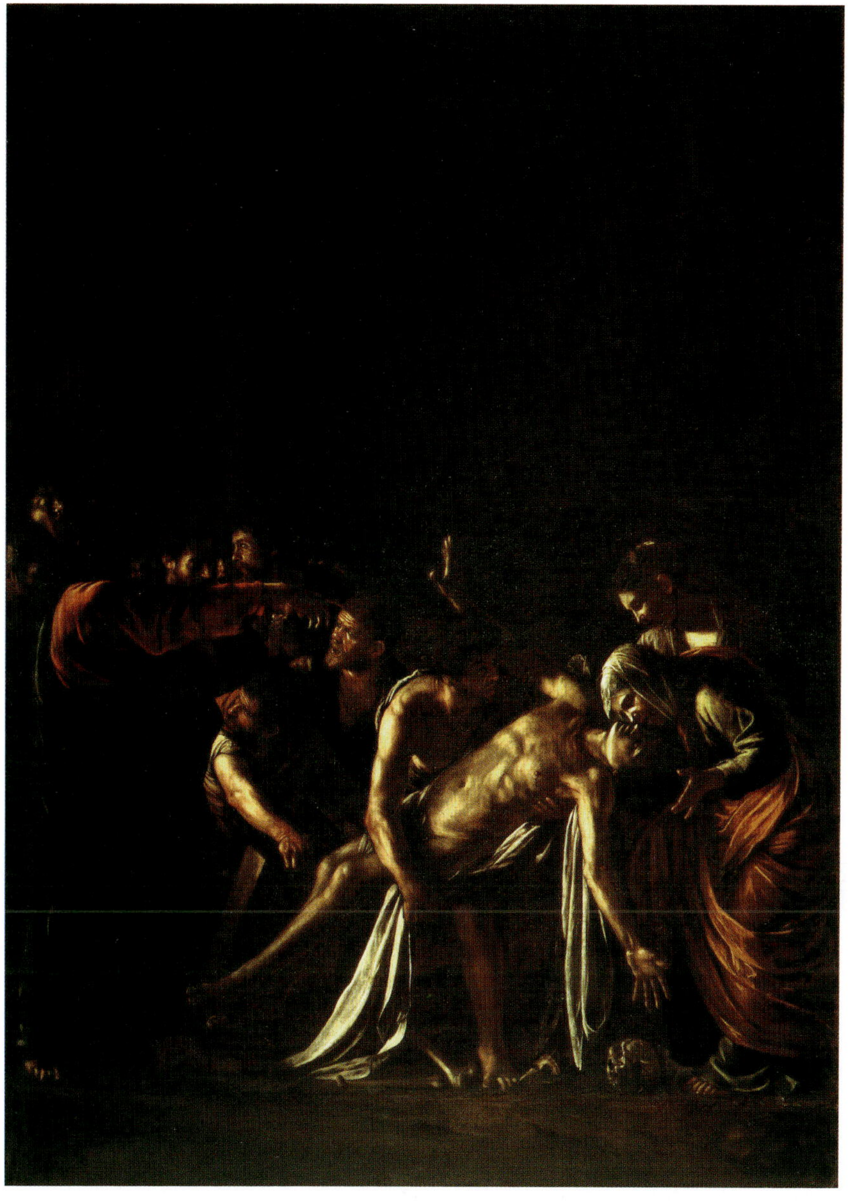

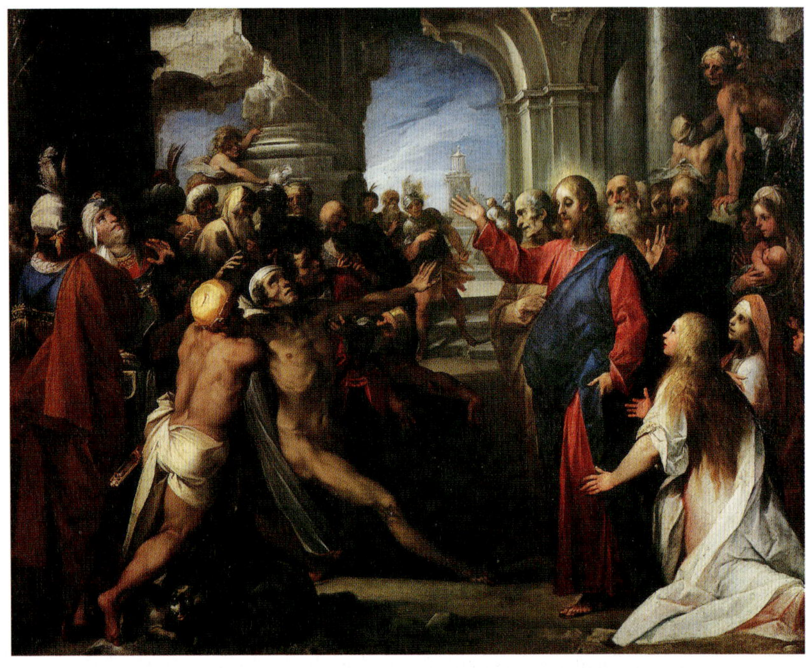

where Lazarus' upper body is vertical, its arms outstretched on the horizontal axis of the painting (with one arm bent at the elbow). Caravaggio's version is far more impressive: both arms are stretched out at right angles to the torso, but the body is laid back diagonally at 60 degrees from the painting's vertical axis. The effect, which is both powerful and disorientating, suggests that Lazarus' body is gripped by rigor mortis, and the composition is intensified by Christ's summoning arm at the left, stretched out horizontally. The circle of figures surrounding Lazarus seems to set the entire composition in a spiralling motion. The disorientation of the viewer is increased by the head of Lazarus' sister Martha. Her face almost touches his, with great emotional feeling, but

63 Giuseppe Cesari, *Resurrection of Lazarus*, c. 1592–3, oil on canvas.

her head is upside down from his point of view. As a counterpoint to all this instability, Caravaggio creates a classical frame for Lazarus with two figures, acting as curving, enclosing parentheses: the man who holds up his body at the left and Martha, who looks into his face at the right. Lazarus's body with outstretched arms forms a crucifix, alluding to Christ's future death on the cross and the promise of resurrection that is prefigured in the present scene. Lazarus's ambivalent physical and psychological struggle as he is caught between death and rebirth is indicated by his opposing hands. His left hand hovers over a skull on the ground, representing death, while his right hand is raised to the divine light and command of Christ. But with his characteristic ambiguity, Caravaggio fails to make clear whether Lazarus is accepting or rejecting resurrection, since the gesture of his right hand could be interpreted either way. As in his *Burial of St Lucy* (see illus. 58) and *Adoration of the Shepherds* (see illus. 64), the top half of the painting is left empty. A possible reason for this may be that Caravaggio was reluctant to paint figures larger than life in big pictures like this one. As were most of his late canvases, this work was painted quickly, with loose brushwork, and the light seems eerily luminescent.

Caravaggio painted two nativity scenes in 1609, and both follow the expectations and conventions for an altarpiece more than most of his works. In the *Adoration of the Shepherds*, all the figures are arranged diagonally, with the three shepherds and Joseph contemplating Mary and the Christ Child, their heads cascading downwards and to the left, like a waterfall. Entirely lacking the problematic and ambiguous figures of his earlier works, this painting shows the act of devotion simply

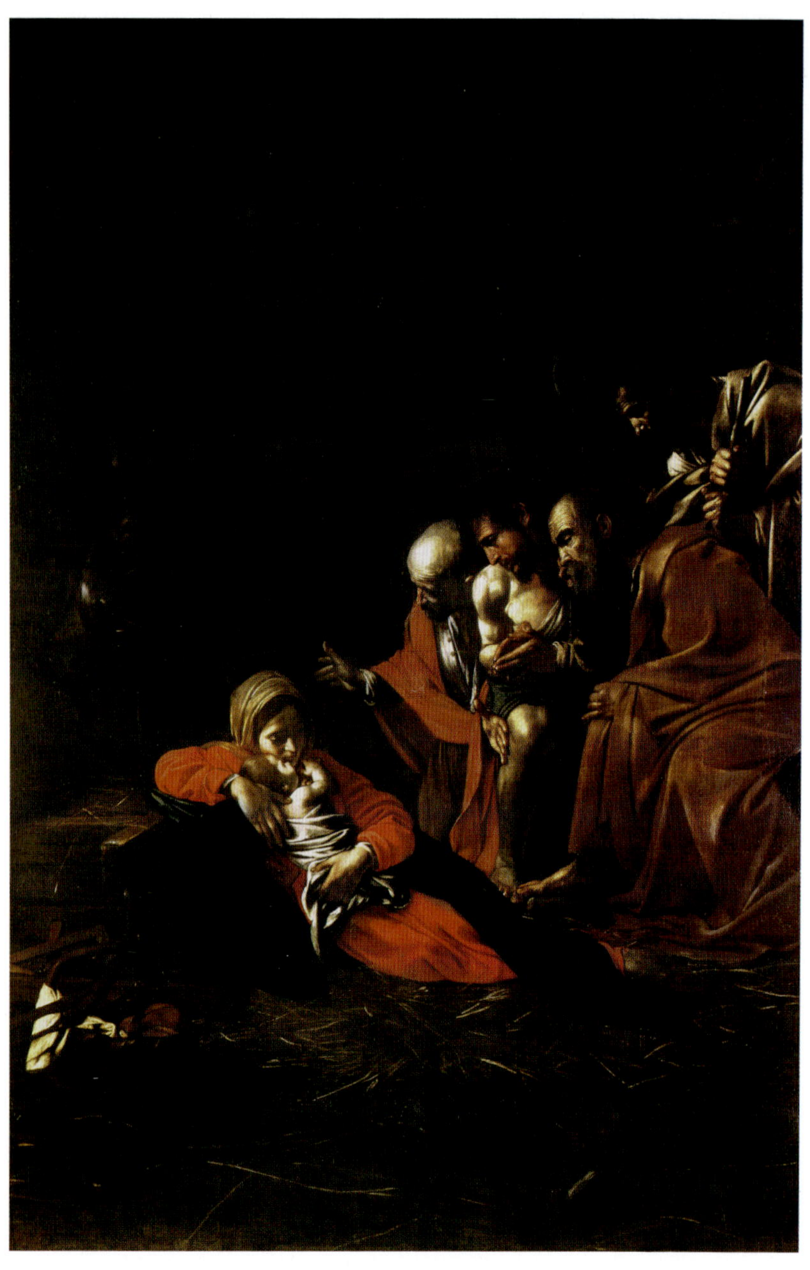

64 Caravaggio, *Adoration of the Shepherds*, 1609, oil on canvas.

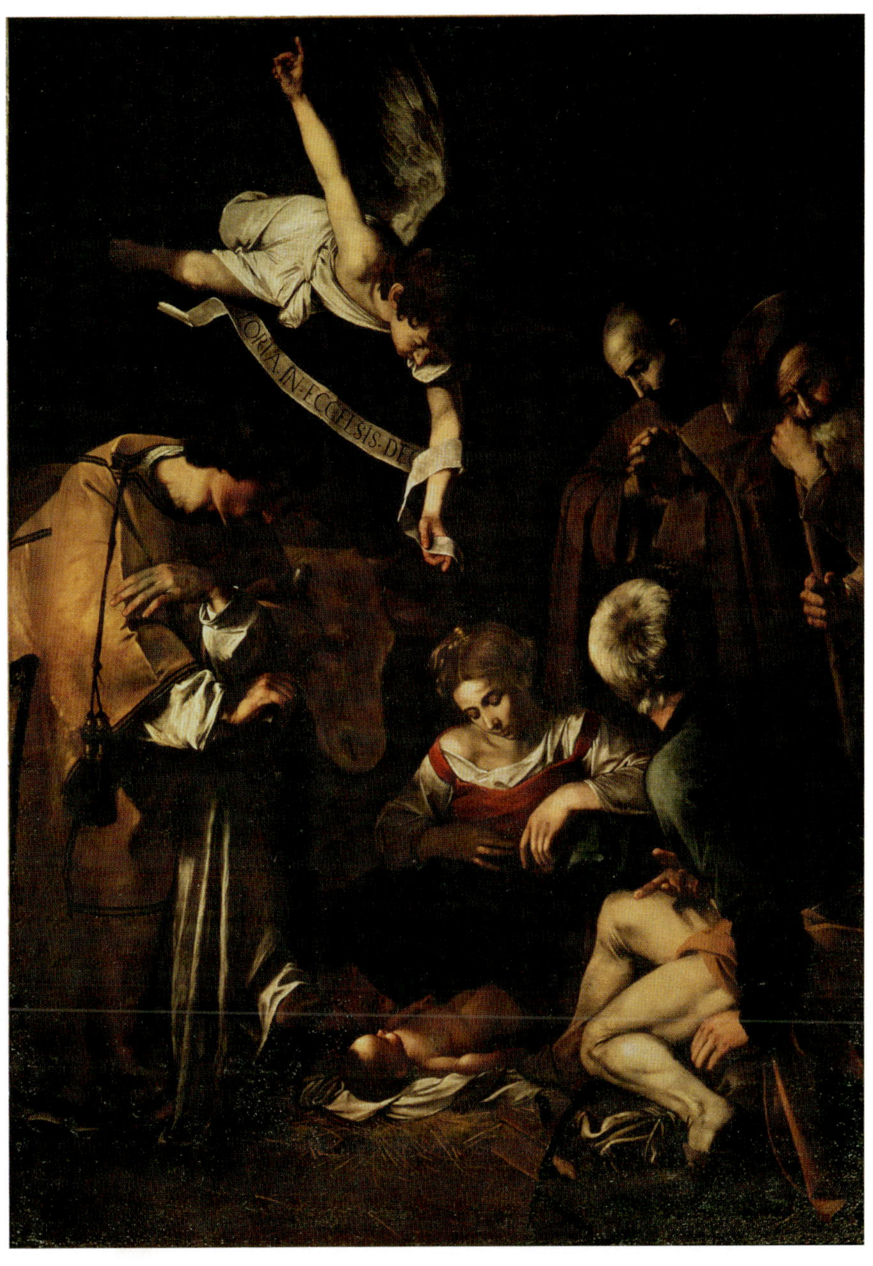

65 Caravaggio, *Nativity with SS Lawrence and Francis*, 1609, oil on canvas.

and reverently. In this case, the spaciousness and relative emptiness of the setting provide an amplitude that enhances the feeling of reverence. Mary sits on the ground as the Madonna of Humility; the theme of poverty is continued in the simplicity of the protagonists and in the still-life of carpenter's tools in the left foreground. The one unconventional aspect of the painting is the ox above Mary: it does not look at the Christ Child to symbolize the Christian faithful, as is customary; its eyes are entirely blocked by the ass.

The other Christmastide scene, the *Nativity with SS Lawrence and Francis* (illus. 65), symbolizes Christ's future passion in the conventional manner by showing the naked baby Jesus lying isolated and exposed on the ground. All the figures seem to meditate quietly and prayerfully on this idea. This time, Caravaggio paid attention to tradition and showed the ox looking down at the Christ Child. As is usual with Caravaggio's angels, this one hurtles forwards into space, seeming to fall. It points to heaven, but, again characteristically for the artist, no hint is given of the empyrean above, nothing but blackness.

Even in these late works that seem most traditional, Caravaggio transcends convention by representing the demeanours and emotions of his protagonists with an eye to the way people actually look and behave. Not only is he faithful to the mien of people, but he expresses their emotions with a depth that is rarely seen in art.

Conclusion: Caravaggio and the Creation of Modernity

ARAVAGGIO PLAYED a critical role in the formation of a modern approach to painting. Previous works of the early modern period had already been open to sophisticated, multivalent interpretations, such as Botticelli's *Primavera* or Michelangelo's *Last Judgment*. But Caravaggio's art marks a new, more complex stage of development during the years around 1600, comparable to the novelties introduced in literature by Cervantes and Shakespeare, who likewise presented reality, layering, startling effects, irony and ambiguity in their works. Caravaggio's new, subjective tendencies that have been described in this book strikingly anticipate later, more mature phases of modernism in the nineteenth and twentieth centuries. Alone in art, he made advances on many fronts simultaneously, introducing a radical kind of painting that revolutionized style as well as social, expressive and religious meaning. The problematic reception of his paintings is itself evidence that Caravaggio had devised oppositional and disruptive strategies. His canvases created tension in their reception that encouraged thoughtful curiosity on the part of the beholder; thus he opened up a modern sense of the viewer's response. He took advantage of changing patterns of patronage and taste at a time when the newly emerging autonomy of the art market encouraged novelty. Indeed, Caravaggio himself was instrumental in bringing about such changes, in his case irrespective of a picture's church setting.

Caravaggio's boldness in creating a new approach to painting was noticed by his early biographers, such as Carel van Mander, who wrote one of the earliest reports on the artist (his manuscript, dated 1603, was published a year later). Van Mander describes Caravaggio's fearlessness in his art:

> There is also a certain Michelangelo da Caravaggio, who is doing extraordinary things in Rome . . . he has climbed up from poverty through hard work and by taking on everything with foresight and courage, as some do who will not be held back by faint-heartedness or lack of courage, but who push themselves forward boldly and fearlessly and who everywhere seek their advantage boldly.[1]

Van Mander's subsequent discussion makes it clear that he was thinking not only of Caravaggio's boldness in creating a new style of realism, but of his equally audacious conception of religious imagery. The unhesitating support given to Caravaggio by wealthy and powerful patrons, even when he was in serious trouble, is testament to their love of his art in all its novelty.

Caravaggio's early works anticipated the unusual presentation of subjects in his mature paintings. His daring approach early on was exemplified by his ambiguous mixing of antique and contemporary genres, by his emphasis on the mood and inner psychology of his protagonists, and by the homoerotic suggestiveness of his paintings of young boys. In his first major public commission for religious paintings, in the Contarelli chapel, he picked up ideas he had tried out in his *Boy Bitten by a Lizard* (see illus. 51), in which he represented an action caught in the moment and the surprised reaction of his subject. In his Contarelli chapel canvases he shows the tax-gatherer's astonished reaction to Christ's summons in the *Calling of St Matthew* (see illus. 18, 29); Matthew's amazement as the angel guides his writing of his Gospel in the first *Inspiration* (see illus. 36, 37); and the sudden appearance of an assassin in the *Martyrdom* (see illus. 31). Slightly later, he repeats the idea of surprise in his *Supper at Emmaus* (see illus. 45) and *Doubting Thomas* (see illus. 28). Caravaggio used surprise in religious paintings in a way that suggested the foreignness or alien aspect of divine revelation rather than the welcoming and naturalized approach to it employed by previous artists.

By 1600, in his mature Roman works, Caravaggio had already succeeded in creating a powerful, new kind of expressiveness in his use of light. The divine nature of the sharp, piercing light in his paintings in the years just after the turn of the century went unnoticed by both the protagonists in his pictures and nearly all his peers writing about his art in the seventeenth century. It was while he was living with Cardinal Del Monte that Caravaggio began to formulate his approach to light, which breaks forth in its full maturity in his paintings for the Contarelli chapel. In these works, he had his first major opportunity to develop metaphors of light in a religious context, across a series of narrative paintings. In these and later pictures he used light to represent human incomprehension and passivity in the face of divine revelation, and darkness to symbolize humankind's isolation in a world that seemed far removed from heaven.

The works Caravaggio painted in southern Italy after 1606 may be called 'late' more than merely in the sense that he died (young) in 1610; they are late because they have qualities that are normally associated with an artist's old-age style. These canvases are characterized by loose brushwork and an unparalleled depth of expressiveness in the human figures, traits that are also found in the late works of Titian and Rembrandt, who lived long lives and had true old-age styles. After 1606 a calmer, more meditative spirituality emerges in Caravaggio's art, along with a deepening of emotion and a directness and economy of style. The spectacular effects of his earlier Roman works are greatly reduced, but even as his art becomes increasingly compliant with religious norms, it grows more profoundly expressive. In his late works he seems to have wanted to demonstrate that he was capable of competing with other artists on their own terms as practitioners of classicism, the style that was pitted against his by critics who held that he was incapable of controlling design and composition. He succeeded in going further than almost any previous artist (with the possible exception of Titian) in the depth of expressiveness of his protagonists; his late works were virtually unprecedented in this respect. He transcended his own achievement in his mature Roman paintings by moving beyond their theatrical and showy effects (illus. 66).

In this book I have focused on the rich complexity of Caravaggio's art that makes it modern, including its uncompromising realism, its privileging of the human over the divine and the poor over the wealthy, and its contrary and

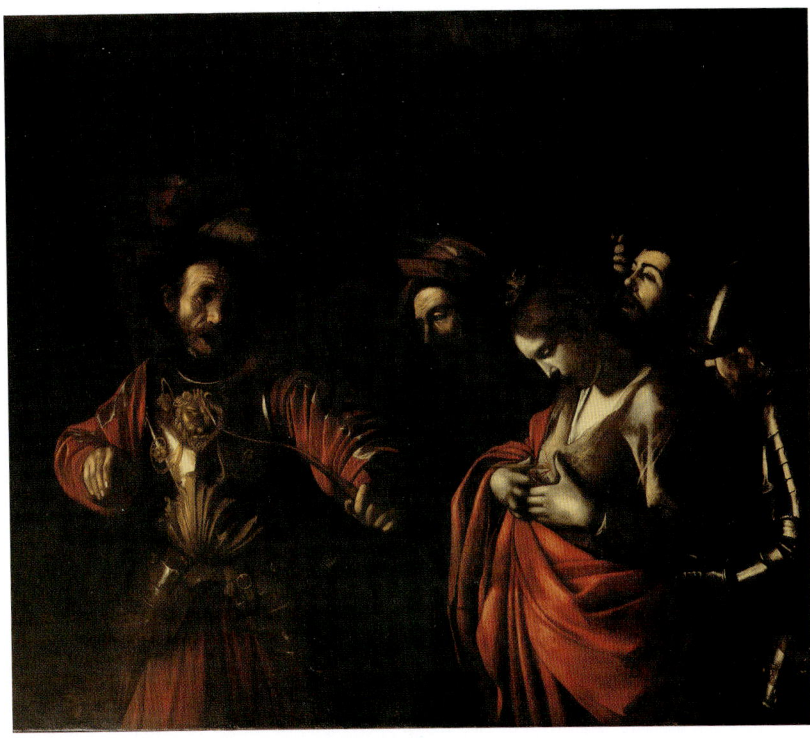

contingent expressiveness. The antinomies of his art embrace the real and the divine, darkness and light, ignorance and revelation, irony and seriousness. The problematical reception of his art grew from his rhetorical strategies, which began with a heretofore unseen, unflinching realism. He had his models re-enact sacred dramas that he devised from a totally fresh point of view, and he conceived an entirely modern outlook in the psychological reactions of his protagonists. His saints reveal human limitations of understanding not previously seen in monumental church art, even if his protagonists' expressions are multivalent and hard to read. In the

66 Caravaggio, *Martyrdom of St Ursula*, 1610, oil on canvas.

anti-idealist rhetoric that he communicated through his figures' realistic reactions to divinity, he posited a critical, oppositional approach to expression and meaning. The ambiguity of his figures' demeanours has given rise to disparate readings of his paintings, beginning with his contemporaries and stretching to today's interpretations. This antinomic character of his art makes it modern. The strangeness of his paintings appealed to a new kind of art market that sought out aesthetic delight and unrestrained novelty more than the artist's illumination of Counter-Reformation theology, even if the latter is implicit at deeper and unanticipated levels in his works. His pessimistic view of humanity in the face of divinity is essentially tragic (illus. 67).

Caravaggio's contemporaries easily detected his realism, but the deeper meaning of his religious expression remained largely hidden to them, or at least was rarely articulated in their writings. Critics of his paintings both past and present have detected unusual and disturbing approaches to religious imagery and meaning. Antipodal readings owing to his paintings' inherently ambiguous expressiveness continue to be put forward in the art-historical literature of today, with some writers endorsing his positive religious approach and others emphasizing his secular outlook. As a serious religious exploration of the limits of human understanding, his imagery deepens for some but undermines for others the sacred aspect of his art.

In confronting the specific objections, both old and new, to Caravaggio's sacred representations, I have proposed in this book iconographic solutions that allow the reader to see how his paintings are conceived within an essentially positive religious frame. Some of the misunderstandings of his art may be resolved through awareness that his visual narrative schemes are based on both historical and contemporary theological ideas. His oppositional strategies created a kind of internal resistance in his paintings that made slow, thoughtful contemplation of them more rewarding than mere notice of their naturalism, on both expressive and aesthetic levels. Caravaggio's novel, anti-idealist rhetorical strategies; his focus on realism and a resolutely human, as opposed to divine, perspective; the antinomies, ambiguities and contingent expressiveness of his art; its focus on the plebeian and

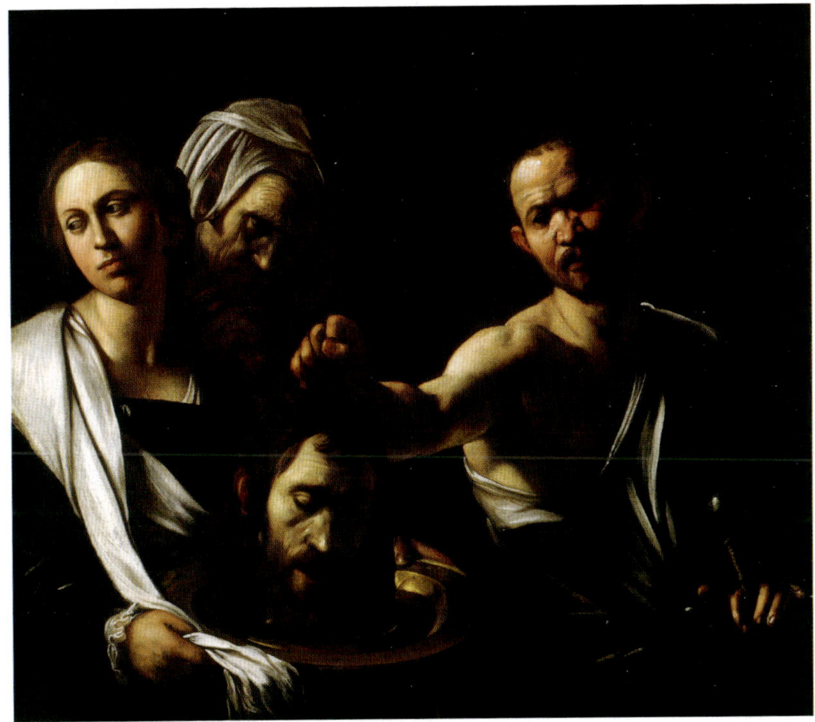

67 Caravaggio, *Salome Receiving the Head of John the Baptist*, c. 1607–9, oil on canvas.

the ordinary; and its rich complexity and reception, all lead to the conclusion that he took essential steps towards modernity. He created a new kind of art that would not be fully realized by other painters for 250 years.

Although in this book I have situated Caravaggio's art in its time, my argument about his modernity nevertheless is relevant to the ways in which he anticipates later developments in painting. His subjective, personal manner of making art was unusual during his lifetime and more typical of later periods of modernity. He prefigures developments in the nineteenth and twentieth centuries, in the works of painters ranging from Gustave Courbet to Pablo Picasso to Anselm Kiefer.[2] His plebeian protagonists with their ambivalent expressiveness look forward to the peasants of Courbet, his ambiguity and complexity are reimagined by Picasso, and his irony and antinomic strategies resurface in Kiefer's postmodern works. It is only in our own time that we are able to appreciate fully Caravaggio's art as embodying qualities that we now recognize as foundational for and characteristic of the modern, but which at the same time are rooted in his cultural moment.

REFERENCES

Introduction

1 Roland Barthes, 'The Reality Effect', *The Rustle of Language*, trans. R. Howard (Oxford, 1986), pp. 141–8.
2 Larry Keith, 'Caravaggio's Painting Technique: A Brief Survey Based on Paintings in the National Gallery, London', in *Caravaggio: Reflections and Refractions*, ed. Lorenzo Pericolo and David M. Stone (Burlington, VT, 2014), p. 35.
3 Giulio Mancini, *Considerazioni sulla pittura* (MS, c. 1617–21), in Howard Hibbard, *Caravaggio* (New York, 1983), p. 350.
4 See chapters 11 and 12 below.

1 Early Life: Milan–Rome, 1571–99

1 Rodolfo Papa, *Caravaggio: Lo stupore nell'arte* (Verona, 2009), p. 27.
2 Stefania Macioce, *Michelangelo Merisi da Caravaggio: Documenti, fonti e inventari 1513–1875*, 2nd edn (Rome, 2010).
3 Giovanni Baglione, *Le vite de' pittori, scultori et architetti . . .* (Rome, 1642), in Howard Hibbard, *Caravaggio* (New York, 1983), pp. 352–6; Giovanni Pietro Bellori, *Le vite de' pittori, scultori e architetti moderni* (Rome, 1672), in Hibbard, *Caravaggio*, pp. 361–74.
4 Giulio Mancini, *Considerazioni sulla pittura* (MS, c. 1617–21), in Hibbard, *Caravaggio*, pp. 346–51.
5 Giacomo Berra, *Il giovane Caravaggio in Lombardia: Ricerche documentarie sui Merisi, gli Aratori e i Marchesi di Caravaggio* (Florence, 2005), pp. 116–19.
6 Francesca Curti, 'Sugli esordi di Caravaggio a Roma: La bottega di Lorenzo Carli e il suo inventario', in *Caravaggio a Roma: Una vita dal*

vero, ed. Michele Di Sivo and Orietta Verdi, exh. cat., Archivio di Stato di Roma, Sant'Ivo alla Sapienza (Rome, 2011), p. 70; Berra, *Il giovane Caravaggio*, pp. 39–41, 45, with further literature.

2 The Modern Art Market; Early Patronage

1 Giovanni Pietro Bellori, *Le vite de' pittori, scultori e architetti moderni* (Rome, 1672), in Howard Hibbard, *Caravaggio* (New York, 1983), p. 361.

2 Ibid., p. 367.

3 Luigi Spezzaferro, 'Caravaggio accettato: Dal rifiuto al mercato', in *Caravaggio nel IV centenario della cappella Contarelli: Convegno internazionale di studi, Roma, 24–26 maggio 2001*, ed. Caterina Volpi (Città di Castello, Italy, 2002), p. 32.

4 Bellori, *Vite*, in Hibbard, *Caravaggio*, p. 363; also Giovanni Baglione, *Le vite de' pittori, scultori et architetti . . .* (Rome, 1642), in Hibbard, *Caravaggio*, p. 353.

5 Baglione, *Vite*, in Hibbard, *Caravaggio*, p. 352; Sandro Corradini and Maurizio Marini, 'The Earliest Account of Caravaggio in Rome', *Burlington Magazine*, CXL (1998), p. 25; Francesca Curti, 'Costantino Spada "regattiero de quadri vecchi" e l'amicizia con Caravaggio', in *'L'essercitio mio è di pittore' Caravaggio e l'ambiente artistico romano*, ed. Francesca Curti, Michele Di Sivo and Orietta Verdi (Rome, 2012), p. 171.

6 Patrizia Cavazzini, *Painting as Business in Early Seventeenth-century Rome* (University Park, PA, 2008), p. 124.

7 Ibid., pp. 20–21, 32, 38, 132, 139.

8 Richard E. Spear and Philip Sohm, *Painting for Profit: The Economic Lives of Seventeenth-Century Italian Painters* (New Haven, CT, and London, 2010), pp. 48, 49.

9 Donald Posner, 'Caravaggio's Homo-erotic Early Works', *Art Quarterly*, XXXIV (1971), pp. 301–24; Christoph L. Frommel, 'Caravaggio und Seine Modelle', *Castrum Peregrini*, XCVI (1971), pp. 21–56.

10 The original Latin of Dirck van Ameyden's undated biography of Del Monte is transcribed by Luigi Spezzaferro, 'La cultura del Cardinal Del Monte e il primo tempo del Caravaggio', *Storia dell'arte*,

IX/10 (1971), p. 60. Creighton Gilbert, *Caravaggio and His Two Cardinals* (University Park, PA, 1995), pp. 204–5, translates relevant passages.

11 Zygmunt Waźbiński, *Il Cardinale Francesco Maria Del Monte 1549–1626* (Florence, 1994), pp. 377, 379.

12 Francis Haskell, *Patrons and Painters: Art and Society in Baroque Italy* (New Haven, CT, and London, 1980), p. 29.

13 Todd Olson, *Caravaggio's Pitiful Relics* (New Haven, CT, and London, 2014), p. 31.

14 Corradini and Marini, 'The Earliest Account of Caravaggio in Rome', pp. 25, 27; Helen Langdon, *Caravaggio: A Life* (New York, 1999), p. 131.

15 Fiora Bellini, 'Tre documenti inediti per Michelangelo da Caravaggio', *Prospettiva*, LXV (1992), p. 70.

3 Early Roman Works, c. 1592–9

1 Giovanni Baglione, *Le vite de' pittori, scultori et architetti . . .* (Rome, 1642), in Howard Hibbard, *Caravaggio* (New York, 1983), p. 352.

2 Ibid.

3 Hibbard, *Caravaggio*, p. 37.

4 Baglione, *Vite*, in Hibbard, *Caravaggio*, p. 352; Giovanni Pietro Bellori, *Le vite de' pittori, scultori, e architetti moderni* (Rome, 1672), in Hibbard, *Caravaggio*, p. 363.

5 Helen Langdon, *Caravaggio: A Life* (New York, 1999), pp. 89–93; Andrew Graham-Dixon, *Caravaggio: A Life Sacred and Profane* (New York, 2011), pp. 97–110.

6 Langdon, *Caravaggio*, p. 87.

7 Todd Olson, *Caravaggio's Pitiful Relics* (New Haven, CT, and London, 2014), p. 37.

8 Bellori, *Vite*, in Hibbard, *Caravaggio*, p. 362.

9 Graham-Dixon, *Caravaggio*, p. 151.

10 Hermann Voss, *La pittura del Barocco a Roma*, ed. Andrea de Marchi, trans. Gunter Schwabe and Gemma Buonanno (Vicenza, 1999), pp. 438, 493 (original edn: *Die Malerei des Barock in Rom*, Berlin, 1924).

11 Frederick Cummings, 'The Meaning of Caravaggio's "Conversion of the Magdalen"', *The Burlington Magazine*, CXVI (1974), pp. 572–8;

Sebastian Schütze, *Caravaggio: The Complete Works* (Cologne, Germany, 2009), pp. 75–6, 255–6, with further literature.

4 A Stark Reality: Life and Mature Roman Works, 1599–1606

1 Giovanni Baglione, *Le vite de' pittori, scultori et architetti . . .* (Rome, 1642), in Howard Hibbard, *Caravaggio* (New York, 1983), p. 353.

2 Helen Langdon, *Caravaggio: A Life* (New York, 1999), p. 176.

3 Giovanni Pietro Bellori, *Le vite de' pittori, scultori e architetti moderni* (Rome, 1672), in Hibbard, *Caravaggio*, p. 371.

4 Giulio Mancini, *Considerazioni sulla pittura* (MS, *c.* 1617–21), in Hibbard, *Caravaggio*, p. 350.

5 Joachim von Sandrart, *Academie der Bau-, Bild- und Mahlerey-Künste von 1675*, ed. Arthur Peltzer (Munich, 1925), in Hibbard, *Caravaggio*, p. 378.

6 Andrew Graham-Dixon, *Caravaggio: A Life Sacred and Profane* (New York, 2011), pp. 210–12.

7 Langdon, *Caravaggio*, p. 273.

8 For Caravaggio's brawls and police record, see chapter 2 above.

9 Graham-Dixon, *Caravaggio*, p. 248.

10 Quoted in Walter Friedlaender, *Caravaggio Studies* (New York, 1969), p. 277.

11 Graham-Dixon, *Caravaggio*, p. 264.

12 John Sherman, *Mannerism* (Harmondsworth, Middlesex, and Baltimore, MD, 1967), p. 17.

13 Bellori, *Le vite*, in Hibbard, *Caravaggio*, p. 364.

14 Quoted in André Félibien, *Entretiens sur les vies et sur les ouvrages des plus excellens peintres anciens et modernes . . .* (Trévoux, France, 1725), vol. IV, p. 194.

15 Bellori, *Le vite*, in Hibbard, *Caravaggio*, p. 364.

16 See the discussion of de Piles and Diderot in Natalia Gozzano, 'La cappella Contarelli nei documenti e nella letteratura artistica', in *La cappella Contarelli in San Luigi dei Francesi: Arte e committenza nella Roma di Caravaggio*, ed. Natalia Gozzano and Patrizia Tosini (Rome, 2005), pp. 90–92.

5 The Divine and the Human

1 For a critique of Giulio Carlo Argan's appeal to Heidegger's *Dasein*
  to explain Caravaggio's realism, see Lorenzo Pericolo, 'Interpreting
  Caravaggio in the Second Half of the Twentieth Century: Between
  Galileo and Heidegger, Giordano Bruno and Laplanche', in
  Caravaggio: Reflections and Refractions, ed. Lorenzo Pericolo and David
  M. Stone (Burlington, VT, 2014), pp. 302–4.
2 Giulio Mancini, *Considerazioni sulla pittura* (MS, c. 1617–21), in
  Howard Hibbard, *Caravaggio* (New York, 1983), p. 349.
3 Andrew Graham-Dixon, *Caravaggio: A Life Sacred and Profane* (New
  York, 2011), pp. 311–12; Frances Gage, 'Caravaggio's "Death of
  the Virgin", Giulio Mancini, and the Madonna Blasphemed', in
  Caravaggio: Reflections and Refractions, pp. 83–104.
4 Todd Olson, *Caravaggio's Pitiful Relics* (New Haven, CT, and London,
  2014), pp. 149–54.
5 Troy Thomas, 'An Augustinian Interpretation of Caravaggio's
  "Calling of St Matthew"', *Studies in Iconography*, XXVII (2006), p. 157.
6 Ibid., pp. 183–4.
7 Erin E. Benay, 'Touching is Believing: Caravaggio's "Doubting
  Thomas" in Counter-Reformatory Rome', in *Caravaggio: Reflections
  and Refractions*, pp. 60, 73–5, 77.
8 Pietro Giacomo Bacci, *The Life of St Philip Neri* (London, 1902),
  vol. I, pp. 282–3 (original edn *Vita di B. Filippo Neri Fiorentino*,
  Rome, 1622).
9 St Ignatius Loyola, *The Spiritual Exercises of St Ignatius*, trans. Anthony
  Mottola (Garden City, NY, 1964), p. 82.
10 Troy Thomas, 'Expressive Aspects of Caravaggio's First "Inspiration
  of St Matthew"', *Art Bulletin*, LXVII (1985), pp. 646–7.

6 Ambiguity

1 Valeska von Rosen, *Caravaggio und die Grenzen des Darstellbaren:
  Ambiguität, Ironie und Performativität in der Malerei um 1600* (Berlin,
  2009), pp. 231–8, 245–54.
2 Peter Burgard, 'The Art of Dissimulation: Caravaggio's "Calling of
  St Matthew"', *Pantheon*, LVI (1998), pp. 95–102.

3 Thomas Puttfarken, 'Caravaggio's "Story of St Matthew": A Challenge to the Conventions of Painting', *Art History*, XXI (1998), p. 171; Andreas Prater, 'Wo ist Matthäus: Beobachtungen zu Caravaggios Anfängen als Monumentalmaler in der Contarelli-Kapelle', *Pantheon*, XLIII (1988), pp. 70–74.

4 Puttfarken, 'Caravaggio's "Story of St Matthew"', p. 172; Andrew Graham-Dixon, *Caravaggio: A Life Sacred and Profane* (New York, 2011), p. 195; Troy Thomas, 'An Augustinian Interpretation of Caravaggio's "Calling of St Matthew"', *Studies in Iconography*, XXVII (2006), pp. 160–62 and 185–7, nn. 4–14, for further literature.

5 Thomas, 'Augustinian Interpretation', pp. 162–3, 164, with illustrations.

6 Rodolfo Papa, *Caravaggio: Lo stupore nell'arte* (Verona, 2009), p. 126; Giovanni Urbani, 'Il restauro delle tele del Caravaggio in S. Luigi dei Francesi', *Bollettino dell'Istituto Centrale del Restauro*, XVII (1966), p. 56; Franca Trinchieri Camiz, 'Death and Rebirth in Caravaggio's "Martyrdom of St Matthew"', *Artibus et Historiae*, XI/22 (1990), pp. 94–102.

7 Commentary on the crudity of Matthew in the first *Inspiration* ranges from Giovanni Pietro Bellori in the seventeenth century to many contemporary art historians, including Sebastian Schütze, *Caravaggio: The Complete Works* (Cologne, Germany, 2009), p. 112, and Howard Hibbard, *Caravaggio* (New York, 1983), p. 144.

8 Gabriele Paleotti, *Discourse on Sacred and Profane Images*, trans. William McCuaig (Los Angeles, 2012), p. 170.

9 Todd Olson, *Caravaggio's Pitiful Relics* (New Haven, CT, and London, 2014), pp. 115, 117.

10 Graham-Dixon, *Caravaggio*, p. 221.

11 Leonard Slatkes, 'Caravaggio's "Pastor Friso"', *Nederlands Kunsthistorisch Jaarboek*, XXIII (1972), pp. 67–72; Creighton Gilbert, *Caravaggio and his Two Cardinals* (University Park, PA, 1995), pp. 1–97; Rodolfo Papa, 'Il sorriso di Dio. Il cosiddetto "San Giovannino" di Caravaggio nella Pinacoteca capitolina', in *Art e Dossier*, XIII/131 (1998), pp. 28–32; Valeska von Rosen, 'Implicit Decontextualization: Visual Discourse of Religious Paintings in Roman Collections circa 1600', in *Sacred Possessions: Collecting Italian*

Religious Art, 1500–1900, ed. Gail Feigenbaum and Sybille Ebert-Schifferer (Los Angeles, 2011), pp. 46–9.

12 Graham-Dixon, *Caravaggio*, p. 228.

13 Jonathan Unglaub, 'Caravaggio and the "Truth in Pointing"', in *Caravaggio: Reflections and Refractions*, ed. Lorenzo Pericolo and David M. Stone (Burlington, VT, 2014), pp. 152, 158–9, 161; Lorenzo Pericolo, *Caravaggio and Pictorial Narrative: Dislocating the Istoria in Early Modern Painting* (London and Turnhout, Belgium, 2011), pp. 209, 211–479.

14 Rosen, *Caravaggio*, pp. 1, 4, 231, 235–8, 245–54, 284, 294–8.

15 Herwarth Röttgen, 'Il Cavalier d'Arpino nella cappella Contarelli', in *La cappella Contarelli in San Luigi dei Francesi: Arte e committenza nella Roma di Caravaggio*, ed. Natalia Gozzano and Patrizia Tosini (Rome, 2005), p. 27.

16 Fabio Simonelli, 'Le fonti archivistiche per la cappella Contarelli: Edizione dei documenti', in *La cappella Contarelli*, pp. 147–51, docs 16, 17; Natalia Gozzano, 'La cappella Contarelli nei documenti e nella letteratura artistica', in ibid., p. 85.

17 Sybille Ebert-Schifferer, in *Caravaggio: The Artist and His Work* (Los Angeles, 2012), pp. 117–19, is the latest scholar to take up Spezzaferro's original proposal that the first version of Caravaggio's *Inspiration of St Matthew* was set up in the Contarelli Chapel in the late 1590s as a temporary altarpiece. See Luigi Spezzaferro, 'Caravaggio rifiutato? I. Il problema della prima versione del "San Matteo"', *Ricerche di storia dell'arte*, X (1980), pp. 49–64.

18 Gozzano, 'La cappella Contarelli', p. 85; Hibbard, *Caravaggio*, p. 303.

7 Oppositional Meanings

 1 The secularist view of Caravaggio's paintings is taken by art historians such as Herwarth Röttgen and Ferdinando Bologna; the religious position, above all, by Maurizio Calvesi. See Herwarth Röttgen, *Il Caravaggio: Ricerche e interpretazioni* (Rome, 1974), pp. 138–9, 142, 227–8, 240; Ferdinando Bologna, 'Il Caravaggio nella cultura e nella società del suo tempo', in *Colloquio sul tema Caravaggio e i Caravaggeschi, organizzato d'intesa con le Accademie di Spagna e di Olanda. Accademia Nazionale dei Lincei, CCCLXXI, Quaderno

n. 205, *Problemi attuali di scienza e di cultura* (Rome, 1974), pp. 149–87;
Maurizio Calvesi, 'Caravaggio', *Art e Dossier*, I (1986), pp. 3–66.

2 Peter Burgard, 'The Art of Dissimulation: Caravaggio's "Calling
of St Matthew"', *Pantheon*, LVI (1998), pp. 95–102; Valeska von
Rosen, *Caravaggio und die Grenzen des Darstellbaren: Ambiguität, Ironie
und Performativität in der Malerei um 1600* (Berlin, 2009), pp. 1, 4,
231, 235–8, 245–54, 284, 294–8; Lorenzo Pericolo, *Caravaggio
and Pictorial Narrative: Dislocating the Istoria in Early Modern Painting*
(London and Turnhout, Belgium, 2011), pp. 93, 141–2, 152–3, 171,
175, 208, 211, 219, 222, 224–5, 237, 278, 284, 288, 444, 475–6, 490.

3 See, for example, Thomas Puttfarken, in 'Caravaggio's "Story of
St Matthew": A Challenge to the Conventions of Painting', *Art
History*, XXI (1998), p. 171, who finds it unacceptable that the
bearded man who questions Christ in the *Calling of St Matthew* could
be identified as the saint.

4 Troy Thomas, 'An Augustinian Interpretation of Caravaggio's
"Calling of St Matthew"', *Studies in Iconography*, XXVII (2006), p. 163.

5 Ibid., pp. 163–75.

6 Ibid.

7 Troy Thomas, 'Expressive Aspects of Caravaggio's First "Inspiration
of St Matthew"', *Art Bulletin*, LXVII (1985), p. 639.

8 Chrysostom 10:4 (*Homil.* 1, 9, 10).

9 Andrew Graham-Dixon, *Caravaggio: A Life Sacred and Profane* (New
York, 2011), p. 238.

10 Helen Langdon, 'Caravaggio: Biography in Paint', in *Caravaggio
and Paintings of Realism in Malta*, ed. Cynthia de Giorgio and Keith
Sciberras (Malta, 2007), p. 64.

11 Giovanni Baglione, *Le vite de' pittori, scultori et architetti . . .* (Rome,
1642), in Howard Hibbard, *Caravaggio* (New York, 1983), p. 354;
Giovanni Pietro Bellori, *Le vite de' pittori, scultori e architetti moderni*
(Rome, 1672), in Hibbard, *Caravaggio*, p. 366.

12 Alessandro Zuccari, 'Caravaggio, i suoi committenti e il culto
laurentano', in *Caravaggio* (Madrid and Bilbao, Spain, 1999),
pp. 63–4.

13 John T. Spike, *Caravaggio*, 2nd revd edn (New York, 2010),
pp. 149–50.

8 The Social Embedded in the Religious

1 Giovanni Pietro Bellori, *Le vite de' pittori, scultori, e architetti moderni* (Rome, 1672), in Howard Hibbard, *Caravaggio* (New York, 1983), p. 372.
2 Jonathan Unglaub, 'Caravaggio and the "Truth in Pointing"', in *Caravaggio: Reflections and Refractions*, ed. Lorenzo Pericolo and David M. Stone (Burlington, VT, 2014), p. 150; Todd Olson, 'The Street Has its Masters: Caravaggio and the Socially Marginal', in *Caravaggio: Realism, Rebellion, Reception*, ed. Genevieve Warwick (Newark, DE, 2006), p. 79.
3 Helen Langdon, *Caravaggio: A Life* (New York, 1999), p. 75.
4 Ibid., pp. 89–93; Andrew Graham-Dixon, *Caravaggio: A Life Sacred and Profane* (New York, 2011), pp. 97–110.
5 Olson, 'The Street Has its Masters', p. 73.
6 Gabriele Paleotti, *Discourse on Sacred and Profane Images*, trans. William McCuaig (Los Angeles, 2012), p. 230.
7 Maurizio Calvesi, *Le realtà del Caravaggio* (Turin, Italy, 1990), pp. 279–84.
8 Roberto Longhi, *Studi caravaggeschi* (Florence, Italy, 1999), vol. 1, p. 198; Roger Hinks, *Michelangelo Merisi da Caravaggio: His Life, His Legend, His Works* (London, 1953), p. 75; Peter Robb, *M: The Man Who Became Caravaggio* (New York, 1999), p. 379; John T. Spike, *Caravaggio*, 2nd revd edn (New York, 2010), pp. 180–84.
9 Charles B. Schmitt and Quentin Skinner, eds, *The Cambridge History of Renaissance Philosophy* (Cambridge, 1988), p. 256.
10 Todd Olson, *Caravaggio's Pitiful Relics* (New Haven, CT, and London, 2014), pp. 146–7, 191–2.
11 See chapter 14 below.

9 The Created Personas of the Self-portraits

1 Caravaggio's self-representations as guises anticipate the recent strategies of postmodern artists such as Cindy Sherman.
2 Maurizio Marini, *Io Michelangelo da Caravaggio* (Rome, 1974), pp. 555–6. See also David Stone, 'Self and Myth in Caravaggio's "David and Goliath"', in *Caravaggio: Realism, Rebellion, Reception*,

ed. Genevieve Warwick (Newark, DE, 2006), p. 46, n. 71, where
the initials on the sword are read as 'M A C O F': '*Michaeli Angeli
Caravaggio Opus Fecit*'. More recently, in David Stone, 'Signature
Killer: Caravaggio and the Poetics of Blood', *Art Bulletin*, XCIV
(2012), p. 583, the author agrees that Marini's transcription is
more likely.

3 No documents connected to this work survive. It is variously dated
1606 or 1609/10; some scholars believe that Caravaggio painted it
for Scipione Borghese, who worked to secure his pardon after he
murdered Tomassoni.

4 For interpretations of the meaning of this painting, see Helen
Langdon, 'Caravaggio: Biography in Paint', in *Caravaggio and
Paintings of Realism in Malta*, ed. Cynthia de Giorgio and Keith
Sciberras (Malta, 2007), p. 64; Stone, 'Self and Myth', p. 38; Sergio
Rossi, 'Peccato e redenzione negli autoritratti del Caravaggio', in
*Michelangelo Merisi da Caravaggio: La vita e le opere attraverso i documenti: Atti
del convegno internazionale di studi*, ed. Stefania Macioce (Rome, 1996),
p. 323; John Varriano, *Caravaggio: The Art of Realism* (University Park,
PA, 2006), p. 83; Howard Hibbard, *Caravaggio* (New York, 1983),
p. 262; Lorenzo Pericolo, *Caravaggio and Pictorial Narrative: Dislocating
the Istoria in Early Modern Painting* (London and Turnhout, Belgium,
2011), p. 328.

5 Giovanni Pietro Bellori, *Le vite de' pittori, scultori e architetti moderni*
(Rome, 1672), in Hibbard, *Caravaggio*, p. 373.

6 Giovanni Battista della Porta, *De humana physiognomonia* (Naples,
1602).

7 Hibbard, *Caravaggio*, pp. 343–87.

8 Helen Langdon, *Caravaggio: A Life* (New York, 1999), pp. 297, 312;
Andrew Graham-Dixon, *Caravaggio: A Life Sacred and Profane* (New
York, 2011), p. 286. See chapter 14 below on the inaccurate claim
that the duel between Caravaggio and Tomassoni began because of
an argument over a wager on a tennis match.

9 Most scholars now accept this idea. See Franca Trinchieri Camiz,
'Death and Rebirth in Caravaggio's "Martyrdom of St Matthew"',
Artibus et Historiae, XI/22 (1990), p. 94.

10 On Caravaggio's character in the *Martyrdom* remaining unbaptized,
see Graham-Dixon, *Caravaggio*, pp. 201–2.

11 On the theme of ambiguity in Caravaggio's narrative paintings, see Pericolo, *Caravaggio and Pictorial Narrative*.

12 Ibid., pp. 314, 328.

13 Irving Lavin, 'Caravaggio Revolutionary or the Impossibility of Seeing', in *Opere e giorni: Studi su mille anni di arte europea dedicati a Max Seidel*, ed. Klaus Bergdolt and Giorgio Bonsanti (Venice, 2001), p. 637.

14 Lucia Corrain, 'Cristo nell'orto di Caravaggio: Un esempio di narrazione prodromica', in *Caravaggio nel iv centenario della cappella Contarelli: Convegno internazionale di studi, Roma*, ed. Caterina Volpi (Città di Castello, Italy, 2002), p. 225.

15 Langdon, 'Caravaggio: Biography in Paint', p. 61.

16 Pericolo, *Caravaggio and Pictorial Narrative*, pp. 468–9.

10 Scepticism, Eroticism, Irony, Wit

1 Richard H. Popkin, *The History of Scepticism from Erasmus to Spinosa* (Berkeley, CA, and Los Angeles, 1979), p. 51.

2 Francisco Sanches, *That Nothing Is Known (Quod Nihil Scitur)*, ed. Elaine Limbrick, trans. Douglas F. S. Thomson (Cambridge, 1988), pp. 224, 240–41, 243, 244–54.

3 Ippolito Falcone, *Narcisso al fonte, cioè l'uomo che si specchia nella propria miseria* (Venice, 1675), p. 88, quoted in Steven F. Ostrow, 'Caravaggio's Angels', in *Caravaggio: Reflections and Refractions*, ed. Lorenzo Pericolo and David M. Stone (Burlington, VT, 2014), p. 125.

4 Troy Thomas, 'Expressive Aspects of Caravaggio's First "Inspiration of St Matthew"', *Art Bulletin*, LXVII (1985), pp. 639–40.

5 Marcia Hall, *The Sacred Image in the Age of Art: Titian, Tintoretto, Barocci, El Greco, Caravaggio* (New Haven, CT, 2011), pp. 258–9.

6 Valeska von Rosen, *Caravaggio und die Grenzen des Darstellbaren: Ambiguität, Ironie und Performativität in der Malerei um 1600* (Berlin, 2009), pp. 7–9.

7 Giovanni Andrea Gilio, *Dialogo degli errori della pittura* (Camerino, Italy, 1564).

8 Howard Hibbard, *Caravaggio* (New York, 1983), illus. 89, 90.

9 Von Rosen, *Caravaggio*, pp. 287–98.

10 Giovanni Baglione, *Le vite de' pittori, scultori et architetti* . . . (Rome, 1642), in Hibbard, *Caravaggio*, p. 353.

11 Darkness and Light

1 For similar views, see Peter Serracino-Inglott, '*Ars Moriendi – Ad Usum Proprium*: Aspects of Dealing with Death in Caravaggio', in *Caravaggio and Paintings of Realism in Malta*, ed. Cynthia de Giorgio and Keith Sciberras (Malta, 2007), p. 95; John Moffitt, *Caravaggio in Context: Learned Naturalism and Renaissance Humanism* (Jefferson, NC, 2004), pp. 39–40.

2 Helen Langdon, 'Caravaggio: Biography in Paint', in *Caravaggio and Paintings of Realism in Malta*, pp. 53–64.

3 Frederick Copleston, *A History of Philosophy: Ockham to Suarez* (Westminster, MD, 1959), vol. III, p. 259.

4 Bernardino Telesio, *De rerum natura iuxta propria principia*, ed. Luigi de Franco (Cosenza and Florence, Italy, 1965), vol. I, p. 26; Bernardino Bonansea, *Tommaso Campanella: Renaissance Pioneer of Modern Thought* (Washington, DC, 1969), p. 15; Henry O. Taylor, *Thought and Expression in the Sixteenth Century* (New York, 1920), vol. II, pp. 347–8.

5 Bonansea, *Tommaso Campanella*, p. 15.

6 Telesio, *De rerum natura*, vol. I, p. 74; Cees Leijenhorst, 'Bernardino Telesio (1509–1588): New Fundamental Principles of Nature', in *Philosophers of the Renaissance*, ed. Paul R. Blum, trans. Brian McNeil (Washington, DC, 2010), p. 171.

7 Telesio, *De rerum natura*, vol. II, p. 52; Leijenhorst, 'Bernardino Telesio', p. 172.

8 Quoted in Moffitt, *Caravaggio in Context*, pp. 39–40.

9 Francesco Patrizi, *Nova de universis philosophia* (Ferrara, 1591), Panarchia 11, p. 23a; 22, pp. 47rb-va; Panaugia, 4, p. 10a; Thomas Leinkauf, 'Francesco Patrizi (1529–1597): New Philosophies of History, Poetry, and the World', in *Philosophers of the Renaissance*, p. 214.

10 Eugenie E. Maechling, 'Light Metaphysics in the Natural Philosophy of Francesco Patrizi da Cherso (1529–1597)', M. Phil. thesis, University of London, 1977, pp. 10, 43–4; Bonansea, *Tommaso Campanella*, pp. 17–18; Benjamin Brickman, *An Introduction to Francesco Patrizi's Nova de Universis Philosophia* (New York, 1941), pp. 27, 56, 60;

John Henry, 'Francesco Patrizi da Cherso's Concept of Space and its Later Influence', *Annals of Science*, XXXVI (1979), pp. 551–2.

11 Maechling, 'Light Metaphysics', pp. 23, 26–8, 31.

12 Brickman, *Introduction to Francesco Patrizi*, pp. 32, 36, 38, 56, 65, 67; Maechling, 'Light Metaphysics', p. 67.

13 Copleston, *History of Philosophy*, p. 259.

14 Brickman, *Introduction to Francesco Patrizi*, pp. 32, 36, 38, 56, 65, 67; Maechling, 'Light Metaphysics', p. 67.

15 Bonansea, *Tommaso Campanella*, p. 116.

16 Maechling, 'Light Metaphysics', pp. 33, 35; Brickman, *Introduction to Francesco Patrizi*, pp. 9, 27, 29, 47, 51–3, 56, 58–9.

17 Quoted in Moffitt, *Caravaggio in Context*, pp. 38–9.

18 Giulio Mancini, *Considerazioni sulla pittura* (MS, c. 1617–21), in Howard Hibbard, *Caravaggio* (New York, 1983), p. 350.

19 Giovanni Pietro Bellori, *Le vite de' pittori, scultori e architetti moderni* (Rome, 1672), in Hibbard, *Caravaggio*, p. 364; Joachim von Sandrart, *Academie der Bau-, Bild- und Mahlerey-Künste von 1675*, ed. Arthur Peltzer (Munich, 1925), in Hibbard, *Caravaggio*, p. 376.

20 Sandro Corradini, *Caravaggio: Materiali per un processo* (Rome, 1993), document 58.

21 Quoted in Troy Thomas, 'Expressive Aspects of Caravaggio's First "Inspiration of St Matthew"', *Art Bulletin*, LXVII (1985), p. 651.

22 Giordano Bruno, *De umbris idearum*, in *Opera latine conscripta*, ed. Francesco Fiorentino et al. (Naples and Florence, 1879–91), vol. II, pp. 20–21; Giordano Bruno, *Ash Wednesday Supper*, ed. and trans. Edward A. Gosselin and Lawrence S. Lerner (Hamden, CT, 1977), p. 48.

23 Giordano Bruno, *Eroici furori* [1585], in *Dialoghi italiani*, ed. Giovanni Aquilecchia, 3rd edn (Florence, 1958), p. 1,123.

24 Paul-Henri Michel, *The Cosmology of Giordano Bruno* (Ithaca, NY, 1973), p. 243.

25 John Harvey, *The Story of Black* (London, 2013), p. 117.

12 The Science of Art

1 Thomas Digges, *A Perfit Description of the Caelestiall Orbes* … (London, 1576), cited in Alexandre Koyré, *From the*

Closed World to the Infinite Universe (Baltimore, MD, 1957), pp. 28–30.

2 John T. Spike, *Caravaggio*, 2nd revd edn (New York, 2010), cat. 13.

3 Examples of Caravaggio's patrons and priests questioning the absence of God, angels and the heavens in his paintings are discussed above, particularly with respect to his *Death of the Virgin* and *Burial of St Lucy*.

4 The clearest and simplest characterization of the confusion over the new world systems is provided by John Donne in 'An Anatomy of the World: The First Anniversary' (1611), in *Complete Verse and Selected Prose*, ed. John Hayward (London, 1972), p. 202.

5 Ibid.

6 Giordano Bruno, *Eroici furori* [1585], in *Dialoghi italiani*, ed. Giovanni Aquilecchia, 3rd edn (Florence, 1958), p. 942.

7 Bernardino Telesio, *De rerum natura iuxta propria principia*, ed. Luigi de Franco (Cosenza and Florence, Italy, 1965), vol. II, p. 168; Cees Leijenhorst, 'Bernardino Telesio (1509–1588): New Fundamental Principles of Nature', in *Philosophers of the Renaissance*, ed. Paul R. Blum, trans. Brian McNeil (Washington, DC, 2010), p. 176; Bernardino Bonansea, *Tommaso Campanella: Renaissance Pioneer of Modern Thought* (Washington, DC, 1969), p. 15.

8 Leijenhorst, 'Telesio', p. 175.

9 Joachim von Sandrart, *Academie der Bau-, Bild- und Mahlerey-Künste von 1675*, ed. Arthur Peltzer (Munich, 1925), in Howard Hibbard, *Caravaggio* (New York, 1983), pp. 375–80.

10 Spike, *Caravaggio*, pp. 106–9.

11 In comparing Caravaggio and Galileo, see the cautionary approach of Lorenzo Pericolo, 'Interpreting Caravaggio in the Second Half of the Twentieth Century: Between Galileo and Heidegger, Giordano Bruno and Laplanche', in *Caravaggio: Reflections and Refractions*, ed. Lorenzo Pericolo and David M. Stone (Burlington, VT, 2014), p. 306.

12 Galileo Galilei, *Dialogue Concerning the Two Chief World Systems*, trans. Stillman Drake, revd edn (Berkeley, CA, and Los Angeles, 1962), p. 39.

13 Luigi Salerno, 'Caravaggio, A Reassessment', *Apollo*, n.s. CXIX (1984), p. 441.

14 Peter Robb, M: *The Man Who Became Caravaggio* (New York, 1999),
   pp. 277, 280.

15 Giovanni Baglione, *Le vite de' pittori, scultori et architetti . . .* (Rome,
   1642), in Hibbard, *Caravaggio*, p. 352; Sandro Corradini and
   Maurizio Marini, 'The Earliest Account of Caravaggio in Rome',
   Burlington Magazine, CXL (1998), pp. 161–76, esp. 163, doc. 57; Clovis
   Whitfield, *Caravaggio's Eye* (London, 2011), p. 230; Spike, *Caravaggio*,
   p. 70.

16 On the controversial idea that Caravaggio used a camera obscura or
   parabolic mirror, see David Hockney, *Secret Knowledge: Rediscovering
   the Lost Techniques of the Old* Masters, 2nd edn (New York, 2006),
   pp. 111–25, 218–27; Spike, *Caravaggio*, pp. 70–72; and Whitfield,
   Caravaggio's Eye, pp. 213–37.

13 The Religious Orders

1 Howard Hibbard, *Caravaggio* (New York, 1983), pp. 129–31.

2 Catherine Puglisi, *Caravaggio* (London, 1998), pp. 248–9; Bert
   Treffers, 'Il Francesco Hartford del Caravaggio e la spiritualità
   francescana alla fine del XVI sec.', *Mitteilungen des Kunsthistorischen
   Institutes in Florenz*, XXXII (1988), pp. 145–71; Bert Treffers,
   'Dogma, esegesi e pittura: Caravaggio nella cappella Contarelli in
   San Luigi dei Francesi', *Storia dell'arte*, LXVII (1989), pp. 241–55;
   Creighton Gilbert, *Caravaggio and His Two Cardinals* (University Park,
   PA, 1995), pp. 135–58; Sergio Benedetti, 'Classical and Religious
   Influences in Caravaggio's Painting', in *Saints and Sinners: Caravaggio
   and the Baroque Image*, exh. cat., McMullen Museum of Art, Boston
   College, ed. Franco Mormando (Chicago, 1999), pp. 222, 230.

3 Walter Friedlaender, *Caravaggio Studies* (New York, 1969), pp. 121–3;
   Joseph Chorpenning, 'Another Look at Caravaggio and Religion',
   Artibus et Historiae, VIII (1987), pp. 149–58.

4 Friedlaender, *Caravaggio Studies*, pp. 123–31; Alessandro Zuccari,
   'La politica culturale dell'Oratorio romano nella seconda metà del
   cinquecento', *Storia dell' arte*, XLI (1981), pp. 77–112.

5 Andrew Graham-Dixon, *Caravaggio: A Life Sacred and Profane* (New
   York, 2011), pp. 115–16; Maurizio Calvesi, *Le realtà del Caravaggio*
   (Turin, Italy, 1990), pp. 248, 284–7.

6 Troy Thomas, 'Caravaggio and the Roman Oratory of St Philip Neri', *Studies in Iconography*, XII (1988), pp. 61–89.

7 Troy Thomas, 'Expressive Aspects of Caravaggio's First "Inspiration of St Matthew"', *Art Bulletin*, LXVII (1985), pp. 641–8, 652.

8 Thomas, 'Caravaggio and the Roman Oratory', p. 67.

9 Troy Thomas, 'An Augustinian Interpretation of Caravaggio's "Calling of St Matthew"', *Studies in Iconography*, XXVII (2006), pp. 163–70.

10 John T. Spike, *Caravaggio*, 2nd rev. edn (New York, 2010), pp. 116–18.

11 Thomas, 'Augustinian Interpretation', p. 157.

12 On the conversion of Jews by the priests of San Luigi dei Francesi, see Adrienne von Lates, 'Caravaggio, Montaigne, and the Conversion of the Jews at San Luigi dei Francesi', *Gazette des Beaux-Arts*, CXXIV (1994), pp. 107–16.

13 For the contracts, see Fabio Simonelli, 'Le fonti archivistiche per la cappella Contarelli: Edizione dei documenti', in *La cappella Contarelli in San Luigi dei Francesi: Arte e committenza nella Roma di Caravaggio*, ed. Natalia Gozzano and Patrizia Tosini (Rome, 2005), pp. 130–31, 140–43.

14 Natalia Gozzano, 'La cappella Contarelli nei documenti e nella letteratura artistica', in *La cappella Contarelli*, p. 83; Simonelli, 'Le fonti archivistiche', pp. 117–18.

15 Thomas, 'Augustinian Interpretation', pp. 163–70.

16 Rose-Marie and Rainer Hagen, *What Great Paintings Say* (Cologne, 2003), vol. 1, p. 221.

17 Gabriele Paleotti, *Discourse on Sacred and Profane Images*, trans. William McCuaig (Los Angeles, 2012), p. 257.

18 Herwarth Röttgen, 'Il Cavalier d'Arpino nella cappella Contarelli', in *La cappella Contarelli*, pp. 27–34; on the history of the chapel, see Gozzano, 'La cappella Contarelli'; Simonelli, 'Le fonti archivistiche'.

19 Hibbard, *Caravaggio*, pp. 128–30.

20 Helen Langdon, 'Caravaggio: Biography in Paint', in *Caravaggio and Paintings of Realism in Malta*, ed. Cynthia de Giorgio and Keith Sciberras (Malta, 2007), p. 64.

21 I hold this view notwithstanding documentation that apparently connects this portrait to Vincenzo Giustiniani's collection, and a technical examination that has linked it to Caravaggio's

painting technique. See Francesco Scannelli, *Il microcosmo della pittura* . . . (Cesena, Italy, 1657), in Hibbard, *Caravaggio*, pp. 359–60; Francesca Cappelletti, '"Beauty from Nature" and Devotion: The Caravaggisti's New Images of the Saints', in *Caravaggio and His Followers in Rome* (New Haven, CT, 2011), p. 236.

22 John Varriano, 'Caravaggio and Religion', in *Saints and Sinners*, p. 191.

23 Francesco Susinno, *Le vite de' pittori messinesi* (MS, 1724), in Hibbard, *Caravaggio*, p. 386.

24 Ibid.

25 Genevieve Warwick, 'Introduction: Caravaggio in History', in *Caravaggio: Realism, Rebellion, Reception*, ed. Genevieve Warwick (Newark, DE, 2006), p. 14; Michael Kitson, *The Complete Paintings of Caravaggio* (New York, 1969), p. 9.

26 Hibbard, *Caravaggio*, p. 296.

27 Varriano, 'Caravaggio and Religion', pp. 191–2.

28 John Gash, *Caravaggio* (London, 1980), p. 16.

14 The Reception of Caravaggio's Art

1 Their *Vite* are gathered together in Howard Hibbard, *Caravaggio* (New York, 1983).

2 Gaetano Cozzi, 'Intorno al cardinale Ottavio Paravicino, a monsignor Paolo Gualdo e a Michelangelo da Caravaggio', *Rivista storica italiana*, LXXIII (1961), pp. 36–68.

3 Troy Thomas, 'Expressive Aspects of Caravaggio's First "Inspiration of St Matthew"', *Art Bulletin*, LXVII (1985), p. 651; Troy Thomas, 'An Augustinian Interpretation of Caravaggio's "Calling of St Matthew"', *Studies in Iconography*, XXVII (2006), pp. 181–2.

4 Herwarth Röttgen, *Il Caravaggio: Ricerche e interpretazioni* (Rome, 1974), pp. 138–9, 142, 227–8, 240; Giulio Carlo Argan, 'Il "realismo" nella poetica del Caravaggio', in *Scritti di storia dell'arte in onore di Lionello Venturi* (Rome, 1956), vol. II, pp. 31, 37; Ferdinando Bologna, 'Il Caravaggio nella cultura e nella società del suo tempo', in *Colloquio sul tema Caravaggio e i Caravaggeschi, organizzato d'intesa con le Accademie di Spagna e di Olanda. Accademia Nazionale dei Lincei, CCCLXXI, Quaderno n. 205, Problemi attuali di scienza e di cultura*

(Rome, 1974), pp. 149–87; Cesare Brandi, *Michelangelo Merisi da Caravaggio* (Rome, 1972–3), pp. 69–73, 96–9, 116.

5 Alessandro Zuccari, 'La politica culturale dell'Oratorio romano nella seconda metà del cinquecento', *Storia dell' arte*, XLI (1981), pp. 92–105; Maurizio Fagiolo dell'Arco, 'Le "opere di misericordia", contributo alla poetica del Caravaggio', *L'Arte*, I (1968), pp. 37–61; Walter Friedlaender, *Caravaggio Studies* (New York, 1969), pp. 120–31; Maurizio Calvesi, 'Caravaggio', *Art e Dossier*, I (1986), pp. 3–66.

6 For further interpretation of Paravicino's letter, see Andrew Graham-Dixon, *Caravaggio: A Life Sacred and Profane* (New York, 2011), pp. 152–3.

7 Giovanni Baglione, *Le vite de' pittori, scultori et architetti . . .* (Rome, 1642), in Hibbard, *Caravaggio*, p. 354.

8 Giovanni Pietro Bellori, *Le vite de' pittori, scultori e architetti moderni* (Rome, 1672), in Hibbard, *Caravaggio*, p. 365.

9 Gabriele Paleotti, *Discourse on Sacred and Profane Images*, trans. William McCuaig (Los Angeles, 2012), pp. 176, 214.

10 Sebastian Schütze, *Caravaggio: The Complete Works* (Cologne, Germany, 2009), pp. 141, 262, 272; Sybille Ebert-Schifferer, *Caravaggio: The Artist and His Work* (Los Angeles, 2012), pp. 132, 135, 187, 189.

11 24 August 1605, in Gian Alberto Dell'Acqua and Mia Cinotti, *Il Caravaggio e le sue grandi opere da San Luigi dei Francesi* (Milan, 1971), p. 159.

12 Mia Cinotti, *Michelangelo Merisi detto Il Caravaggio: Tutte le opera* (Bergamo, Italy, 1983), vol. I (I pittori bergamaschi: Il Seicento), p. 571.

13 Giulio Mancini, *Considerazioni sulla pittura* (MS, *c.* 1617–21), in Hibbard, *Caravaggio*, p. 349.

14 Filippo Baldinucci, *Notizie de' professori del disegno da Cimabue in qua* [1681–1728] (Florence, Italy, 1846), vol. III, p. 277.

15 Graham-Dixon, *Caravaggio*, p. 318.

16 Denis Mahon, *Studies in Seicento Art and Theory* (London, 1947), pp. 109–54, 193–229, 231–75.

17 Graham-Dixon, *Caravaggio*, pp. 273, 292; Bellori, *Le vite*, in Hibbard, *Caravaggio*, p. 372.

18 Todd Olson, *Caravaggio's Pitiful Relics* (New Haven, CT, and London, 2014), pp. 196–8.
19 Graham-Dixon, *Caravaggio*, pp. 307, 309, 340, 345.
20 Roberto Longhi, *Caravaggio* (Rome, 1977).

15 Life in Southern Italy, 1606–10

1 Helen Langdon, *Caravaggio: A Life* (New York, 1999), pp. 355–6.
2 Keith Sciberras, '"Frater Michael Angelus in Tumult": The Cause of Caravaggio's Imprisonment in Malta', *Burlington Magazine*, CXLIV (2002), pp. 229–32.
3 Langdon, *Caravaggio*, p. 362.
4 Francesco Susinno, *Le vite de' pittori messinesi* (MS, 1724), in Howard Hibbard, *Caravaggio* (New York, 1983), p. 386.
5 Ibid., p. 382.
6 Giovanni Baglione, *Le vite de' pittori, scultori, et architetti* . . . (Rome, 1642), in Hibbard, *Caravaggio*, p. 355; Andrew Graham-Dixon, *Caravaggio: A Life Sacred and Profane* (New York, 2011), p. 420.
7 Langdon, *Caravaggio*, p. 388.
8 Ibid.
9 Ibid., pp. 389–90.
10 Graham-Dixon, *Caravaggio*, p. 429.
11 Baglione, *Le vite*, in Hibbard, *Caravaggio*, pp. 354–5.
12 For the probable negative reaction of ordinary people to Caravaggio's *Madonna di Loreto*, see ibid., p. 354.

16 Reconciliation and Spirituality

1 Giulio Mancini, *Considerazioni sulla pittura* (MS, c. 1617–21), in Howard Hibbard, *Caravaggio* (New York, 1983), p. 348; Giovanni Baglione, *Le vite de' pittori, scultori, et architetti* . . . (Rome, 1642), in Hibbard, *Caravaggio*, p. 355.

17 Late Works, 1606–10

1 Helen Langdon, *Caravaggio: A Life* (New York, 1999), p. 357.

Conclusion: Caravaggio and the Creation of Modernity

1 Carel van Mander, *Het Schilder-Boeck* (Haarlem, 1604), in Howard Hibbard, *Caravaggio* (New York, 1983), p. 344.

2 Even if Roger Fry, in *Transformations* (London, 1926), p. 117, declared Caravaggio to be the first modern painter, my conception of him, based on situating the artist in his historical frame as an early modernist, is quite different from his. See also André Berne-Joffroy, *Le Dossier Caravage* (Paris, 1959), p. 10, who wrote that 'what begins in the work of Caravaggio is, quite simply, modern painting.'

SELECT BIBLIOGRAPHY

Cassani, Silvia, Maria Sapio et al., eds, *Caravaggio: The Final Years* (Naples, 2005)

De Giorgio, Cynthia, and Keith Sciberras, eds, *Caravaggio and Paintings of Realism in Malta* (Valletta, Malta, 2007)

Ebert-Schifferer, Sybille, *Caravaggio: The Artist and His Work* (Los Angeles, 2012)

Friedlaender, Walter, *Caravaggio Studies* (New York, 1969)

Gilbert, Creighton, *Caravaggio and His Two Cardinals* (University Park, PA, 1995)

Gozzano, Natalia, and Patrizia Tosini, eds, *La cappella Contarelli in San Luigi dei Francesi, arte e committenza nella Roma di Caravaggio* (Rome, 2005)

Graham-Dixon, Andrew, *Caravaggio: A Life Sacred and Profane* (New York, 2011)

Hibbard, Howard, *Caravaggio* (New York, 1983)

Langdon, Helen, *Caravaggio: A Life* (New York, 1999)

Macioce, Stefania, *Michelangelo Merisi da Caravaggio, Documenti, fonti e inventari 1513–1875. Il edizione corretta, integrata e aggiornata* (Rome, 2010)

Mormando, Franco, ed., *Saints and Sinners: Caravaggio and the Baroque Image*, exh. cat., McMullen Museum of Art, Boston College (Chicago, 1999)

Olson, Todd, *Caravaggio's Pitiful Relics* (New Haven, CT, and London, 2014)

Pericolo, Lorenzo, *Caravaggio and Pictorial Narrative: Dislocating the 'Istoria' in Early Modern Painting* (London and Turnhout, 2011)

—, and David M. Stone, eds, *Caravaggio: Reflections and Refractions* (Burlington, VT, 2014)

Puglisi, Catherine, *Caravaggio* (London, 1998)

Rosen, Valeska von, *Caravaggio und die Grenzen des Darstellbaren: Ambiguität, Ironie und Performativität in der Malerei um 1600* (Berlin, 2009)

Schütze, Sebastian, *Caravaggio: The Complete Works* (Cologne, 2009)

Scibberas, Keith, and David M. Stone, *Caravaggio: Art, Knighthood, and Malta* (Valletta, Malta, 2006)

Spike, John T., *Caravaggio*, 2nd revd edn (New York, 2010)

Varriano, John, *Caravaggio: The Art of Realism* (University Park, PA, 2006)

Vodret, Rossella, *Caravaggio: The Complete Works* (Milan, 2010)

Warwick, Genevieve, ed., *Caravaggio: Realism, Rebellion, Reception* (Newark, DE, 2006)

ACKNOWLEDGEMENTS

I wish to thank Dr Gregory Crawford, Interim Director of the School of Humanities, and Dr Susannah Gal, Associate Dean for Research and Outreach, both of the Pennsylvania State University, Harrisburg, for grants from their offices supporting the publication of this book. For an additional generous grant, I give my thanks to the Institute for the Arts and Humanities, the Pennsylvania State University, University Park, and its director, Dr Michael Bérubé. My heartfelt thanks go to scholars whose publications in recent years have increased my understanding of Caravaggio, especially Valeska von Rosen, Stefania Macioce, Helen Langdon, Andrew Graham-Dixon, Todd Olson, David Stone and Lorenzo Pericolo. This book would not have been possible without the encouragement of Michael Leaman, Publisher at Reaktion Books, who first suggested that I revise a previous book project to fit the format of the Renaissance Lives series. His continued advice and support have been invaluable. To François Quiviger, Editor of the Renaissance Lives series, I owe a debt of gratitude for his thoughtful suggestions to improve my text, and for his corrections of several errors. I am also grateful to Martha Jay, Managing Editor at Reaktion Books, for her advice and careful review of my manuscript. In addition, I thank the helpful staffs of the following libraries where I carried out much of my research: the Pennsylvania State University; Marquand Library of Art and Archeology, Princeton University; the Library of Congress; the Warburg Institute, University of London; the Bibliotheca Hertziana, Rome; and the Vatican Library. I presented a version of my chapter on 'The Created Personas of the Self-portraits' at the annual meeting of the Renaissance Society of America, San Diego, California, 4–6 April 2013.

PHOTO ACKNOWLEDGEMENTS

The author and publishers wish to express their thanks to the below sources of illustrative material and/or permission to reproduce it. Some locations of works are given below rather than in the captions.

Photo akg-images/Cameraphoto: 57 (private collection, Rome); photo akg-images/De Agostini Picture Library/V. Pirozzi: 63 (Galleria Nazionale d'Arte Antica di Palazzo Corsini, Rome); photo Alinari/ Bridgeman Images: 32 (Gemäldegalerie, Staatliche Museen, Preussischer Kulturbesitz, Berlin-Dahlem); photo bpk, Berlin/Stiftung Preussische Schlösser und Gärten, Sanssouci/Gerhard Murza, Bildergalerie, Potsdam/ Art Resource, NY: 28 (Bildergalerie von Sanssouci, Stiftung Preussische Schlösser und Gärten Berlin-Brandenburg, Potsdam); photos Bridgeman Images: 14 (Galleria Doria-Pamphilj, Rome), 17 (Galleria Nazionale d'Arte Antica, Palazzo Barberini, Rome), 26 (Musée du Louvre, Paris), 35 (Cappella Contarelli, San Luigi dei Francesi, Rome), 45 (National Gallery, London), 48 (Pinacoteca di Brera, Milan), 50 (gift of the Kresge Foundation and Mrs Edsel B. Ford, Detroit Institute of Arts, Detroit), 51 (National Gallery, London), 64 (Museo Nazionale, Messina); photo De Agostini Picture Library/Bridgeman Images: 13 (Galleria Doria-Pamphilj, Rome); photos De Agostini Picture Library/G. Nimatallah/Bridgeman Images: 16 (Museo Thyssen-Bornemisza, Madrid), 67 (National Gallery, London); photo Foto Marburg/Art Resource, NY: 36, 37 (destroyed; formerly Gemäldegalerie, Kaiser-Friedrich-Museum, Berlin); photo Kimbell Art Museum, Fort Worth, Texas: 9 (AP 1987.06, Kimbell Art Museum, Fort Worth); photo Leonard C. Hanna, Jr. Fund/Bridgeman Images: 54 (Cleveland Museum of Art, Cleveland); photo Erich Lessing/

Art Resource, NY: 39 (Kunsthistorisches Museum, Vienna); image © The Metropolitan Museum of Art/Art Resource, NY: 10 (The Metropolitan Museum of Art, Rogers Fund, 1952 [52.81]), 44; photos Mondadori Portfolio/Electa/Art Resource, NY: 3 (San Fedele, Milan), 66 (Palazzo Zevallos Stigliano, Banca Intesa Sanpaolo Collection, Naples); photo Mondadori Portfolio/Electa/Mario Berardi/Bridgeman Images: 30 (Pinacoteca, Bologna); photo courtesy the National Gallery of Ireland: 42 (National Gallery of Ireland, Dublin); photo Allen Phillips/Wadsworth Atheneum, courtesy the Ella Gallup Sumner and Mary Catlin Sumner Collection Fund: 15 (Wadsworth Atheneum Museum of Art, Hartford); photos © RMN-Grand Palais/Art Resource, NY: 7 (Musée du Louvre, Paris), 56 (Musée du Louvre, Paris); photo San Luigi dei Francesi, Rome: 52 (Cappella Contarelli, San Luigi dei Francesi, Rome); photo Santa Maria della Concezione, Rome: 43 (Santa Maria della Concezione, Rome); photo Santo Stefano Rotundo, Rome: 22; photos Scala/Art Resource, NY: 4 (Pinacoteca di Brera, Milan), 5 (Cappella del Crocifisso, Santa Maria in Vallicella, Rome), 6 (State Hermitage Museum, St Petersburg), 8 (Pinacoteca Capitolina, Rome), 11 (Galleria degli Uffizi, Florence), 18 (Cappella Contarelli, San Luigi dei Francesi, Rome), 19 (Cappella Cerasi, Santa Maria del Popolo, Rome), 20 (Cappella Cerasi, Santa Maria del Popolo, Rome), 21 (Cappella Cerasi, Santa Maria del Popolo, Rome), 23 (Galleria degli Uffizi, Florence), 24, 25, 27 (Cappella dell'Assunta, Santa Maria della Scala, Rome), 29 (Cappella Contarelli, San Luigi dei Francesi, Rome), 31 (Cappella Contarelli, San Luigi dei Francesi, Rome), 33 (Pinacoteca Capitolina, Rome), 34 (Santissima Trinità dei Pellegrini, Rome), 38 (Cappella Cavalletti, Sant'Agostino, Rome), 41 (Cappella Contarelli, San Luigi dei Francesi, Rome), 46 (Cappella Contarelli, San Luigi dei Francesi, Rome), 47 (Pinacoteca Vaticana, Rome), 49 (Cappella Cerasi, Santa Maria del Popolo, Rome), 53 (Galleria Borghese, Rome), 58 (Santa Lucia al Sepolcro, Syracuse), 59 (Cathedral Museum, Valletta, Malta), 60 (Pio Monte della Misericordia, Naples), 61 (Oratorio di San Giovanni Battista dei Cavalieri, Valletta, Malta), 62 (Museo Nazionale, Messina), 65 (stolen in 1969, formerly Oratorio di San Lorenzo, Palermo); and photos Scala/Ministero per i Beni e le Attività culturali/Art Resource, NY: 1 (Galleria Borghese, Rome), 2 (Galleria Borghese, Rome), 12 (Galleria degli Uffizi, Florence), 40 (Galleria Borghese, Rome), 55 (Museo Nazionale di Capodimonte, Naples).

INDEX

Illustration numbers are indicated by *italics*.